T0222593

Lecture Notes in Artificial Intelligence 8903

Subseries of Lecture Notes in Computer Science

More information about this series at http://www.springer.com/series/1244

Silvia Miksch · David Riaño
Annette ten Teije (Eds.)

Knowledge Representation for Health Care

6th International Workshop, KR4HC 2014
Held as Part of the Vienna Summer of Logic, VSL 2014
Vienna, Austria, July 21, 2014
Revised Selected Papers

 Springer

Editors
Silvia Miksch
Vienna University of Technology
Vienna
Austria

Annette ten Teije
Vrije Universiteit Amsterdam
Amsterdam
The Netherlands

David Riaño
Universitat Rovira i Virgili
Tarragona
Spain

ISSN 0302-9743   ISSN 1611-3349 (electronic)
Lecture Notes in Artificial Intelligence
ISBN 978-3-319-13280-8   ISBN 978-3-319-13281-5   (eBook)
DOI 10.1007/978-3-319-13281-5

Library of Congress Control Number: 2014956509

LNCS Sublibrary: SL7 – Artificial Intelligence

Springer Cham Heidelberg New York Dordrecht London

Printed on acid-free paper

Springer International Publishing AG Switzerland is part of Springer Science+Business Media
(www.springer.com)

Preface

As computerized healthcare support systems are rapidly becoming more knowledge intensive, the representation of medical knowledge in a form that enables reasoning is growing in relevance and taking a more central role in the area of Medical Informatics. In order to achieve a successful decision support and knowledge management approach to medical knowledge representation, the scientific community has to provide efficient representations, technologies, and tools to integrate all the important elements that healthcare providers work with: electronic health records and healthcare information systems, clinical practice guidelines and standardized medical technologies, codification standards, etc.

Synergies to integrate the above-mentioned elements and types of knowledge must be sought both in the medical problems (e.g., prevention, diagnosis, therapy, prognosis, etc.) and in the Computer Science and Artificial Intelligence technologies (e.g., natural language processing, digital libraries, knowledge representation, knowledge integration and merging, decision support systems, machine learning, e-learning, etc.). The sixth international KR4HC workshop aimed at attracting the interest of novel research and advances contributing in the definition, representation, and exploitation of healthcare knowledge in medical informatics.

Historical Remark of the Workshop: The first KR4HC workshop, held in conjunction with the 12th Artificial Intelligence in Medicine conference (AIME09), brought together members of two existing communities: the clinical guidelines and protocols community, which held a line of four workshops (European Workshop on Computerized Guidelines and Protocols CPG2000 and CPG2004; AI Techniques in Health Care: Evidence-based Guidelines and Protocols 2006, and Computer-based Clinical Guidelines and Protocols 2008), and a related community which held a series of three workshops devoted to the formalization, organization, and deployment of procedural knowledge in health care (CBMS07 Special Track on Machine Learning and Management of Health Care Procedural Knowledge 2007; From Medical Knowledge to Global Health Care 2007; Knowledge Management for Health Care Procedures 2008). Since then, two more KR4HC workshops were held KR4HC 2010 and KR4HC 2011, in conjunction with the ECAI10 and the AIME11 conferences. In 2012, the fourth KR4HC workshop was organized in conjunction with ProHealth as part of the BPM12 conference. We are continuing the efforts with a second Joint Workshop on Knowledge Representation for Health Care and Process-Oriented Information Systems in Health Care (KR4HC/ProHealth) in the 14th Artificial Intelligence in Medicine conference (AIME13).

The Sixth International Workshop on Knowledge Representation for Heath Care was organized together with the 14th International Conference on Principles of Knowledge Representation and Reasoning (KR14), within the Vienna Summer of Logic 2014.

Twenty-six papers were submitted to KR4HC 2014, among which eighteen were full research papers, and eight were short papers describing short research, position papers, problem analyses, or demonstrations of implemented systems. Seven were selected for full presentation (39%) and nine for short presentation, among which four where short papers (50%) and five were full research papers (28%). One of the accepted long papers was withdrawn by the authors.

We would also like to acknowledge Stefania Montani (Università degli Studi del Piemonte Orientale "Amedeo Avogadro") for her implication in the proposal and preparation of the keynote talk. Unfortunately she finally had to excuse her participation. This drove us to agree on Giorgio Leonardi (Università degli Studi del Piemonte Orientale "Amedeo Avogadro") to present Stefania's talk, which resulted on a challenging presentation under the title "Knowledge-Intensive Medical Process Similarity."

This volume contains a selection of the 11 best papers presented in the KR4HC 2014 workshop, together with a paper by the keynote speaker.

September 2014

Silvia Miksch
David Riaño
Annette ten Teije

Organization

KR4HC 2014 was organized by Silvia Miksch, Vienna University of Technology, Austria, David Riaño, Universitat Rovira i Virgili, Spain, and Annette ten Teije, Vrije Universiteit Amsterdam, The Netherlands.

Program Committee

Samina Abidi	Dalhousie University, Canada
Syed Sibte Raza Abidi	Dalhousie University, Canada
Roberta Annicchiarico	IRCCS Fondazione Santa Lucia, Italy
Luca Anselma	Università di Torino, Italy
Joseph Barjis	Delft University of Technology, The Netherlands
Paul De Clercq	Medecs BV, The Netherlands
Arturo Gonzlez Ferrer	University of Haifa, Israel
Adela Grando	Arizona State University, USA
Robert Greenes	Arizona State University, USA
Femida Gwadry-Sridhar	University of Western Ontario, Canada
David Isern	Universitat Rovira i Virgili, Spain
Patty Kostkova	City University, UK
Vassilis Koutkias	INSERM, France
Peter Lucas Radboud	University Nijmegen, The Netherlands
Wendy MacCaull	St. Francis Xavier University, Canada
Ronny Mans	Eindhoven University of Technology, The Netherlands
Mar Marcos	Universitat Jaume I, Spain
Stefania Montani	Università degli Studi del Piemonte Orientale "Amedeo Avogadro", Italy
Leon Osterweil	University of Massachusetts Amherst, USA
Mor Peleg	University of Haifa, Israel
Manfred Reichert	University of Ulm, Germany
Hajo A. Reijers	Eindhoven University of Technology, The Netherlands
Danielle Sent	AMC/UvA, The Netherlands
Brigitte Seroussi	Hôpitaux de Paris, France
Andreas Seyfang	Vienna University of Technology, Austria
Paolo Terenziani	Università degli Studi del Piemonte Orientale "Amedeo Avogadro", Italy
Frank van Harmelen	Vrije Universiteit Amsterdam, The Netherlands
Dongwen Wang	University of Rochester, USA

Contents

Methods and Applications

Knowledge-Intensive Medical Process Similarity

Stefania Montani[1]([⊠]), Giorgio Leonardi[1], Silvana Quaglini[2], Anna Cavallini[3], and Giuseppe Micieli[3]

[1] Dipartimento di Scienze e Innovazione Tecnologica, Computer Science Institute, Università del Piemonte Orientale, Viale Michel 11, 15121 Alessandria, Italy
stefania.montani@di.unipmn.it
[2] Department of Electrical, Computer and Biomedical Engineering, Università di Pavia, Via Ferrata 1, 27100 Pavia, Italy
[3] on behalf of the Stroke Unit Network (SUN) collaborating centers, Istituto di Ricovero e Cura a Carattere Scientifico Fondazione "C. Mondino", Via Mondino 2, 27100 Pavia, Italy

Abstract. Process model comparison and similar processes retrieval are key issues to be addressed in many real world situations, and particularly relevant ones in medical applications, where similarity quantification can be exploited to accomplish goals such as conformance checking, local process adaptation analysis, and hospital ranking.

In recent years, we have implemented a framework which allows to: (i) extract the actual process model from the available process execution traces, through process mining techniques; and (ii) compare (mined) process models, by relying on a novel distance measure. Our distance measure is **knowledge-intensive**, in the sense that it explicitly makes use of domain knowledge, and can be properly adapted on the basis of the available knowledge representation formalism. We also exploit all the available mined information (e.g., temporal information about delays between activities). Interestingly, our metric explicitly takes into account complex **control flow information** too, which is often neglected in the literature.

The framework has been successfully tested in stroke management.

1 Introduction

Process model comparison is a key issue to be addressed in many real world situations. For example, when two companies are merged, process engineers need to compare processes originating from the two companies, in order to analyze their possible overlaps, and to identify areas for consolidation. Particularly interesting is the case of medical process model comparison, where similarity quantification can be exploited in a quality assessment perspective. Indeed, the process model actually implemented at a given healthcare organization can be compared to the existing reference clinical guideline, e.g., to check conformance, or to understand the level of adaptation to local constraints that may have been required. A quantification of these differences (and maybe a ranking of the hospitals derived from it) can be exploited for several purposes, like, e.g., legal purposes, performance evaluation and funding distribution.

S. Miksch et al. (Eds.): KR4HC 2014, LNAI 8903, pp. 1–13, 2014.
DOI: 10.1007/978-3-319-13281-5_1

The actual process models are not always explicitly available at an organization. However, a database of process execution traces (also called the "event log") can often be reconstructed starting from the data that the organization collects, through its information system, or, in the best case, by means of the workflow technology. In these situations, process mining techniques [3] can be exploited, to extract process related information (e.g., process models) from log data.

Stemming from these considerations, we have recently implemented a framework, which allows the user to:

1. mine the actual process model from the available event log, through process mining techniques; and
2. perform process model comparison, to fulfill the objectives described above.

In task 1, we extract process models in the form of graphs, where nodes represent activities, and edges represent control flow relations. These graphs may also include gateway nodes, that provide information about parallel or mutually exclusive execution of activities. Indeed, we are able to operate with several graph structures, such as heuristic [16] and multi-phase graphs [15] (see Sect. 2 for more details). In task 2, we compare process models. Process model comparison is a non trivial issue, since hospital models can be extremely complex (see, e.g., Fig. 1). To address this challenge, we rely on a novel metric, whose distinguishing characteristics can be summarized as follows:

– our metric is **knowledge-intensive**, since it makes use of domain knowledge, and of all the information that can be extracted through process mining or through statistics on the event log, such as temporal information, and it can be properly adapted on the basis of the available knowledge representation formalism (e.g., taxonomy vs. semantic network with different characteristics);
– moreover, our metric takes into account complex **control flow information** (other than sequence), which is often neglected in the literature, by explicitly dealing with gateway nodes.

We are currently applying our framework to stroke management. In this domain, our metric has proved to outperform other literature approaches, and to generate outputs that are closer to those provided by a stroke management expert.

The paper is organized as follows. Sect. 2 summarizes our approach, and discusses its novelty with respect to related literature contributions. Sect. 3 showcases experimental results. Sect. 4 illustrates our conclusions and future research directions.

2   Methods

As described in the Introduction, our framework allows the user to: extract the actual process model from the available medical process execution traces; and perform medical process model comparison.

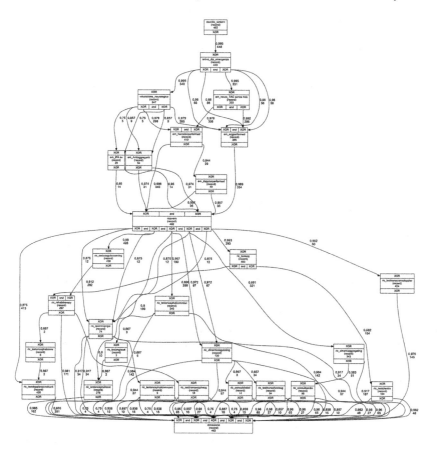

Fig. 1. An example process model.

The first task relies on *process mining* techniques. Process mining describes a family of a-posteriori analysis techniques exploiting the information recorded in event logs, to extract process related information (e.g., process models).

In our work, we are currently relying on mining algorithms available within ProM [14], an open source tool which supports a wide variety of process mining and data mining activities.

In particular, we have mainly exploited ProM's *heuristic miner* [16] and *multi-phase miner* [15] for mining the process models.

Heuristic miner takes in input the event log, and generates a graph, where nodes represent activities, and edges represent control flow information. Control flow relations other than sequence are not explicitly provided in the form of gateway nodes, but can be derived. Heuristic miner labels edges with several mined information, that we are considering in process comparison. Heuristic miner is known to be tolerant to noise, a problem that may affect many real world event logs (e.g., in medicine sometimes the logging may be incomplete).

Multi-phase miner, on the other hand, provides in output an Event-driven Process Chain (EPC), i.e., a graph that contains three types of nodes: activities, gateway nodes, events. Events describe the situation before/after the execution of an activity; they don't provide additional information about the process control flow. We have therefore ignored events in distance calculation. On the other hand, we explicitly consider gateway nodes.

As a future work, we would also like to define a new mining algorithm, able to overcome some of the limitations of the existing approaches (see Sect. 4).

The second task implemented by our framework (i.e., process model comparison), is independent of the chosen mining algorithm; it only requires to receive two graphs as an input, and different graph structures can be managed (since they are all converted to a common syntactic representation before process model comparison is performed).

Process model comparison is the most significant contribution of our work, as it relies on a novel metric. Since mined process models are represented in the form of graphs, we define a metric based on the notion of graph edit distance [2]. Such a notion calculates the minimal cost of mapping one graph to another by applying edit operations, i.e., insertions/deletions and substitutions of nodes, and insertions/deletions of edges. While string edit distance looks for an *alignment* that minimizes the cost of transforming one string into another by means of edit operations, in graph edit distance a *mapping* has to be looked for. A mapping is a function that matches nodes to nodes, and edges to edges. Among all possible mappings, graph edit distance will select the one that leads to the minimal cost, having properly quantified the cost of every type of edit operation. Like in string edit distance, there is no procedure to identify which nodes/edges in the first graph correspond to which nodes/edges in the second one; all possible matches are tried, and the minimal cost ones are applied. Computational cost of this all-to-all match is typically contained by means of dynamic programming solutions or, as in our case, of greedy approaches.

With respect to the classical graph edit distance definition in [2], and to the available literature approaches, we have however introduced two innovative contributions:

1. we operate in a **knowledge-intensive** way in calculating the cost of activity node substitution. Indeed, we exploit domain knowledge to represent activities and their relationships, and then use this semantic information when substituting one activity to another: the more two activities are similar (e.g., anti-coagulant vs anti-aggregant drugs, whose effect is comparable, and that can be both provided in a stroke emergency), the less we pay for their substitution.

   We also allow for the use of different metrics to calculate the cost of activity node substitution, on the basis of the available *knowledge representation formalisms* (e.g., a taxonomy vs a different kind of semantic network).

   Moreover, we add a cost contribution related to edge substitution, able to exploit information learned through process mining, like, e.g., the percentage of traces that cross a given edge in the mined model, and some statistics about the temporal duration of a given edge. For instance, we are able to penalize the presence of different time delays between the very same sequence of two activities, in the two graphs being compared[1].

2. we consider complex **control flow information** (i.e., other than sequence) between the mined process activities. This information, in our approach, is made explicit in the form of gateway nodes (e.g., AND joins/splits) in the graph. In calculating graph edit distance, we only map activity nodes to activity nodes, and gateway nodes to gateway nodes. Our metric is then able to explicitly take into account the cost of gateway node substitution, on the basis of their type (AND vs. XOR), and of the activities and other gateways they directly connect. To compare the connected activity nodes, we rely again on domain knowledge, as explained in item 1. For instance, the AND of two activities in the first graph will be considered as very similar to the AND of two activities in the second graph, if the activities themselves are semantically very similar.

The technical details and formulas of the approach have been published elsewhere. The interested reader can refer to [9–11].

The goal of comparing objects with a complex structure (i.e., graphs) entails the definition of a nontrivial notion of distance. The issue of providing a proper graph distance definition has been afforded in the literature, following three main directions, i.e.:

1. relying on a local notion of similarity (two subgraphs are similar if their neighboring nodes are similar), as in the similarity flooding algorithm [6];
2. relying on subgraph isomorphism, e.g., to find maximum common sub-graphs [13], and
3. adapting the edit distance notion to graphs [2].

We are currently following direction 3, but directions 1 and 2 could be considered in our future work for comparison.

The closest works with respect to our approach are [4] and [5] (which extends [4]). Indeed, these works have been considered in our experiments for comparison (see Sect. 3).

Specifically, [4] provides a normalized version of graph edit distance for comparing business process models, and defines syntactical edit operation costs for activity node substitution, activity node insertion/deletion, and edge insertion/deletion.

With respect to [4], we have introduced several novel contributions:

(a) we have moved towards a *knowledge-intensive* approach in activity node substitutions, by allowing the exploitation of domain knowledge. The work in [4], on the other hand, relies on edit distance between activity node names;
(b) always in the *knowledge-intensive* perspective, we have explicitly considered edge substitutions, which was disregarded in [4];

---

[1] Deletion and insertion costs, on the other hand, are simply based on the count of mapped vs. unmapped items.

(c) the work in [4] does not take into account control flow elements other than sequence, so that gateway nodes are not represented in the graph, and not used in distance calculation. On the contrary, we have considered this issue as well in our contribution.

The work in [5] extends the work in [4] specifically by dealing with issue (c) (but not with (a) and (b)): indeed, the authors explicitly represent gateway nodes, in order to describe, e.g., parallelism and mutual exclusion. With respect to our approach, Ref. [5] simplifies the treatment of incoming/outgoing activity nodes with respect to a gateway node: in comparing two gateway nodes, it only calculates the fraction of their incoming (respectively, outgoing) activity nodes that were mapped; it does not consider the cost of their substitution, i.e., how similar this mapped activity nodes are. On the other hand, we explicitly use domain knowledge in this phase of distance calculation as well, as described in [9]. The work in [5] also considers activity nodes that are connected to the gateway node at hand indirectly. On the contrary, we limit our comparison to incoming/outgoing activity nodes that are directly connected to the gateway node we want to examine. In [5] incoming/outgoing gateway nodes to the gateway nodes being compared are completely disregarded.

Experimental comparisons between our approach and the contributions in [4] and [5] are provided in Sect. 3.

3   Experiments

We have applied our framework to stroke management processes. In the following subsections, we will describe the experimental setting, and provide our results.

3.1   Experimental Setting

A stroke is the rapidly developing loss of brain function(s) due to disturbance in the blood supply to the brain. This can be due to ischemia (lack of glucose and oxygen supply) caused by a thrombosis or embolism, or to a hemorrhage. As a result, the affected area of the brain is unable to function, leading to inability to move one or more limbs on one side of the body, inability to understand or formulate speech, or inability to see one side of the visual field. A stroke is a medical emergency and can cause permanent neurological damage, complications, and death. It is the leading cause of adult disability in the United States and Europe and the number two cause of death worldwide.

In our experiments, we could rely on a database of 9929 traces, collected at 16 stroke units of the Stroke Unit Network (SUN) of Regione Lombardia, Italy [7]. The number of traces varies from 1149 to 266. Traces are composed of 13 activities on average, with no repeated activities. Data refer to the period 2009-2012.

Our co-author Dr. Anna Cavallini, an experienced physician in stroke patient management, has also provided us with the domain knowledge to define the taxonomy partially reported in Fig. 2. The taxonomy, which was developed by using the Protégé ontology editor[2], is composed of 111 classes, organized in a hierarchy of six levels, and defined on the basis of their goal. First, the taxonomy divides the activities into two main classes: activities that take place in the emergency phase (EM - generally performed in the emergency room), and activities that take place during the hospitalization phase (H - generally performed in the stroke unit). These two main classes correspond to two main goals, which are: (1) to face the stroke emergency as quickly as possible, and (2) to plan the patient's monitoring and secondary prevention. Moreover, these classes are further refined in subclasses, according to more specific goals. This refinement continues to the leaves, where the most specific activities are represented.

Some subclasses (e.g., diagnostic procedures and therapy) are repeated in both main classes, but their goal is very different: for example, a computerized tomography (CT) or a magnetic resonance (MR) in the emergency phase have the main goal of excluding a hemorrhagic stroke, while the same examinations in the hospitalization phase are performed to monitor stroke evolution and refine the etiopathogenetic diagnosis. Thus, the activities "H brain CT" and "H brain MR" (see Fig. 2), which are put together in the brain parenchyma evaluation node of the hospitalization (H) phase, although based on very different technologies, are closer than "H brain CT" and "EM brain CT", because these are executed to investigate brain parenchyma in the two different EM and H phases. The organization of the taxonomy also makes the distance between "H brain CT" and "'H brain MR" smaller than the one between "H brain CT" and 'H transthoracic echocardiogram" because, even if these last two activities are performed in the same phase (hospitalization), their goal is completely different (monitoring changes in the brain parenchyma vs. cardiologic diagnosis).

In our distance calculation, Palmer's taxonomic distance was used [12] to calculate the cost of activity node substitution. This distance allows us to exploit the hierarchical structure, since the distance between two activities is set to the normalized number of arcs on the path between the two activities themselves in the taxonomy.

We asked a stroke management expert (other than our co-authors) to provide a ranking of the SUN stroke units (see Table 1, column 2), on the basis of the quality of care they provide. Quality of care was established referring to the available guidelines. This ranking has then been used as a "golden" standard for our evaluation results. The first hospital in the ranking (H0) is a stroke unit in which top-level human and technological resources are available, and positive clinical outcomes (e.g., number of stroke patients who survive and/or improve after care) are very high on average. Moreover, this hospital is the one where the largest number of traces was collected (1149), and it is therefore the one from which the most reliable process mining results could be obtained. The expert identified 6 hospitals (H1-H6) with a high similarity level with respect to H0; 5 hospitals (H6-H11) with a medium similarity level with respect to H0; and 4 hospitals (H12-H15) with a low similarity level with respect to H0. According to the expert, the ordering of the hospitals within one specific similarity level is not

---

[2] http://protege.stanford.edu/ (accessed on 4/11/2014).

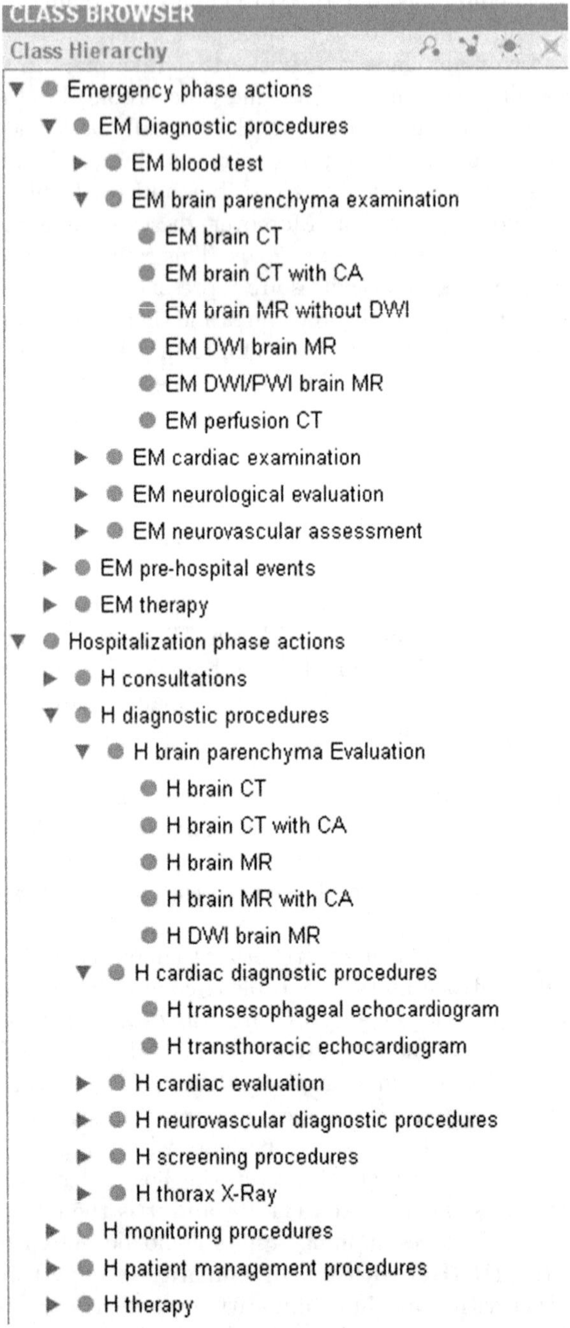

Fig. 2. An excerpt from the domain taxonomy. EM: emergency phase (usually managed in an emergency room); H: hospitalization phase (usually managed in a stroke unit).

very relevant. It is instead important to distinguish between different similarity levels.

We set up six different experimental configurations, where two different miners were exploited in task 1 (process mining), and three different metrics were relied upon in task 2 (process model comparison):

1. heuristic miner + the distance in [4];
2. heuristic miner + the distance in [5];
3. heuristic miner + the new distance described in this paper;
4. multi-phase miner + the distance in [4];
5. multi-phase miner + the distance in [5];
6. multi-phase miner + the new distance described in this paper.

Specifically, first we mined the process models according to heuristic miner, and to multi-phase miner. We then ordered the two available process model sets with respect to H0, resorting to the new distance defined in this paper, and to the distance in [4,5], globally obtaining six rankings.

3.2   Results

Experimental results are shown in Tables 1 (for heuristic miner) and 2 (for multi-phase miner).

In both tables, column 1 shows the levels of similarity with respect to the reference hospital. Column 2 shows the ranking according to the stroke medical expert; columns 3, 4 and 5 show the results obtained relying on the distance in [4] (Dijkman), the distance in [5] (LaRosa), and the distance defined in this paper (KI dist. - where KI stands for Knowledge Intensive), respectively.

As already observed, according to the expert, the ordering of the hospitals within one specific similarity level is not very relevant, so that classical metrics for comparing ranked sets are not useful to assess the ranking quality. It is only important to distinguish between different similarity levels.

When exploiting heuristic miner (see Table 1), the distance in [4] correctly rates 5 process models in the high similarity group, 3 process models in the medium similarity group, and 3 process models in the low similarity group (column 3, Table 1).

The distance in [5], on the other hand, correctly rates 4 process models in the high similarity group, 3 process models in the medium similarity group, and 3 process models in the low similarity group (column 4, Table 2).

The distance defined in this paper correctly rates 5 process models in the high similarity group, 4 process models in the medium similarity group, and 3 process models in the low similarity group (column 5, Table 1).

When exploiting multi-phase miner (see Table 2), the distance in [4] correctly rates 5 process models in the high similarity group, 2 process models in the medium similarity group, and 2 process models in the low similarity group (column 3, Table 2).

Table 1. Ordering of 15 hospitals, with respect to a given reference model, when relying on heuristic miner. Incorrect positions in the rankings with respect to the expert's qualitative similarity levels are highlighted in bold.

Similarity	Medical expert	Dijkman	LaRosa	KI dist.
High	H1	H1	H4	H4
High	H2	H4	H3	H1
High	H3	H2	H1	H2
High	H4	H3	H2	H5
High	H5	H6	**H9**	**H8**
High	H6	**H7**	**H10**	H3
Medium	H7	H8	H7	H6
Medium	H8	H11	**H14**	H11
Medium	H9	H10	**H6**	**H13**
Medium	H10	**H5**	H11	H7
Medium	H11	**H12**	H8	H10
Low	H12	**H9**	**H5**	**H9**
Low	H13	H14	H12	H12
Low	H14	H13	H13	H15
Low	H15	H15	H15	H14

The distance in [5], on the other hand, correctly rates 4 process models in the high similarity group, 2 process models in the medium similarity group, and 2 process models in the low similarity group (column 4, Table 2).

The distance defined in this paper correctly rates 5 process models in the high similarity group, 4 process models in the medium similarity group, and 3 process models in the low similarity group (column 5, Table 2).

Thus, our distance produces results that are closer to the qualitative ranking provided by the human expert. Very interestingly, this situation holds both when relying on heuristic miner, and when relying on multi-phase miner. In the case of multi-phase miner, the performance of the distances in [4] and in [5] are particularly poor.

In conclusion, our knowledge-intensive approach to distance calculation has proved to be able to provide a reliable process model comparison in practice. As such, it could be confidently used for comparing medical processes in a quality evaluation perspective, at least when comparing hospitals that are equipped with similar resources, as it was the case in our experiments.

4   Conclusions and Future Work

In this paper, we have described a novel framework for process comparison. In particular, we resort to a **knowledge-intensive** distance definition, in the sense

Table 2. Ordering of 15 hospitals, with respect to a given reference model, when relying on multi-phase miner. Incorrect positions in the rankings with respect to the expert's qualitative similarity levels are highlighted in bold.

Similarity	Medical expert	Dijkman	LaRosa	KI dist.
High	H1	H1	**H14**	H2
High	H2	H4	H4	H1
High	H3	H2	H1	H3
High	H4	H3	H3	H4
High	H5	H6	H6	**H8**
High	H6	**H8**	**H11**	H6
Medium	H7	H11	**H5**	H11
Medium	H8	**H5**	**H13**	H9
Medium	H9	**H12**	**H2**	**H12**
Medium	H10	H9	H8	H10
Medium	H11	**H14**	H9	H7
Low	H12	**H10**	H12	H13
Low	H13	H13	**H10**	**H5**
Low	H14	H15	H15	H14
Low	H15	**H7**	**H7**	H15

that it explicitly makes use of domain knowledge, and can be properly adapted on the basis of the available knowledge representation formalism. We also exploit all the information that can be mined from the event log, including temporal information. Our distance also explicitly takes into account complex **control flow information**, which is often neglected in the literature. This obviously makes distance calculation more general, and closer to the semantic meaning of the mined process model.

Experimental results in stroke management have favored our contribution, in comparison to the distance definitions reported in [4,5], the most similar already published works with respect to our approach. Indeed our metric, that could take advantage of domain knowledge, in the form of a taxonomy, outperformed the works in [4] and in [5] on a real world stroke management event log, and provided results that were closer to those of a human expert. This held both when relying on heuristic miner to learn process models, and when relying on multi-phase miner.

We believe that our metric could therefore be confidently used for comparing medical processes in a quality evaluation perspective. Indeed, when domain knowledge is available, rich and well consolidated, as is often the case in medicine, its exploitation can surely improve the quality of any automated support to the expert's work - including process comparison (see e.g., [1]). Moreover, we made an explicit use of temporal information, and time is in fact a very important parameter in medical applications (particularly when referring to emergency medicine, as it is in the case of stroke).

In the future, we plan to complement the framework by introducing a new process mining algorithm, able to overcome some of the limitations characterizing most of the approaches described in the literature. In particular, it may happen that the existing approaches generate a process model that includes a path never recorded as a trace in the event log. This can be very harmful in some applications (like, e.g., patient management/disease treatment), and, generally, in all those cases in which the quality of the process has to be assessed. We plan to define a new algorithm that does not incur in this problem, and provides process mining results correct and reliable as much as possible, in order to facilitate the work of medical decision makers.

We also plan to further optimize the process mining task by means of a pre-processing step, in which log traces are properly clustered, along the lines described in [8].

Acknowlegements. We would like to thank Dr. I. Canavero for her independent work in the experimental phase.

This research is partially supported by the GINSENG Project, Compagnia di San Paolo.

References

1. Basu, R., Archer, N., Mukherjee, B.: Intelligent decision support in healthcare. Analytics **33–38**, 2012 (2012)
2. Bunke, H.: On a relation between graph edit distance and maximum common subgraph. Pattern Recogn. Lett. **18**(8), 689694 (1997)
3. Van der Aalst, W., van Dongen, B., Herbst, J., Maruster, L., Schimm, G., Weijters, A.: Workflow mining: a survey of issues and approaches. Data Knowl. Eng. **47**, 237–267 (2003)
4. Dijkman, R., Dumas, M., García-Bañuelos, L.: Graph matching algorithms for business process model similarity search. In: Dayal, U., Eder, J., Koehler, J., Reijers, H.A. (eds.) BPM 2009. LNCS, vol. 5701, pp. 48–63. Springer, Heidelberg (2009)
5. LaRosa, M., Dumas, M., Uba, R., Dijkman, R.: Business process model merging: an approach to business process consolidation. ACM Trans. Softw. Eng. Methodol. **22**(2), 11 (2013)
6. Melnik, S., Garcia-Molina, H., Rahm, E.: Similarity flooding: a versatile graph matching algorithm and its application to schema matching. IEEE, USA (2002)
7. Micieli, G., Cavallini, A., Quaglini, S., Fontana, G., Duè, M.: The Lombardia stroke unit registry: 1-year experience of a web-based hospital stroke registry. Neurol. Sci. **31**(5), 555–564 (2010)
8. Montani, S., Leonardi, G.: Retrieval and clustering for supporting business process adjustment and analysis. Inf. Syst. **40**, 128–141 (2014)
9. Montani, S., Leonardi, G., Quaglini, S., Baudi, A.: Improving process model retrieval by accounting for gateway nodes: an ongoing work. In: volume 1101 of CEUR Workshop Proceedings, pp. 31–40. CEUR-WS.org (2013)

10. Montani, S., Leonardi, G., Quaglini, S., Cavallini, A., Micieli, G.: Mining and retrieving medical processes to assess the quality of care. In: Delany, S.J., Ontañón, S. (eds.) ICCBR 2013. LNCS, vol. 7969, pp. 233–240. Springer, Heidelberg (2013)
11. Montani, S., Leonardi, G., Quaglini, S., Cavallini, A., Micieli, G.: Improving structural medical process comparison by exploiting domain knowledge and mined information. Artif. Intell. Med. **62**, 33–45 (2014)
12. Palmer, M., Wu, Z.: Verb semantics for English-Chinese translation. Mach. Transl. **10**, 59–92 (1995)
13. Valiente, G.: Algorithms on Trees and Graphs. Springer, Berlin (2002)
14. van Dongen, B.F., de Medeiros, A.K.A., Verbeek, H.M.W.E., Weijters, A.J.M.M.T., Van der Aalst, W.M.P.: The ProM framework: a new era in process mining tool support. In: Ciardo, G., Darondeau, P. (eds.) ICATPN 2005. LNCS, vol. 3536, pp. 444–454. Springer, Heidelberg (2005)
15. van Dongen, Boudewijn F., van der Aalst, Wil M.P.: Multi-phase process mining: building instance graphs. In: Atzeni, P., Chu, W., Lu, H., Zhou, S., Ling, T.W. (eds.) ER 2004. LNCS, vol. 3288, pp. 362–376. Springer, Heidelberg (2004)
16. Weijters, A., Van der Aalst, W., Alves de Medeiros, A.: Process Mining with the Heuristic Miner Algorithm, WP 166. Eindhoven University of Technology, Eindhoven (2006)

Preliminary Result on Finding Treatments for Patients with Comorbidity

Yuanlin Zhang[1]([⊠]) and Zhizheng Zhang[2]

[1] Texas Tech University, Lubbock, USA
y.zhang@ttu.edu
[2] Southeast University, Nanjing, China
seu_zzz@seu.edu.cn

Abstract. According to some research, comorbidity is reported in 35 to 80 % of all ill people [1]. Multiple guidelines are needed for patients with comorbid diseases. However, it is still a challenging problem to automate the application of multiple guidelines to patients because of redundancy, contraindicated, potentially discordant recommendations. In this paper, we propose a mathematical model for the problem. It formalizes and generalizes a recent approach proposed by Wilk and colleagues. We also demonstrate that our model can be encoded, in a straightforward and simple manner, in Answer Set Programming (ASP) – a class of Knowledge Representation languages. Our preliminary experiment also shows our ASP based implementation is efficient enough to process the examples used in the literature.

Keywords: Answer set programming · Clinical practice guidelines · Knowledge representation · Comorbidity

1 Introduction

Clinical practice guidelines (CPGs) [2], created by experts and supported by medical evidences, are documents guiding the decisions in specific areas/conditions of healthcare. It is generally agreed that the use of guidelines can greatly improve the outcome of clinical medical care. To promote the use of CPGs and increase their accessibility, an important effort is to build systems that can automatically execute the guidelines given patients' information. Most of the early systems are based on the representation languages such as Asbru, GLIF, GUIDE, EON, PROforma [3–5]. CPGs are usually developed to target a single disease [3], and thus these systems and languages were focusing on single diseases too.

It has been noted that the majority of elderly patients have multiple comorbidities and medications that must be addressed by their patient care team [6]. When applying multiple CPGs to comorbid patients, as pointed out by Sittig et al. [7], "the challenge is to create mechanisms to identify and eliminate redundant, contraindicated, potentially discordant, or mutually exclusive guideline based recommendations for patients presenting with comorbid conditions or multiple medications."

© Springer International Publishing Switzerland 2014
S. Miksch et al. (Eds.): KR4HC 2014, LNAI 8903, pp. 14–28, 2014.
DOI: 10.1007/978-3-319-13281-5_2

As an example, consider an ulcer patient with transient stroke. According to the ulcer CPG, *stop aspirin* is a necessary activity in the treatment of ulcer while *start aspirin*, according to the transient stroke CPG, is also a necessary activity under certain situations. In this case, it is desirable for a CPG based system to identify the inconsistency of the *stop aspirin* and *start aspirin* activities resulted from two distinct CPGs, and then remove the inconsistency by replacing the activity of *start aspirin* by *start clopidogrel.*

Recently several attempts [8–10] have been made to attack the problem (or a part of it). We are particularly interested in the approach proposed by Wilk and colleagues [10–12] which consists of two steps. The first step is to identify the adverse and contradictory activities, i.e., inconsistencies, that are obtained by applying the CPG to each of the several diseases a patient has. The second step is to mitigate the inconsistencies. We call the problem introduced by Wilk et al. *guideline reconciling problem.*

Wilk and colleagues offered one of the first few automated solutions for the concurrent application of CPGs to two diseases. However, they only gave a solution for the problem, based on Constraint Logic Programming program and pseudo code algorithms, but did not give a mathematical definition of the problem. As a result of the lack of problem definition, it is not easy to evaluate how closely this problem models the real problems on the application of two or more CPGs, and the solution to the reconciling problem may be unnecessarily restricted (e.g., to the approach used in their work) too.

In the research reported here, we make the following contributions to improve Wilk and colleagues' work.

We separate the reconciling problem from its solution(s). We find that graph theory provides a handy tool for us to develop an explicit mathematical definition for the reconciling problem. Compared with Wilk et al.'s work, our definition does not depend on an programming languages or algorithms. We expect the definition to be more accessible to researchers in the medical area (maybe with help of computer scientists) and thus makes it easier for them to evaluate its capacity of modeling the real situation. On the other hand, once the problem is (mathematically) defined, computer scientists can focus on finding better ways to solve the problem, without worrying too much about the required medical background.

In our definition, we also generalize the problem implied by Wilk et al's algorithms by allowing OR decision nodes.

Once the problem is defined, there are many immediate ways to solve the problem under both declarative and imperative programming paradigms. As an example, we present a solution based on Answer Set Programming (ASP), a declarative programming paradigm. ASP is a well developed non-monotonic logic programming paradigm in the knowledge representation community. The logic rules of ASP are natural because a good amount of knowledge in guidelines are in the form of rules. More important, rules in CPGs usually involve exceptions, which can be addressed very well by the non-monotonicity property of ASP. Thanks to its declarativeness and non-monotonicity, ASP is elaboration tolerant

[13,14] (which means that it is convenient to modify a set of facts expressed in ASP to take into account new phenomena or changed circumstances in the domain of concern), which is particularly amenable to the constant revision of guidelines driven by the growth of our knowledge on all aspects of diseases. Equally important to the expressiveness of ASP, several efficient ASP inference engines or solvers such as DLV [15] and CLASP [16] have been developed and maintained in the last decade. They enable the development of efficient ASP based solutions to application problems. An important note in our decision of using ASP is there are many aspects of the problem (as a mathematical model for reconciling CPGs) that need to be improved to address the real life problems. Those improvements can very well make the problem NP-hard. So, we are not interested in ad hoc algorithm(s) specifically designed for the problem defined in its current form.

The encoding of the problem using ASP is natural and simple, almost a straightforward translation of the problem definition. Our preliminary experiment also shows that the examples mentioned in [10] can be solved efficiently. As far as we are aware of, there is no system available on applying multiple CPGs to several diseases. Our ASP program is available publicly and downloadable at http://redwood.cs.ttu.edu/~yzhang/temp/KR-14/code-coMorbidity-dlv.lp.

The rest of this paper is organized as follows. We first review the activity graph representation of clinical practice guidelines and answer set programming in Sect. 2. The formal definition of the problem of concurrent application of CPGs to a patient's comorbid diseases is given in Sect. 3. In Sect. 4, an answer set programming based solution is presented. We then present the implementation of the ASP approach and the preliminary evaluation of the program in Sect. 5. Finally, conclusion is made in the last section of the paper.

2 Preliminary

The work reported in [11,12] focuses on the activity graphs that are used to represent a major portion of a CPG (e.g., in SAGE [17]). We will recall activity graphs in the first subsection, and introduce some background knowledge about Answer Set Programming in the second subsection.

2.1 Activity Graph for CPGs

An activity graph (AG) is a directed graph that consists of context, action and decision nodes. A context node is the root node of the AG and it defines a clinical context where the CPG is applied to. As an example, "patient diagnosed with TIA" is the root node of the AG for transient ischemic attack (TIA) (Fig. 1 right). An action is a clinical action to be performed according to the guideline. An example is "take aspirin." A decision step represents a decision point in a guideline. For example, a decision step in the guideline for TIA is whether hypoglycaemia is present. Decision nodes can be further divided into OR or XOR nodes. The former indicates more than one alternative can be resulted

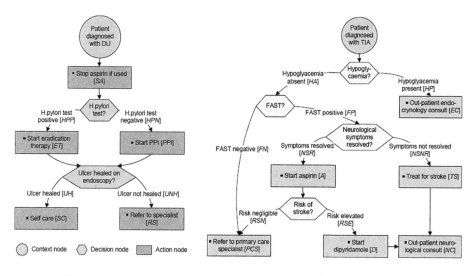

Fig. 1. Activity Graphes for DU (left) and TIA (right) (from [12])

from a decision node while the later means that only one alternative can be resulted from the decision node. Figure 1 left shows an example of the AGs for duodenal ulcer (DU) and TIA. For every disease (clinical context) we assume there is one and only one clinical practice guideline for it and one and only one activity graph for it.

2.2   Answer Set Programming

We now give a brief introduction of answer set programming and refer the interested reader to the book [14] for more details.

Answer set programming originates from non-monotonic logic and logic programming. It is a logic programming paradigm based on the answer set semantics [14,18], which particularly offers an elegant declarative semantics to the negation as failure operator in Prolog. An ASP program consists of *rules* in the form:

$$l_0 | \ldots | l_k \ :- \ l_{k+1}, \ldots, l_m, not\ l_{m+1}, \ldots, not\ l_n.$$

where each l_i for $i \in [0..n]$ is a literal of some signature, i.e., an expression of the form $p(t)$ or $\neg p(t)$ where p is a predicate and t is a term, and *not* is called *negation as failure* or *default negation* and | epistemic disjunction. A rule without body is called a *fact*, and a rule without head is called a *denial*. The rule is read as: if one believes $l_{k+1}, \ldots$, and l_m and there is no reason to believe $l_{m+1}, \ldots$, and l_n, one must believe $l_0, l_1, \ldots$, or l_k. The answer set semantics of a program P assigns to P a collection of answer sets, i.e., interpretations of the signature of P corresponding to possible sets of beliefs (i.e., literals). These beliefs can be built by a rational reasoner by following the principles that the rules of P must be satisfied and that one shall not believe anything unless one is forced to believe.

There have been several research groups developing and maintaining high quality efficient ASP solvers. Examples include DLV [15], and Clasp [16]. These solvers have been employed to successfully solve problems ranging from monitoring elderly people in nursing homes [19] to decision support systems for the space shuttle controllers [20].

3   Definition of the Reconciling Problem

In this section, based on graphs, we define the reconciling problem in the concurrent application of CPGs to a patient with two diseases. We first define activity graph obtainable from the CPG for a disease, candidate treatment for a disease using the activity graph, and valid treatment. We then define point of contention, i.e., conflicts, among candidate treatments and the mitigation operation to remove the conflicts. Finally, we define the reconciling problem.

3.1   Candidate Treatment

Definition 1 (Activity Graph). *An* activity graph *of a CPG of a disease is a directed graph with labels on some edges* $(CN \cup AN \cup DN_o \cup DN_{xor}, E, l : E \to L)$ *where*

- $CN, AN, DN_o, DN_{xor}, L$ *are disjoint sets,*
- $CN = \{x\}$ *and* x *is called the* context node,
- *Elements of* AN, DN_o, DN_{xor}, L *are called* action nodes, or-decision nodes, xor-decision nodes, *and* labels *respectively,*
- $E \subseteq V \times V$, *where* $V = CN \cup AN \cup DN_o \cup DN_{xor}$ *and an element* (x, y) *of* E *is called* an edge, *an* incoming edge *of* y *and an* outgoing edge *of* x, *such that there is no incoming edge for the context node and for any non decision node there is at most one outgoing edge,*
- l, *called a* labeling function, *is a partial function from edges to labels such that* $l((x, y))$ *is always defined if* x *is a decision node.*

The activity graph shown in the left of Fig. 1 is as follows: $CN = \{du\}$ where du is the shorthand for "Patient diagnosed with DU" for convenience, $AN = \{sa, et, ppi, sc, rs\}$ (note that these names in the figure are in capital letters), $DN_o = \emptyset$, $DN_{xor} = \{htest, uhe\}$ where $htest$ is for "H. pylori test?" and uhe for "Ulcer healed on endoscopy?"

$$E = \{(du, sa), (sa, htest), (htest, et), (htest, ppi),$$
$$(et, uhe), (ppi, uhe), (uhe, sc), (uhe, rs)\},$$

$L = \{hpp, hpn, uh, unh\}$, and the labeling function l labels outgoing edges of decision nodes as follows: $l((htest, et)) = hpp$, $l((htest, ppi)) = hpn$, $l((uhe, sc)) = uh$, $l((uhe, rs)) = unh$.

For treatment oriented CPGs, an important task is to follow them to find a treatment with the given patient information. We now define the candidate treatment with respect to a CPG of a disease.

Definition 2 (Candidate Treatment). *A candidate treatment is the collection of actions of a subgraph H of G such that*

- *the context node of G belongs to H,*
- *every node of H is reachable from the context node wrt H,*
- *for every node x of H, there is a node y of H that is a leaf node of G such that y is reachable from x in H, and*
- *for every xor-decision-node x of H, its outgoing degree wrt H is one.*

H *is called an* underlying graph *of the candidate treatment.*

It is worth noting that or-decision may cause two or more decision options to be satisfied. Therefore, in our definition of candidate treatment we allow parallel outgoing edges from an or-decision node. We also note an interpretation of or-decision is that external preference information is usually used to help choose one of the several outgoing edges. With preference information given, the underlying graph of a candidate treatment is reduced to a path in the activity graph.

For simplicity, we assume that for any candidate treatment, there is a unique underlying graph without loss of generality. The majority of CPGs have xor-decision-node only. In this case, a candidate treatment is a path from the context node to a leaf node. In the left graph of Fig. 1, there are totally four candidate treatments for patients diagnosed with DU (chronic condition):

- T_1^{du}: $\{sa, et, sc\}$ with the underlying path $du \to sa \to hpt \to uhd \to et \to sc$.
- T_2^{du}: $\{sa, ppi, sc\}$ with the underlying path $du \to sa \to hpt \to uhd \to ppi \to sc$.
- T_3^{du}: $\{sa, et, rs\}$ with the underlying path $du \to sa \to hpt \to uhd \to et \to rs$.
- T_4^{du}: $\{sa, ppi, rs\}$ with the underlying path $du \to sa \to hpt \to uhd \to ppi \to rs$.

The right graph of Fig. 1 presents five candidate treatments for patients with TIA where *tia* is for "Patient diagnosed with TIA," *hc* is for "Hypoglycaemia?" *nsrtest* for "Neurological symptoms resolved?" and *rstest* for "Risk of stroke?"

- T_1^{tia}: $\{ec\}$ with the underlying path $tia \to ec$.
- T_2^{tia}: $\{pcs\}$ with the underlying path $tia \to hc \to fast \to pcs$.
- T_3^{tia}: $\{a, pcs\}$ with the underlying path $tia \to hc \to fast \to nsrtest \to a \to rstest \to pcs$.
- T_4^{tia}: $\{a, d, nc\}$ with the underlying path $tia \to hc \to fast \to nsrtest \to a \to rstest \to d \to nc$.
- T_5^{tia}: $\{ts, nc\}$ with the underlying path $tia \to hc \to fast \to nsrtest \to ts \to nc$.

3.2   Valid Treatment

For a patient with comorbid diseases, inconsistencies are often introduced in the possible treatments because of the amalgamation of multiple guidelines. We give the definition of the related concepts as follows.

Given two candidate treatments T_1, T_2 wrt two activity graphs G_1 and G_2 respectively, and a collection I of sets, called *incompatible sets*[1], of actions, a

---

[1] Many incompatible sets are known facts are directly from the medical field.

set AS of actions is a *point of contention* (POC for short) between T_1 and T_2 if every action of AS is an action of T_1 or T_2 and $AS \in I$.

For example, start aspirin a and stop aspirin sa form an incompatible set[2] $\{sa, a\}$. Suppose there is an ulcer patient diagnosed with transient ischemic attack. A point of contention between T_1^{du} and T_3^{tia} is $\{sa, a\}$.

When there are point of contentions between candidate treatments for two diseases, one can find ways to mitigate the point of contention. Mitigation operator is defined by Wilk et al. [12] as follows.

A *mitigation operator* (MO) for disease d_1 and d_2 is a tuple (d_1, d_2, *contentions, LHS, RHS, toBeRemoved*) where

- d_1 is called a *base disease* and d_2 a *target disease*,
- *contentions* is a set of actions from the activity graphs for d_1 and d_2,
- *LHS* and *RHS* are a set of elements, called *action literals* of the form *pos(A)* or *neg(A)* where A is a medical action that may or may not be an action of activity graphes of d_1 or d_2,
- toBeRemoved is a set of actions of activity graph of d_2.

For example, the following MO1 and MO2 are MOs for TIA and UD addressing the point of contention $\{a, sa\}$.

- MO1: (*tia, du,* $\{sa, a\}$, $\{pos(a), neg(d)\}$,$\{neg(a), pos(cl)\}$, $\{sa\}$).
- MO2: (*tia, du,* $\{sa, a\}$, $\{pos(a), pos(d)\}$,$\{pos(a), pos(d), pos(ppi)\}$, $\{sa\}$).

Given candidate treatment T_1 and T_2 wrt activity graph G_1 of disease d_1 and activity graph G_2 of disease d_2, an MO $\alpha=(d_1, d_2,$ *contentions, LHS, RHS, toBeRemoved*) for d_1 and d_2 is *relevant* to T_1 and T_2 if *contentions* is a subset of $T_1 \cup T_2$. An MO is *applicable to* T_1 and T_2 if it is relevant and for every *pos(A)* $\in LHS$, action $A \in T_1$, and for every *neg(A)* $\in LHS$, action $A \notin T_1$. Suppose α is applicable to T_1 and T_2, the *modified treatment* by applying α to T_1 and T_2 is T_1' and T_2' where

- $T_1' = \{A : pos(A) \in RHS$or $(A \in T_1$ but A occurs neither in LHS nor RHS)$\}$, and
- $T_2' = T_2 - toBeRemoved$.

Continue the example above. For T_1^{du} and T_3^{tia}, there is a point of contention $\{a, sa\}$ between them. MO1 is applicable and can be used to modify T_1^{du} and T_3^{tia}. By definition, the modified treatments of applying MO1 to T_1^{du} and T_3^{tia} are as follows: $T_3^{tia'}$: $\{cl, pcs\}$ and $T_1^{du'} = \{et, sc\}$.

We next define treatments targeting a specific patient's situation.

Definition 3 (Patient Information). *We define* Patient Information *(PI) as a set of pairs* (decision, value) *where* decision *is a decision node and* value *is a label of an outgoing edge of the node* decision *in G. A candidate treatment T agrees with* patient information I, *if for every decision node x and every edge (x, y) of the underlying graph of T, $(x, val) \in I$ where val is the label of (x, y).*

---

[2] They are logically inconsistent.

For example, both T_3^{tia} and T_4^{tia} agree with PI $\{(hc, ha), (fast, fp), (nsrtest, nsr)\}$ (for ha, fp, see the right graph of Fig. 1).

Definition 4 (Valid Treatment). *Given PI I of a patient, with two diseases, and candidate treatments T_1 and T_2 for these diseases respectively, $T_1 \cup T_2$ is a valid treatment with respect to I if T_1 and T_2 agree with I, and there is no point of contention between T_1 and T_2.*

Definition 5 (Reconciling Problem). *Given PI I of a patient with diseases D_1 and D_2 and a set of MOs for D_1 and D_2, the reconciling problem is to find a valid treatment with respect to I if there exists one, and otherwise find if there are candidate treatment T_1 and T_2 such that their modified treatment T_1' and T_2' by applying some of the MOs are valid.*

For example, let the PI of an ulcer patient diagnosed with transient stroke be $\{(hc, ha), (fast, fp), (nsrtest, nsr)\}$. Clearly, the candidate treatments for ulcer and transient stroke that agree with PI are T_3^{tia}, T_4^{tia} and $T_1^{du}, T_2^{du}, T_3^{du}, T_4^{du}$ respectively. There is no valid treatment for the patient because of a point of contention $\{sa, a\}$ between each pair of the candidate treatments. By applying MO1 to T_3^{tia} and T_1^{du}, we get a valid modified treatment $T_3^{tia'} \cup T_1^{du'}$ where $T_3^{tia'} = \{cl, pcs\}$ and $T_1^{du'} = \{et, sc\}$ as illustrated in the earlier example.

4   ASP Based Solution

In this section, we present an ASP based solution of finding a valid (modified) treatment for patients with comorbid diseases according to the CPGs for these diseases and mitigation operators.

Representation of an Activity Graph. We first introduce the predicates needed to represent the activity graph g for a disease d: cNode(g,ct) – ct is the context node of g, aNode(g,Action) – *Action* is an action node of g, oNode(g,N) – N is an or decision node, xNode(g,N) – N is an xor decision node, edge(g, X, Y) – (X, Y) is an edge of g, label(g, X, Y, L) – the label on the edge (X, Y) is L. A given activity graph will be represented as facts using the predicates above.

Define Candidate Treatments. To specify a valid (modified) treatment, we first need to define a candidate treatment. In turn we need to construct a subgraph H of an activity graph G by Definition 2. By candidateEdge(G, X, Y), we mean the edge (X, Y) is in H. The following rule is to define H:

```
candidateEdge(G, X, Y) | ¬candidateEdge(G, X, Y)
        :- node(G,X), not decisionNode(G, X).
```

which reads that any edge (X, Y) of G can be an edge of H. We will next present ASP rules to make sure H is the underlying graph of a candidate treatment by Definition 2.

First, the context node of an activity graph G must be a node of H. Note that we know only edges of H but not the nodes of H. Now we need a predicate nodeInH(G, N) to denote N is a node of H. It can be defined as:

```
nodeInH(G, X) :- candidateEdge(G, X, Y).
nodeInH(G, Y) :- candidateEdge(G, X, Y).
```

which can be read as any end of an edge (X, Y) of H is a node of H.

Now the rule :- cNode(G, CN), not nodeInH(G, CN). says that if CN is a context node, it must be in H.

Second, every node of H is reachable from the context node in H. We first define the reachability (reachable(G, X, Y) denotes that node Y is reachable from X in H) in a standard way:

```
reachable(G, X, X):- cNode(G,X).
reachable(G, X, Y):- candidateEdge(G,X,Y).
reachable(G, X, Y):- reachable(G,X,Z), candidateEdge(G,Z,Y).
```

The rule below restricts that for every node X of H, X must be reachable from the context node Cn:

```
:- nodeInH(G, X), cNode(G, Cn), not reachable(H, Cn, X).
```

Thirdly, every node of H reaches a leaf node. It is not hard to define a leaf node and use reachable to express this constraints. Rules are omitted here due to lack of space.

Finally, for every *xor* node of H, its outgoing degree must be one. We first define the existence of an outgoing edge for a node X:

```
existsOutgoingEdge(G, X) :- candidateEdge(G, X, Y).
```

Since there is at most one outgoing edge from an action node in any activity graph, the rule

```
:- nodeInH(G, X), xNode(G, X),
   not existsOutgoingEdge(H, X).
```

is sufficient to restrict that for any node X of H, it has one outgoing edge.

Now we are in a position to define a candidate treatment using H. It is not hard to write a rule to define action InH(G, X) which holds if X is an action node of H. We omit the rule here.

Define Valid Treatments. Given a patient information I, we present the ASP rules that encode patient information, the agreement of a candidate treatment to patient information, and the points of contention and finally a valid treatment, in terms of the corresponding definitions given in the previous section.

Patient Information. We use bDisease(d_1) to denote that d_1 is the base disease, tDdisease(d_2) to denote d_2 is the target disease, and patientInfo(x,l) to denote the value of the decision node x is l. The patient information is represented as facts using the predicates above.

Agreement of a Candidate Treatment to the Patient Information. For every decision node, it should agree with the patient information on this node, i.e., for any or-decision node X and any `patientInfo(X, L)` with `(X, Y)` labeled by L, `(X, Y)` must be a candidate edge:

```
:- decision Node(G, X), nodeInH(G, X), patientInfo(X,L),
     label(AG, X, Y, L), not candidateEdge(G, X, Y).
```

Note here for any or-decision node, its outgoing edges in H correspond to a superset of the values on this node given by the patient information.

Incompatible Sets. For every incompatible set, we assign an id (index) for it and include in the program the fact `incompSet(index)`. For every action a in the incompatible set with id `index`, we have the fact `ncompSetAction(index, a)`.

POC of Two Treatments. We need a notion of active action here. An action is *active* if it is in a candidate treatment wrt a disease:

```
active(X):- action InH (H, X).
```

An incompatible set is *active* if all its actions are active. Clearly, an active incompatible set is a POC. We first define a non active incompatible set **non ActiveIncompSet** which is then used to define POC using default negation.

```
nonActiveIncompSet(Index) :-
     not active(X),
     incompSetAction(Index, X).

isPOC(Index) :-
     incompSet(Index),
     not nonActiveIncompSet(Index).
```

We use `existsPOC` to denote the occurrence of a POC between two candidate treatments:

```
existsPOC :- isPOC(Index).
```

Valid Treatment. The last condition for candidate treatments to be valid is that they are POC free:

```
:~ existsPOC.
```

Here we use a new ASP construct called *weak constraints* first introduced in DLV. This weak constraint means that there should not be `existsPOC` in any answer set if it is possible at all. However, `existsPOC` is allowed to be in an answer set if there is no other choice.

Valid Modified Treatments. In this part, we present the ASP rules that apply mitigation operators to eliminate the points of contention between two candidate treatments.

Represent an MO. For every mitigation operator of the form (bD, tD, POC= {a1, ..., ak}, LHS={aL1, ..., aLn}, RHS={aR1, ..., aRm}, toBeRemoved={a11, ..., a1i}), we associate a unique identifier id for it, which is represented by the fact: `moId(id)`. The base disease and target disease in the MO with id are represented by: moBD(id, bD) and moTD(id, tD) respectively. For every action in the POC of the MO with id, we have moPOC(id, a). For every action literal aL of LHS and aR of RHS of the MO with id, we have moLHS(id, aL) and moRHS(id, aR). For every action a in toBeRemoved of the MO with id, we have moToBeRemoved(id, a).

A Relevant MO. We use a method similar to that for active POC to define relevant MO's. The rules are omitted here. We use relevant(I, ID) to denote that the active POC with id I is relevant to the MO with id ID.

Applicability of an MO. Atom applicable(I, ID) denotes that an MO with id ID is applicable to a POC with id of I. The method for defining active POC can be used to define the applicability too. Rules again are not included here due to lack of space.

Generate MO's to Address POC. Let atom applyMO(I, ID) denote that the MO with id ID will be applied to mitigate the POC with id I. It is defined by

    1{applyMO(I, ID): applicable(I, ID)}1 :- isPOC(I).

The new ASP construct 1{applyMO(I, ID): applicable(I, ID)}1 means that for a POC I, we may choose to apply any applicable MO to the POC with id I.

Apply an MO to the Candidate Treatments. Since we do not know the POC beforehand, our generator will "guess" an MO to apply to the POC if there is any. Atom applyMO(I, ID) denotes that the MO with id ID will be applied to mitigate the POC with id I. We use modifiedTreatment(D, A) to denote that A is an action for the disease D after applying the MOs. By the definition of modified treatment, we have the rule for the modified treatment for the target disease (rules for base disease are omitted):

```
modifiedTreatment(TD, Action)  :-
        actionInH (TD, Action),
        applyMO(Index, MOID),
        moTD(MOID, TD),
        not moToBeRemoved(MOID, Action).
```

Valid Modified Treatments. Similarly to the definition of the POCs of candidate treatments, we can write similar rules to define POCs between the modified treatments. Rules are omitted here. Let existsPOC_M denote the existence of POC between modified treatments. To have free POCs between modified treatments, we need rule:

        :- existsPOC_M.

Proposition 3. Given patient information I of a patient with diseases d_1 and d_2, let Π be the program obtained from the discussion above. Assume there is no valid treatment for d_1 and d_2. T_1' and T_2', without any POC between them, are the modified treatment resulted from the application of some MOs to some candidate treatments T_1 and T_2 which agree with I, if and only if there is an answer set S of Π such that $T_1' = \{a : modifiedTreatment(d_1, a)\} \in S$, and $T_2' = \{a : modifiedTreatment(d_2, a) \in S\}$.

5   Evaluation

We have implemented the proposed ASP approach using DLV. A major reason to use DLV, instead of other ASP solvers, is its capacity to represent weak constraints which are convenient for this application. However, since DLV does not support choice rules yet, in our implementation, we have translated the choice rules using epistemic disjunctions. The translation technique is well known in the ASP community [21].

The program consists of two parts. The first part is the general knowledge, shared by all CPGs, to generate candidate treatments, identify POC's, and find relevant and applicable MO's, if there is a POC, and apply them to obtain a valid modified treatment. The second part consists of the representation of activity graphs of the CPGs, MO's, and patient information.

The DLV implementation of the ASP solution is straightforward. In contrast, we are not aware of experimental results in the existing work.

To evaluate the program, we consider the CPGs for duodenal ulcer (DU) and transient ischemic attack (TIA) that are used by Wilk et al. in [12]. These CPGs (Fig. 1) include only the crucial actions and decision nodes of the guidelines published by the National Institute for Health and Clinical Excellence, UK (NICE) [10].

As for mitigated operators for patients with both DU and TIA, we use MO1 and MO2, in the section of the definition of the reconciling problem, in our implementation.

We assume a patient has both conditions of DU and TIA. We consider two scenarios based on the report in [10]. The first is that the patient has a positive result for the H. Pylori test, negative result for hypoglycemia test, and negtive result for the FAST test. In this scenario, there is no POC. Our program output one valid treatment (by guessing a result for decision nodes whose result is unknown) for DU: {sa (stop aspirin if used), et (start eradication therapy), sc (self care)}, and one valid treatment for TIA:

{pcs (refer to primary care specialist)}.

In the second scenario, some adverse interaction is present. The patient has a negative result for the H. pylori test, negative result for the hypoglycemia test, positive result for the FAST test, and has had neurological symptoms resolved. In this scenario, there is an adverse interaction between the actions of *stopping aspirin* and *starting aspirin*. Some relevant mitigation operator has to be employed to find a new valid treatment. A valid treatment found by our program for DU is {ppi (start PPI), sc (self care)}, and that for TIA is {cl (clopidogrel), pcs (refer to primary care specialist)} where aspirin is replaced by clopidogrel.

We run the program on a Sony Vaio laptop with Intel i5 CPU at 2.53GHz, 4GB memory and Windows 7. The DLV solver we used is the version of *build BEN/Dec 21 2011*. The real time to run the above two scenarios is 0 second (i.e., not detectable by DLV solver).

The program together with the two scenarios is downloadable at http://redwood.cs.ttu.edu/~yzhang/temp/KR-14/code-coMorbidity-dlv.lp.

6   Related Work and Conclusion

We note some recent work on the study of treatment of comorbid patients. The first one by Riano and Collado [22] focuses on using rules to represent the MO's and acquiring these rules for Hypertension, Diabetes Mellitus and Heart Failure. In both Wilk et al's and our work, we assume the MO's are given. The second one is by Lopez-Vallverdu et al. [23]. They propose a model combining treatments based on the seriousness, evolution and acuteness of the patients' condition and examine a specific case for Hypertension and Heart Failure. However, they did not cover POC's and their mitigation.

The main ideas underlying the reported work here are from Wilk et al.'s work in identifying the point of contention between two treatments and employing MO's to mitigate the contention [10,12].

The major difference between our work and Wilk et al.'s lies in the separation of the definition of the problem from programming languages and algorithms. Specifically, we present a mathematical definition of the problem of mitigating the point of contention that may occur in treatments for two diseases when two CPGs for these diseases are used. We then offer a purely declarative ASP based solution which naturally models the original problem. The major advantages of our proposal is as follows. First, it is more accessible for the medical researchers to evaluate how closely the defined problem models the real problems involved in comorbidities. Second, the formal definition of the problem allows the discussion of the correctness of the proposed solutions. Our ASP based solution facilitates the proof of its correctness. Thirdly, our ASP based solution will benefit from the the well developed and maintained efficient ASP solvers. Fourthly, some key issues, such as dealing with more parallel paths, raised by Wilk et al. [10] can be addressed in a natural way by our approach. For example, the parallel paths problem has been addressed in our current problem definition and solution.

The proposed ASP based solution is easy to implement and efficient to address some scenarios reported in the literature. Clearly the current definition of the reconciling problem does not include the temporal information and how to balance the treatment to maximize the patients' outcome. In the next step, we will work with medical professionals to refine the problem definition to better reflect the real practice in solving the problems related to comorbidity issues. We also plan to write ASP program for a complete CPG, which will help us further understand the limitations of the ASP approach and investigate how to address those challenges.

Acknowlegment. We would like to thank Michael Gelfond and Samson Tu for discussions on this subject. Yuanlin Zhang's work is partially supported by the NSF grants IIS-1018031 and CNS-1359359. Zhizheng Zhang's work is partially supported by Project 60803061 and 61272378 sponsored by National Natural Science Foundation of China, and Project BK2008293 by Natural Science Foundation of Jiangsu.

References

1. Jakovljević, M., Ostojić, L.: Comorbidity and multimorbidity in medicine today: challenges and opportunities for bringing separated branches of medicine closer to each other. Psychiatr. Danub. **1**, 18–28 (2013)
2. Field, M.J., Lohr, K.N., et al.: Guidelines for Clinical Practice: From Development to Use. National Academies Press, Washington (1992)
3. Peleg, M., Tu, S., Bury, J., Ciccarese, P., Fox, J., Greenes, R.A., Hall, R., Johnson, P.D., Jones, N., Kumar, A., et al.: Comparing computer-interpretable guideline models: a case-study approach. J. Am. Med. Inf. Assoc. **10**(1), 52–68 (2003)
4. de Clercq, P.A., Blom, J.A., Korsten, H.H., Hasman, A.: Approaches for creating computer-interpretable guidelines that facilitate decision support. Artif. Intell. Med. **31**(1), 1–27 (2004)
5. Isern, D., Moreno, A.: Computer-based execution of clinical guidelines: a review. Int. J. Med. Inf. **77**(12), 787–808 (2008)
6. Boyd, C.M., Darer, J., Boult, C., Fried, L.P., Boult, L., Wu, A.W.: Clinical practice guidelines and quality of care for older patients with multiple comorbid diseases. JAMA J. Am. Med. Assoc. **294**(6), 716–724 (2005)
7. Sittig, D.F., Wright, A., Osheroff, J.A., Middleton, B., Teich, J.M., Ash, J.S., Campbell, E., Bates, D.W.: Grand challenges in clinical decision support. J. Biomed. Inf. **41**(2), 387–392 (2008)
8. Real, F., Riaño, D.: An autonomous algorithm for generating and merging clinical algorithms. In: Riaño, D. (ed.) K4HelP 2008. LNCS, vol. 5626, pp. 13–24. Springer, Heidelberg (2009)
9. Abidi, S.R., Abidi, S.S.R.: Towards the merging of multiple clinical protocols and guidelines via ontology-driven modeling. In: Combi, C., Shahar, Y., Abu-Hanna, A. (eds.) AIME 2009. LNCS, vol. 5651, pp. 81–85. Springer, Heidelberg (2009)
10. Wilk, S., Michalowski, W., Michalowski, M., Farion, K., Hing, M.M., Mohapatra, S., et al.: Mitigation of adverse interactions in pairs of clinical practice guidelines using constraint logic programming. J. Biomed. Inf. **46**(2), 341–353 (2013)
11. Michalowski, M., Mainegra Hing, M., Wilk, S., Michalowski, W., Farion, K.: A constraint logic programming approach to identifying inconsistencies in clinical practice guidelines for patients with comorbidity. In: Peleg, M., Lavrač, N., Combi, C. (eds.) AIME 2011. LNCS, vol. 6747, pp. 296–301. Springer, Heidelberg (2011)
12. Wilk, S., Michalowski, M., Michalowski, W., Hing, M.M., Farion, K.: Reconciling pairs of concurrently used clinical practice guidelines using constraint logic programming. In: AMIA Annual Symposium Proceedings. American Medical Informatics Association, vol. 2011, p. 944 (2011)
13. McCarthy, J.: Elaboration tolerance. In: Common Sense, vol. 98, Citeseer (1998)
14. Gelfond, M., Kahl, Y.: Knowledge Representation, Reasoning, and the Design of Intelligent Agents. Manuscript (2013)
15. Faber, W., Pfeifer, G., Leone, N., Dell'armi, T., Ielpa, G.: Design and implementation of aggregate functions in the dlv system. Theory. Pract. Log. Program. **8**(5–6), 545–580 (2008)
16. Gebser, M., Kaufmann, B., Schaub, T.: Conflict-driven answer set solving: from theory to practice. Artif. Intell. **187–188**, 52–89 (2012)
17. Tu, S.W., Campbell, J.R., Glasgow, J., Nyman, M.A., McClure, R., McClay, J., Parker, C., Hrabak, K.M., Berg, D., Weida, T., et al.: The sage guideline model: achievements and overview. J. Am. Med. Inf. Assoc. **14**(5), 589–598 (2007)

18. Gelfond, M., Lifschitz, V.: The stable model semantics for logic programming. In: Proceedings of ICLP-88, pp. 1070–1080 (1988)
19. Mileo, A., Merico, D., Pinardi, S., Bisiani, R.: A logical approach to home health-care with intelligent sensor-network support. Comput. J. **53**(8), 1257–1276 (2010)
20. Nogueira, M., Balduccini, M., Gelfond, M., Watson, R., Barry, M.: An A-Prolog decision support system for the Space Shuttle. In: Provetti, A., Son, T.C. (eds.) Answer Set Programming: Towards Efficient and Scalable Knowledge Representation and Reasoning. AAAI 2001 Spring Symposium Series, March 2001
21. Baral, C.: Knowledge Representation, Reasoning, and Declarative Problem Solving. Cambridge University Press, Cambridge (2003)
22. Riaño, D., Collado, A.: Model-based combination of treatments for the management of chronic comorbid patients. In: Peek, N., Marín Morales, R., Peleg, M. (eds.) AIME 2013. LNCS, vol. 7885, pp. 11–16. Springer, Heidelberg (2013)
23. López-Vallverdú, J.A., Riaño, D., Collado, A.: Rule-based combination of comorbid treatments for chronic diseases applied to hypertension, diabetes mellitus and heart failure. In: Lenz, R., Miksch, S., Peleg, M., Reichert, M., Riaño, D., ten Teije, A. (eds.) ProHealth 2012 and KR4HC 2012. LNCS, vol. 7738, pp. 30–41. Springer, Heidelberg (2013)

Towards a Conceptual Model for Enhancing Reasoning About Clinical Guidelines
A Case-Study on Comorbidity

Veruska Zamborlini[1,2]([✉]), Marcos da Silveira[2], Cédric Pruski[2],
Annette ten Teije[1], and Frank van Harmelen[1]

[1] VU University Amsterdam, Amsterdam, The Netherlands
{annette,frank.van.harmelen}@cs.vu.nl
[2] Public Research Center Henri Tudor, Esch-sur-Alzette, Luxembourg
v.carrettazamborlini@vu.nl, marcos.dasilveira@cs.vu.nl,
cedric.pruski@tudor.lu

Abstract. Computer-Interpretable Guidelines (CIGs) are representations of Clinical Guidelines (CGs) in computer interpretable languages. CIGs have been pointed as an alternative to deal with the various limitations of paper based CGs to support healthcare activities. Although the improvements offered by existing CIG languages, the complexity of the medical domain requires advanced features in order to reuse, share, update, combine or personalize their contents. We propose a conceptual model for representing the content of CGs as a result from an iterative approach that take into account the content of real CGs, CIGs languages and foundational ontologies in order to enhance the reasoning capabilities required to address CIG use-cases. In particular, we apply our approach to the comorbidity use-case and illustrate the model with a realistic case study (Duodenal Ulcer and Transient Ischemic Attack) and compare the results against an existing approach.

1 Introduction

Clinical guidelines (CGs) assemble statements provided by the best available evidences. Their goal is to assist healthcare professionals on the definition of the appropriate treatment and care for people with specific diseases and conditions. A formalised representation of CGs, called computer-interpretable guideline (CIGs), has been proposed to overcome some limitations of paper based CGs using dedicated languages (e.g., PROforma [13], GLIF [3], Asbru [8]). It can be integrated to health information systems to support health professionals in their daily practice. Although being expressive, existing CIG specification languages are designed for one main objective: to execute the guideline.

However, the evolving requirements from the medical field combined with the properties of information systems, demand other advanced features. These new

Veruska Zamborlini — Funded by CNPq (Brazilian National Council for Scientific and Technological Development) within the program Science without Borders.

S. Miksch et al. (Eds.): KR4HC 2014, LNAI 8903, pp. 29–44, 2014.
DOI: 10.1007/978-3-319-13281-5_3

requirements are mainly motivated to tackle problems like comorbidity (combining guidelines to define appropriate treatments for patients suffering from several diseases), CG update (taking into account new findings from clinical studies) or treatment personalization (taking into account patients preferences).

To cope with these kind of problems, CIGs must be improved in order to offer more *reasoning capabilities*. For instance, considering a patient that suffers from Duodenum Ulcer (DU) and from Transient Ischemic Attack (TIA). Two different guidelines need to be combined to define a treatment. But, a closer analysis of them shows that these guidelines lead to adverse interactions when combined. CIGs combinations, detections of conflicts, and inclusions of information have not been the focus of existing CIGs description languages and their underling editing and execution tools. Therefore, a representation language is needed that enables reasoning over CG information for several tasks like combining or updating CIGs.

In this paper, we introduce a new conceptual model to enhance the reasoning capabilities of CIGs. The elements of the proposed model are identified following an iterative approach to explicitly represent the semantics of recommendations and medical actions. The reasoning capabilities of the proposed model have been assessed on a realistic case study dealing with conflicts detection and solving in case of comorbidity. The remainder of the paper is structured as follows: Sect. 2 presents the analysis of the related work. In Sect. 3 we propose a conceptualization of our model before applying it to the comorbidity use case in general, and then to a particular case study (stroke + ulcer). In Sect. 4 we discuss the results and future work and wrap up with concluding remarks in Sect. 5.

2   Related Work

Several CIGs description languages are proposed in the literature. They provide different methods to model the content of CGs into CIGs. Studies comparing these languages had highlighted the qualities and the scope of each one [5,9]. They mainly analysed three aspects: (1) the edition and execution of CIGs, (2) the capacity to collaborate with other systems, and (3) the dissemination properties. Isern and Moreno [5] centred their study on the editing and execution tools. They underline that the interoperability between systems is the most important barrier to overcome in order to promote CIGs. A standard description language and a standard electronic health record (EHR) would help the progress in this domain and avoid development of ad hoc solutions.

However, Peleg [9] pointed out the difficulty to define a standard language that integrate the different components of each language, and proposes to start by splitting CIGs into small size knowledge chunks. She argues that defining small chunks of decision logics will contribute to cope with three complex and important problems: sharing/reusing, combining and maintaining knowledge. In this paper, we propose a model that is meant to address those problems, though we focus on the comorbidity issue.

With the increasing of aged population and the frequency of comorbidities, this subject has been considered as an important topic of research in the medical domain. Consequently, there is a high demand for computer systems that support medical researches in comorbidity. Recent publications propose semi-automatic combinations of CIGs, some of which we summarize hereafter. Authors claim that existing languages were not designed to address this problem and they propose new CIG representation formalisms for it.

Jafarpour and Abidi [6] adopted OWL to describe CIGs. They also built a merging representation ontology to capture merging criteria in order to achieve the combination of CIGs. SWRL rules were used to identify potential conflicts during the merging process. All conditions related to the merging process need to be described by the rules, increasing the effort to maintain the system up-to-date, and reducing the possibility of sharing knowledge. However, some related problems were not yet (completely) addressed in their work, for instance, potential contradictions between rules, the scalability of the merging model to combine several CIGs, and how the ontology/rules are maintained up-to-date.

A different approach was proposed by Wilk et al. [15]. They describe CIGs as an activity graph and propose to use constraint logic programming (CLP) to identify conflicts associated with potentially contradictory and adverse activities resulting from applying two CGs to the same patient. The goal is to use this approach to alert physicians about potential conflicts during the definition of the treatment plan. The temporal aspect is not considered, thus the approach can only be applied to specific situations (e.g. acute diseases diagnosed during a single patient-physician encounter). Although their model allows reasoning over a subset of the CIGs content (the conditions) and propose possible conflict solutions, the whole work of combining CIGs remains manual. This approach also considers that all predicates use the same terminology and that they can have only two states (true or false). The case study used to demonstrate the applicability of the approach in [15] shows the complexity of combining CIGs and the necessity of external knowledge sources for taking decisions. Inspired on this case study we evaluate the applicability of our model in the comorbidity use case.

Another method to address the CIGs combination problem is proposed by Riano and Collado [11]. They define a language to describe CIGs as actions blocks and decision tables. A generic treatment model is proposed to decide which action is appropriate to a chronically comorbid patient, taking into account three criteria: seriousness, evolution, and acuteness. The expressivity of this language is intentionally limited in order to have a lightweight decision system. The combination of CIGs is the result of pairwise combination of CIGs entities (i.e., actions and decisions table) according to a set of rules that allow identifying conflicts and reorganising or merging actions (in specific and predefined situations). The simplified CIGs representation and the specification of more general rules (for merging tasks) increase the reasoning capability of the system and reduce the maintenance work effort. However, reorganising care actions can raise some problems, especially those related to the clinical validity of modifications. In this case, the evidence-based medicine must be assured in the rules of the generic treatment model. An alternative to this problem is to associate intentions and goals to the actions, as proposed by Latoszek-Berendsen et al. [7]. However, they do not consider combining CIGs and evaluating the role of intentions in this process.

The idea of evaluating pairwise actions associated to goals is exploited in the work of Sanchez-Garzon et al. [12]. They adopt the HTN plan description language to describe CIGs, and they use multi-agents techniques to generate treatment plans and identify potential conflicts between care actions. Treatment goals are considered to solve conflicts, but the assumption of all effects of an action is observed in the patient (and included in the patient data) limits the applicability of their approach. A probabilistic representation of effects would be closer to observations from evidence-based studies, but it would increase the complexity of the reasoning. Although the good preliminary results claimed by the authors, the low interoperability and the complexity of maintenance of agents has been underlined in several publications as a challenge of the domain.

In the referred approaches the care actions are represented as textual information (or labels) and their semantics is not clearly defined, for example, "*Start Aspirin*" and "*Stop Aspirin*" are represented as unrelated actions, what confirms the outcomes of Bonacin et al. [1]. Consequently a specific rule is required to define them as conflicting actions, while it could be automatically detected by reasoning over the meaning of the actions.

Moreover, few evidences about how these actions impact the patients' health state are formalized. For instance, the intention of an action for a specific treatment, their potential effects (desired and side-effects) and the situation (describing the context). Understanding the semantics of the care actions and the related impacts is considered as an important source of information to increase the reasoning capabilities and better explain the causes of conflict [1].

Another potential advantage of having less constraints and more detailed actions is the reduction of required maintenance efforts. New findings about one action can easily be integrated to the CIGs without requiring a whole analysis of the impact of these changes. Collaborative work to specify care actions can also promote the reuse of knowledge chunks, facilitating CIGs construction/update. In this paper we aim to provide a more detailed semantics for care actions and recommendations, and to evaluate the benefits for the use-case of comorbidity.

3   The TMR Model

We present in this section the Transition-based Medical Recommendation (TMR) Model for Clinical Guidelines, a conceptual model designed to capture the core knowledge structure for CGs. The purpose is to favor the reasoning capabilities required by different CIG use cases, like combining CIGs to deal with comorbidity. On what follows we present the conceptualization adopted for our model and its application to the comorbidity use case.

3.1 Conceptualization

In order to investigate the knowledge structure in the CGs domain, we adopted an approach that involves studying several CGs, CIG languages, CIG use-cases and foundational ontologies. We adapted two example recommendations from a CG for Peptic Ulcer[1] to illustrate the concepts and issues to be handled:

- **Section 5**
  1. For patients with ulcer not associated with Helicobacter Pylori (HP), maximal dose of proton pump inhibitors (PPI) is recommended;
  2. For patients with ulcer caused by NSAID (non-steroid anti-inflammatory drugs), NSAID use should be discontinued.

According to Peleg [9], all current GIG languages provide some structure for representing **Actions** and **Decisions**. Considering a structure "if ... then ..." for representing the decision and the corresponding action, a representation for the mentioned example would be: (1) if *"ulcer is not caused by HP"* then *"administer PPI on maximum dose"*; and (2) if *"ulcer is caused by NSAID"* then *"do not administer NSAID"*. While the **Actions** represent the tasks described in a CG, the **Decisions** regard mainly the evaluation of context (Pre-Situations) that would enable to choose the appropriate actions. Moreover, few languages also provide support for expressing the potential effects of actions (Post-Situations) like Asbru and Proforma.

Some representation issues can be observed in the aforementioned example: (i) how to identify and represent the information that is implicit in the CG text itself, like the expected outcome for a recommended action; and (ii) how to represent "negative" actions such as in the example recommendation 2. A proper solution for these issues may enhance the capability of reasoning over the knowledge structure (the dosage is out of the scope in this work).

In order to guide our interpretation of the CG knowledge structure we use foundational (top-level) ontologies (such as UFO [4]) that define generic entities and its relations, e.g. actions and situations. Those theories provide means to justify the modeling choices made in a model. Although the study of those theories is an important part of our approach, it is not the goal of this paper to provide a precise ontologically-founded definition for the concepts.

In this work we select some entities in CG context as a small/core knowledge chunk to be analyzed and combined to represent more complex scenarios. The main concepts adopted in the TMR model for CG domain are summarized in Table 1, namely Situation Type, Care Action Type, Transition and Recommendation. We consider those concepts as being atomic, since the study of their compositionality is not in the scope of this work.

The aforementioned example is instantiated in Fig. 1 according to the TMR Model, also considering the implicit information required. An arrow connecting a **Recommendation** to a **Transition** means that the latter is recommended, whilst an arrow ended with a cross means that the **Transition** is non-recommended.

---

[1] http://www.aiha.com/en/WhatWeDo/PracticeGuidelines_CPGPI.asp

Table 1. TMR concepts summary

Situation type	Represents a property, which characterizes a patient, and its admissible values
Care action type	Represents the action types that can be performed by health care agents in order to change a situation
Transition	Represents the possibility of changing a situation regarding a patient by performing a care action type
Recommendation	Represents a suggestion to either pursue or avoid a transition promoted by a care action type

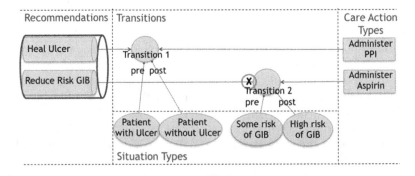

Fig. 1. Instance schema for the TMR model

The named dotted lines from a **Transition** to the **Situation Types** represent its **Pre/Post-Situation Types**, while an arrow between a **Care Action Type** and a **Transition** represent the possibility of achieving the referred post-situation by performing that action when the pre-situation is verified. Therefore, the recommendation named *heal ulcer* recommends for *"patients with ulcer"* the transition promoted by *"administer PPI"* in order to be *"(patient) without ulcer"*, while the recommendation named *"reduce risk GIB (gastrointestinal bleeding)"* non-recommends for *"(patients with) some risk of GIB"* the transition promoted by *"administer aspirin"* to avoid *"(patients with) high risk GIB"*.

We hereafter explain our modeling choices. Firstly we distinguish between instance (individual) and type (universal) levels. The instance level regards, for example, the action occurrence *"John takes PPI"* that leads from a pre-situation *"John with ulcer"* to a post-situation *"John without ulcer"*. The recommendations in CGs, however, do not regard the instance level, i.e. the factual situations and action occurrences, but the type level, i.e. the **Care Action Types** and **Situation Types**, as well as the relations between them. An example of care action type is *"Administer Aspirin"*, which can be performed by health care agents such as a physician, a nurse, or the patient itself, while an example of situation type is *"Patient with some risk of Gastro-Intestinal Bleeding (GIB)"*.

If in one hand an action occurrence directly relates pre and post-situations according to the promoted change, on the other hand an **Action Type** is expected to be related with one or more pairs of **Pre/Post Situation Types**. Indeed, Textor [14] mention the need of a space of outcomes for an action type (e.g. throwing a dice have 6 possible outcomes). Although in the medical domain the outcomes of an action type usually cannot be precisely and completely defined, they constitute the core knowledge that underlies the clinical recommendations. Indeed, the different changes that can be promoted by a care action type must be taken into account as desired or side-effects for a patient (type). For example, administering aspirin has two possible effects: anti-prostaglandin (anti-inflammation, fever-reducing, pain reliever) and anti-platelet ("blood thinner") agent. By inhibiting the formation of prostaglandins, aspirin deplete the protective barrier in the stomach against the acid substances, leading to peptic ulcers. Thus, for patients with bleeding risks or duodenal ulcer, aspirin may have a negative effect, while for patients with cardiovascular events risk, aspirin will have a positive impact.

Aligned to this idea, we introduce the concept **Transition** to relate a **Care Action Type** to **Pre/Post-Situation Types** and represents the possibility of achieving that change by performing the referred action. Thus, by assigning different transitions to a care action type, we define its *"space of transitions"*. Finally, the **Recommendation** can be seen as a commitment for health care agents to either pursue or avoid a transition, whilst the **Guideline** contains a set of recommended or non-recommended transitions.

Moreover, we can classify the situation types involved in a transition as: (i) **Non-Transformable Pre-Situation Type** regards a property that is not to be changed in that specific transition, but is needed as a filter condition (*Patient is a woman*); (ii) **Transformable Pre-Situation Type** regards a property and value that is to be changed in the transition (*Patient with ulcer*); (iii) **Post-Situation Type** regards the expected value for the property that is to be changed in the transition (*Patient without ulcer*).

The aforementioned concepts and relations are represented in an UML class diagram in Fig. 2. While one Guideline is an aggregation of two or more Recommendations, the latter can be part of one or more Guidelines. A Recommendation either recommends or non-recommends one Transition. The latter is promoted by one Care Action Type, which in turn can promote one or more Transitions. Situation Types can be Pre or Post-Situation Type in the context of different Transitions, which must have one Transformable Situation Type, one expected Transformable Situation Type and may have as filter condition some Non-Transformable Situation Types.

Finally, the situation types can also be classified either from the perspective of the patient health condition or of the Health Care System (HCS) as follows: (i) **Patient Health Condition Type**: regards the properties that define the patient health condition (*Patient with ulcer*); (ii) **HCS Epistemic State Type**: regards the knowledge about the patient properties by the HCS (*H. Pylori presence is unknown*); and (iii) **HCS Patient Status Type**: regards the status of

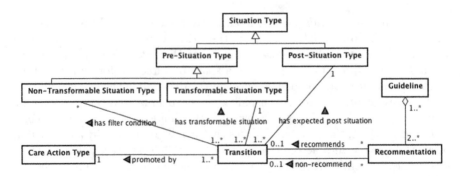

Fig. 2. UML class diagram for the TMR model

a patient in a HCS (*Patient is forwarded*). The transitions regarding these situation types can be classified according to the same criteria, as well as the action type that promotes the transition and the recommendation itself. The concepts here defined are further illustrated in the case study presented in Sect. 3.3.

3.2   TMR Application to the Comorbidity Use-Case

We evaluate the proposed model by reasoning on CIGs combined due to comorbidity, which regards taking into account more than one disease that a patient might have when defining a new treatment plan. If this issue is not correctly addressed the patient will possibly have an inadequate treatment. In consequence it is necessary to combine CIGs and/or treatment plans related to the different diseases in order to identify and solve the issues that eventually appears in the process of treating comorbid patients.

As mentioned in Sect. 2, since the current CIG languages do not properly address this problem, some approaches have being proposed to this end. Jafarpour and Abidi [6] mention two classification for the approaches, namely: (i) Pre-Execution Level Merging: issues are handled during the treatment prescription; and (ii) Execution Level Merging: issues are handled after the treatment prescription. We introduce here an extension for this classification as follows:

Guideline-level Verification aims to handle the combining issues at the guideline level (before execution). The result is a combined version of CIGs in which guideline-level issues are addressed. (e.g. in [15] the authors combine the CIGs before executing, though their goal is to produce a treatment for a specific patient).

On-Prescription Verification aims to handle the combining issues during the prescription of the treatment. The result is a merged treatment free of treatment-level issues. It can be applied between CIGs or between CIGs and existent treatments (e.g. [12]).

After-Prescription Verification aims to handle the combining issues among treatments. The result is a merged treatment applicable free of treatment-level issues (e.g. [11]).

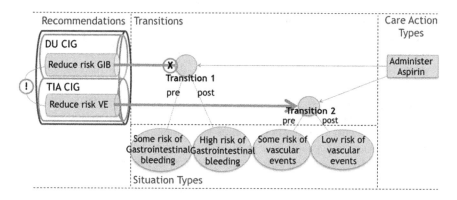

Fig. 3. Comorbidity example according to the TMR model

On-Treatment-Execution Verification aims to handle the issues that cannot
be foreseen, since they happen during the treatment execution. The result
can be an alert to interrupt the treatment execution (e.g. [2]).

We believe that these types of approaches are complementary, since on the
one hand it is useful to anticipate the issues when possible, but on the other
hand it is complex (maybe not possible) to anticipate all of them. The work
presented in this paper fits to the Guideline-level Verification, since we aim to
produce a combined version of CIGs that addresses guideline-level issues and
can be applied to many patients.

A simple scenario for the *Comorbidity* use-case is presented in Fig. 3 according to the TMR Model. When the recommendations from DU CIG and TIA CIG
are combined, it can be identified an interaction between the recommendations
Reduce risk GIB and *Reduce risk VE* (represented in the figure as an exclamation punctuation connecting the recommendations). In this case it regards
recommending and non-recommending transitions promoted by the same care
action type, namely, *Administer Aspirin.*

Note that by applying the TMR model it is possible to detect interactions
among recommendations, but not yet the conflicts. In order to identify conflicts, we would need both: (i) check if the interaction is unavoidable, i.e. no
alternative path that can be derived (for the same purpose/context) and (ii)
consult external knowledge base in order to check for overdoses or incompatibil-
ities. However, the scope of this paper is restricted to identify the interactions,
which could lead to conflicts or require attention from the experts. Moreover, we
consider that the interactions are not all unwelcome (e.g. the recommendations
to inverse transitions may be desirable and the alternative ones are useful to
avoid conflicts) although they could still require some attention (e.g. defining
which alternative recommendation is preferred). Therefore, we distinguish the
following interactions:

Contradictory recommendations: set of recommendations that can lead to
an undesired (non-recommended) final situation.

- *Opposed recommendations to the same care action:* when a care action is recommended in a CG and non-recommended in another, i.e. the execution of a care action may lead both to a desired and an undesired post-situations (e.g. *Adm. Aspirin* reduce the risk of vascular events but also increase the risk of gastrointestinal bleeding).
- *Opposed recommendations to similar transitions:* when a situation is the post-condition of transitions promoted by different care actions that are one recommended and another non-recommended, i.e. the execution of a care action will promote a post-situation that had also been stated as undesired (e.g. recommending *Adm. ACE inhibitor* to lower blood pressure while also non-recommending similar effect promoted by *Adm. Beta-blockers*).

Optmizable recommendations: set of recommendations that are susceptible to optimization.

- *Repeated recommendations to the same care action*: More than one recommendation regarding one Care Action (e.g.: *Perform Blood Exam* is recommended twice).
- *Recommendations to inverse transitions*: two recommendations that revert each other effect (e.g.: *Adm. Midodrine* is recommended to increase blood pressure and *Administer ACE inhibitor* to decrease it).

Alternative recommendations: set of recommendations that holds as alternatives.

- *Repeated recommendations to the similar transitions promoted by different care action*: recommendations that can promote similar effects (e.g. both *Adm. Aspirin* and *Adm. Clopidogrel* may reduce the risk of vascular events).
- *Non-recommended transition whose inverse transition is recommended*: when the undesired effect of a non-recommended transition can be undone by another recommended transition (e.g. the undesired effect of *Adm. Aspirin* on increasing the risk of gastrointestinal bleeding can be undone by *Adm. PPI*, which decreases that risk).

We compared the aforementioned classifications with the ones proposed in GLINDA Project[2]. For example, the *Opposed recommendations to similar transitions* could be mapped both to GLINDA *Cumulative Number Constraint* and *Inconsistent Goals*. We intend to further investigate the matching to the GLINDA classification for conflicts.

3.3   Evaluation on Comorbidity Case Study

In this section we apply our model to a case study on the comorbidity task. We repeat the experiment done by Wilk et al. [15] by modeling the CGs for Duodenal Ulcer (DU) and Transient Ischemic Attack (TIA) and merging them into a combined DU-TIA CIG. However, since the CIGs presented in the referred work do not provide all information that we need in the TMR model, we made

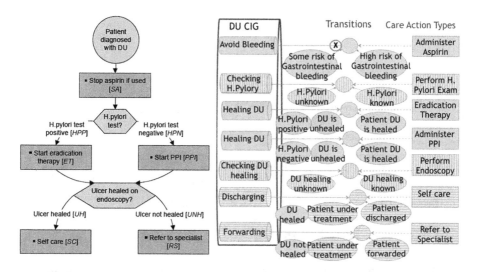

Fig. 4. DU CIG according to [15] (left side) and to TMR Model (right side)

some assumptions based on related CGs or common sense. Figure 4 presents the DU CIG both according to [15] and according to the TMR Model.

The action *"Stop aspirin if used"* in the original CIG is represented in the TMR CIG as a recommendation named *"Avoid Bleeding"* that admonish the transition promoted by the care action *"Administer Aspirin"*. The undesired transition can lead from the situation *"Some risk of gastrointestinal bleeding"* to *"High risk of gastrointestinal bleeding"*. The following decision point *"H.Pylori test?"* in the original CIG is separated in the TMR CIG as: (i) a recommendation to the transition promoted by the care action *"Perfoming H.Pylori exam"* when the infection must be revealed; and (ii) filter pre-situation types for that enables one of the recommendations named *"Healing DU"*. When *"H.Pylori is positive"* the care action *"Eradication Therapy"* can lead from the pre-situation *"DU is unhealed"* to the post-situation *"DU is healed"*. When *"H.Pylori is negative"* instead the care action *"Administer PPI"* can lead from the situation *"DU is unhealed"* to *"DU is healed"*. The two recommendations aforementioned represents the actions *"Start Eradication Therapy"* and *"Start PPI"* from the original CIG. A similar procedure were applied for the other actions and decisions.

Moreover, the different classifications for the Situations Types are distinguished in Fig. 4(right side) by different backgrounds: (i) Patient Health Conditions - filled background; (ii) HCS Epistemic Situations - vertical lines background; and (iii) HCS Patient Status - horizontal lines background. The corresponding classification for Transitions, Actions and Recommendations follows the same pattern in the figure. Moreover, the Pre-Situation Types not directly connected to the Transitions are the Filter Situation Types (e.g. *"H.Pylori is*

---

[2] http://glinda-project.stanford.edu/guidelineinteractionontology.html

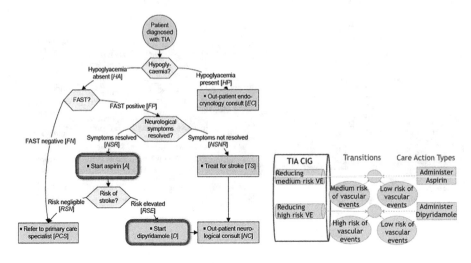

Fig. 5. TIA CIG according to [15] (left side) and to TMR Model (right side)

positive"), whilst those connected are the Pre/Post Situation Types (e.g. *"DU is unhealed"*).

Figure 5 presents the TIA CIG both according to [15] and to the TMR Model (a partial version). We present in the figure only two recommendations that regards Health Condition Transitions and are relevant for this case study (highlighted in Fig. 5). The actions *"Start Aspirin"* and *"Start Dipyridamole"* in the original CIG are represented as the recommendations named *"Reducing Medium Risk VE"* and *"Reducing High Risk VE"*. They recommends respectively the transitions promoted by the care actions *"Administer Aspirin"*, which that leads from *"Medium risk of vascular events (VE)"* to *"Low risk of vascular events"*, and the transition promoted by the care action *"Administer Dipyridamole"* that leads from *"High risk of VE"* to *"Low risk of VE"*.

Finally, when combining the CIGs, the authors identified in [15] a conflict by consulting a restriction in a Medical Background Knowledge (MBK). It states that the recommendations *"Stop aspirin if used"* and *"Start Aspirin"* cannot coexist, while it indeed occurs in the combined version of both CIGs. In order solve the conflict, the authors had two possibilities derived from the MBK: (i) substitute aspirin by clopidogrel; and (ii) combine aspirin treatment with PPI. They choose the second option and introduced it in the merged CIG as *"Start PPI"* when the risk of stroke is elevated, and they also excluded the recommendation *"Stop aspirin if used"* in order to avoid the conflict. Since their final goal was not to produce a generic combined version of guidelines, but to prescribe a treatment for a specific patient, they proposed a solution that is applicable to a specific patient.

Counterwise, the TMR Model allows to identify the interactions among recommendations, depicted in Fig. 6 as letters followed by an exclamation punctuation. The letters refers to the type of interaction: C - Contradictory, O - Optimizable, A - Alternative. Firstly the contradictory recommendations *"Avoid*

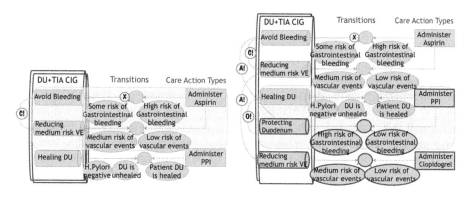

Fig. 6. The left side (a) presents a (partial) combined DU+TIA CIG according to TMR model where contractitory recommendations are highlighted. In the right side (b) the alternatives are introduced and optimizable recommendations are highlighted.

bleeding" and "*Reducing medium risk VE*" are identified since they regard recommending and non-recommending transitions that are promoted by the same Action Type, highlighted in Fig. 6a. Then we introduce in the resultant CIG both mitigation alternatives proposed to address the issue, without excluding the recommendation "*Avoid Bleeding*". The alternatives are named "*Protecting Duodenum*" and "*Reducing Medium Risk of VE*" and represented in Fig. 6b with a darker borderline. Finally, we can also identify an interaction between an existent recommendation and one of alternatives introduced, namely "*Protecting Duodenum*" and "*Healing DU*", since they are both promoted by the action "*Administer PPI*" and may require an optimization (highlighted in Fig. 6b).

Therefore, the combined DU-TIA CIG that we produced does not eliminate the original conflict but allow it to be avoided by introducing alternative recommendations for patients that present both *medium risk of VE* and *some risk of GIB*. Actually the recommendation for *avoiding high risk of GIB* promoted by *aspirin* is not eliminated since it is a restriction that holds for DU patients regardless what else disease they could have. Indeed, the resultant CIG is designed with the purpose of both (i) being applicable to many patients and (ii) being liable to further combination with other guidelines or treatments that the patient already follows. Finally, the contradictory, optimizable and alternative recommendations can be identified by relying on the described semantics for the referred care actions without consulting a MKB.

4 Discussion and Future Work

In this paper we propose the TMR model with the purpose of addressing other CIG use-cases rather than CIG execution, besides applying the model to the comorbidity use-case and comparing to the approach presented in [15]. On what follows we discuss the proposed model, its positive aspects, limitations and future issues to be addressed according to the following perspectives: (i) the model itself (Sect. 4.1) and (ii) its application to the comorbidity use-case (Sect. 4.2).

4.1   The TMR Model

The main contribution of the TMR model consists in an enriched core knowledge structure for CGs that explicitly represents both (i) the care action types with the possible transitions between situations types that can be promoted and (ii) the recommendations as declarative suggestions to pursue or avoid such transitions. We advocate that the TMR model, by providing a more detailed semantics for a small "CG knowledge chunk", can be a step towards addressing important problems like sharing/reusing, combining and maintaining knowledge such as argued by Peleg [9]. Although there is still place for investigations, we achieved some improvements addressing the combining issue at the guideline level (discussed in Sect. 4.2). We intend to apply the TMR model to other use-cases such as adapting and updating CIGs and analyse through the results if the current model is applicable as it is or if it requires adaptations.

Unlike in most CIG languages, TMR does not define sequence among the recommendations, but further investigation on this issue is necessary. Indeed, while for some recommendations sequence is not necessary or desirable (e.g. *do not administer aspirin*), for other ones the sequence can be derived by matching Post and Pre Situation Types (e.g. *If H.Pylori is negative then Administer PPI for healing the DU* and *If DU is healed then discharge the patient*). We also reconsider other two common constructs of current CIG languages, namely the Decision Point and Enquiry (demand of information). The former is implicit in the evaluation of the pre-situations, while the enquiry is represented as a recommendation regarding the HCS Epistemic State. We intend to investigate how to address the known/unknown values for epistemic situations.

We intend to pursue compatibility with current CIG approaches by studying their underlying models and checking for a possible mapping to the TMR Model. In particular, the SDA approach by Riano [10] proposes a non-deterministic model for CIG that is composed of States, Decisions and Actions (SDA), but which is not meant for representing the semantics of the actions. We also plan to use biomedical terminologies/ontologies (e.g. SNOMED, ICD) in the Care Action and Situation Types.

Further improvements that we intend to investigate are (i) the compositionality of the situations, actions, transitions and recommendations, (ii) the inclusion of new concepts (specially goals), (iii) the study of the recommendations as commitments and (iv) addressing temporality, probability and other features that characterize the domain and can enrich the TMR model. In summary, our future work is iteratively (re)apply improved versions of the TMR model to CIG use-cases. Beside extending the TMR model two important goals are: (1) providing formalized version of the TMR model such that we can formally verify and validate the model, and (2) an implementation of the model and it's use-case.

4.2   Application to the Comorbidity Use-Case

We applied the TMR model to the comorbidity use-case and evaluated it by comparing with a related work [15]. We classify our approach as begin designed

Table 2. Comparison to a related work

	Wilk et al. [15]	TMR Model
Core concepts	Actions and decisions	Actions, situations, transitions, recommendations
Description of care actions	Abstract/textual, does not favor reasoning	Detailed, favor reasoning
Knowledge format	Procedural	Declarative
	Sequenced actions and decisions	Non-sequenced recommendations
Language	Workflow and CLP	Graphical notation
Combining issues	Use an MKB for identifying and solving conflicts	Interactions among recommendations can be identified without MKB
Purpose	Introduce ONE alternative to produce a combined CIG for a SPECIFIC patient	Introduce MANY alternatives to produce a combined CIG applicable for MANY patients

to address the combining issues at the guideline level, i.e. to produce a combined version of the CIG that can be applied to many patients and further combined with other CIGs. Then we explore the ability to identify interactions among recommendations, which could lead to conflicts or require attention from the experts, by relying on the CIG internal information rather than external knowledge bases. Table 2 summarizes the comparison with the related work considering different aspects.

As future work on comorbidity we intend to (i) investigate the formalization/automatization for identification of interactions and conflicts, as well as suggesting solutions, (ii) reapply improved versions of the TMR Model (according to the previously improvements mentioned) and (iii) evaluate it on more comorbidity case studies. In particular, we intend to investigate and evaluate the ability to identify interactions among several recommendations in several CGs in the context of multimorbidity.

5 Conclusion

The main contribution of this paper is the TMR Model for representing CGs. This core model enhance some reasoning capabilities with respect to the current CIG languages, required to address other CIG use-cases rather than CIG execution. It explicitly represents both (i) the (space of possible) transitions between situations types promoted by the care actions types and (ii) recommendations as declarative suggestions to pursue or avoid transitions. By reasoning over such knowledge structure we are able to demonstrate improvements on addressing the use case of comorbidity, particularly by repeating an experiment from the literature and comparing the results. We intend to iteratively improve the model and evaluate it by (re)applying it to CIG use-cases (such as sharing, reusing, adapting and updating) at both conceptual and formal levels.

References

1. Bonacin, R., Pruski, C., Da Silveira, M.: Architecture and services for formalising and evaluating care actions from computer-interpretable guidelines. IJMEI Int. J. Med. Eng. Inform. **5**, 253–268 (2013)
2. Bottrighi, A., Chesani, F., Mello, P., Montali, M., Montani, S., Terenziani, P.: Conformance checking of executed clinical guidelines in presence of basic medical knowledge. In: Daniel, F., Barkaoui, K., Dustdar, S. (eds.) BPM Workshops 2011, Part II. LNBIP, vol. 100, pp. 200–211. Springer, Heidelberg (2012)
3. Boxwala, A.A., Peleg, M., Tu, S.W., Ogunyemi, O., Zeng, Q.T., Wang, D., Patel, V.L., Greenes, R.A., Shortliffe, E.H.: GLIF3: a representation format for sharable computer-interpretable clinical practice guidelines. J. Biomed. Inform. **37**(3), 147–161 (2004)
4. Guizzardi, G.: Ontological foundations for structural conceptual models. Ph.D. thesis, CTIT, Centre for Telematics and Information Technology, Enschede (2005)
5. Isern, D., Moreno, A.: Computer-based execution of clinical guidelines: a review. Int. J. Med. Inform. **77**(12), 787–808 (2008)
6. Jafarpour, B., Abidi, S.S.R.: Merging disease-specific clinical guidelines to handle comorbidities in a clinical decision support setting. In: Peek, N., Marín Morales, R., Peleg, M. (eds.) AIME 2013. LNCS, vol. 7885, pp. 28–32. Springer, Heidelberg (2013)
7. Latoszek-Berendsen, A., Talmon, J., de Clercq, P., Hasman, A.: With good intentions. Int. J. Med. Inform. **76**, S440–S446 (2007)
8. Shahar, Y., Miksch, S., Johnson, P.: Asbru: a task-specifc, intention-based, and time-oriented language for representing skeletal plans. In: Keravnou, E.T., Baud, R.H., Garbay, C., Wyatt, J.C. (eds.) AIME 1997. LNCS, vol. 1211. Springer, Heidelberg (1997)
9. Peleg, M.: Computer-interpretable clinical guidelines: a methodological review. J. Biomed. Inform. **46**(4), 744–763 (2013)
10. Riano, D.: The SDA model: a set theory approach. In: 20th IEEE International Symposium on Computer-Based Medical Systems (CBMS'07), pp. 563–568. IEEE (2007)
11. Riaño, D., Collado, A.: Model-based combination of treatments for the management of chronic comorbid patients. In: Peek, N., Marín Morales, R., Peleg, M. (eds.) AIME 2013. LNCS, vol. 7885, pp. 11–16. Springer, Heidelberg (2013)
12. Sánchez-Garzón, I., Fdez-Olivares, J., Onaindía, E., Milla, G., Jordán, J., Castejón, P.: A multi-agent planning approach for the generation of personalized treatment plans of comorbid patients. In: Peek, N., Marín Morales, R., Peleg, M. (eds.) AIME 2013. LNCS, vol. 7885, pp. 23–27. Springer, Heidelberg (2013)
13. Sutton, D.R., Fox, J.: The syntax and semantics of the PROforma guideline modeling language. J. AMIA **10**, 433–443 (2003)
14. Textor, M.: States of affairs. In: Zalta, E. (ed.) The Stanford Encyclopedia of Philosophy, 201 edn. (2012). http://plato.stanford.edu/archives/sum2012/entries/states-of-affairs/
15. Wilk, S., Michalowski, M., Michalowski, W., Hing, M.M., Farion, K.: Reconciling pairs of concurrently used clinical practice guidelines using Constraint Logic Programming. In: AMIA Annual Symposium Proceedings, p. 944. AMIA (2011)

Using First-Order Logic to Represent Clinical Practice Guidelines and to Mitigate Adverse Interactions

Szymon Wilk[1]([⊠]), Martin Michalowski[2], Xing Tan[3], and Wojtek Michalowski[3]

[1] Institute of Computing Science, Poznan University of Technology, Poznan, Poland
Szymon.Wilk@cs.put.poznan.pl
[2] Adventium Labs, Minneapolis, USA
[3] Telfer School of Management, University of Ottawa, Ottawa, Canada

Abstract. Clinical practice guidelines (CPGs) were originally designed to help with evidence-based management of a single disease and such single disease focus has impacted research on CPG computerization. This computerization is mostly concerned with supporting different representation formats and identifying potential inconsistencies in the definitions of CPGs. However, one of the biggest challenges facing physicians is the application of multiple CPGs to comorbid patients. While various research initiatives propose ways of mitigating adverse interactions in concurrently applied CPGs, there are no attempts to develop a generalized framework for mitigation that captures generic characteristics of the problem, while handling nuances such as precedence relationships. In this paper we present our research towards developing a mitigation framework that relies on a first-order logic-based representation and related theorem proving and model finding techniques. The application of the proposed framework is illustrated with a simple clinical example.

1 Introduction

A clinical practice guideline (CPG) codifies the evidence-based best practice in prescribing the most appropriate disease-specific therapy to patients, subject to available patient data and possible diagnoses [16]. Since the scope of each guideline is limited to a single disease, the evidence-based management of a comorbid patient according to the recommendations concurrently coming from multiple CPGs is difficult and can result in inconsistent and potentially harmful therapies. Often the derivation of a combined therapy directly from the guidelines (even for properly diagnosed comorbid conditions) is incorrect due to adverse interactions between the treatments associated with individual therapies. These interactions manifest directly as contradictory recommendations (e.g., use of steroids is recommended by one CPG and prohibited by the other), or they may correspond to drug-drug or drug-disease adverse interactions resulting in actions that cannot be taken concurrently.

As a matter of fact, concurrent application of two or more CPGs is challenging – it requires designing a sophisticated mechanism for identifying and

© Springer International Publishing Switzerland 2014
S. Miksch et al. (Eds.): KR4HC 2014, LNAI 8903, pp. 45–61, 2014.
DOI: 10.1007/978-3-319-13281-5_4

eliminating potential redundancy in the tests or procedures, identifying contradictions (direct adverse interactions), and for managing discordance (indirect, drug-drug or drug-disease interactions) [17]. As such, it is believed that executing multiple CPGs concurrently requires a new, "combinatorial, logical, or semantic" methodological approach [2].

Our previous research [7,8,19] proposes such an approach by introducing and formally defining logical models of CPGs and developing a mitigation algorithm that operates on these models. The algorithm relies on secondary clinical knowledge (i.e., knowledge that goes beyond the primary knowledge encoded in CPGs and that comes from domain experts, textbooks, or repositories of clinical evidence) that is encoded as interaction and revision operators. The operators characterize adverse interactions associated with the concurrent application of CPGs and describe revisions to logical models required to address these interactions. The algorithm employs the constraint logic programming (CLP) paradigm to efficiently solve the logical models, where a solution represents a combined therapy free of adverse interactions.

In the research described here, we move further towards developing a general framework for mitigation by enriching the representation of CPGs using first-order logic (FOL) theories and relying on theorem proving and model finding techniques to process these theories. This expansion is dictated by the following limitations of our previous research:

- Restricted expressive power of the CLP-based approach that does not allow for explicit representation of properties of objects (e.g., a dosage associated with a specific CPG action) and relationships between objects (e.g., precedence between CPG actions),
- Limited interpretability of solutions returned by CLP solvers and consequently the need to assign real-world semantics to truth-value assignment of the propositional symbols in the CLP-based model.

FOL significantly improves the expressiveness of our approach by introducing predicates to represent properties and relationships in the domain (in fact, relationships are only first-order definable). Moreover, predicates impose semantics on solutions, facilitating their interpretation from a clinical perspective.

This paper is organized as follows. We start with a brief review of related work. Then, we present the foundations of FOL, theorem proving and model finding that are relevant to our research. Next, we describe the proposed framework – we start with the underlying FOL theories and then present an overview of the mitigation process. We proceed with a simple clinical example that illustrates the application of the framework. Finally, we provide conclusions and directions for our future research.

2   Related Work

Peleg in her recent methodological review [12] divided the research on computer-interpretable CPGs into eight themes: (1) modeling, (2) acquisition and specification, (3) integration in combination with electronic patient record, (4) validation and verification, (5) execution, (6) exception handling, (7) maintenance, and finally (8) sharing. According to such categorization, our research discussed here belongs to the validation and verification theme. This theme is further subdivided into three problems: (1) checking for internal consistency and existence of anomalies, (2) checking for existence of desired properties and (3) checking for the inconsistencies between multiple CPGs applied to a comorbid patient.

The first problem from the above list was addressed for example in [1], where the authors proposed a knowledge-based detection method for checking the consistency of a CPG represented in ASBRU. The second problem was described in [14], where model checking was applied for authoring and verification of CPGs represented in UML. Moreover, in [18] theorem proving techniques were used to check whether a guideline for managing jaundice in newborns complies with certain properties. Finally, [13] described a comprehensive framework employing ontological domain knowledge and abductive reasoning to evaluate the completeness and appropriateness of a CPG, and to assess the compliance of physician's actions with this CPG.

The research related to the last verification problem is still in its relatively early stages despite its clinical importance. Proposed solutions vary from manual interventions, where human experts verify and combine multiple CPGs using a specialized editing tool [15], through semi-automatic approaches, where experts resolve automatically discovered conflicts [3], to fully automatic techniques [4,5]. In [4] the authors proposed an approach that operates on ontological models of CPGs and applies ontology merging techniques to combine these models so that medical, work-flow, institutional and temporal constraints are satisfied. A different approach was described in [5], where individual CPGs are merged according to the combination rules that capture possible drug-drug interactions and prescribe ways of avoiding them.

3   Background

3.1   Foundations of FOL

The formal language of FOL relies on *logical* and *non-logical* symbols. The logical symbols (connectives, quantifiers, variables) are those that have a fixed meaning in a language. The non-logical symbols are those that have an application-dependent meaning (e.g., symbols needed to represent a CPG in FOL) and they are further categorized into *function* symbols and *predicate* symbols. Each non-logical symbol has an *arity*, indicating how many arguments it requires. A function symbol with arity 0 is called a *constant* and a predicate symbol with arity 0 is called a *propositional symbol*.

FOL allows for two types of syntactic expressions: *terms* (made of variables, constants and functions) and *formulas* (composed of terms, predicates and connectives). Formulas with variables bounded by quantifiers and formulas without variables (i.e., grounded formulas) are called *sentences*. A FOL *theory* $\mathcal{D}$ is a collection of sentences.

An *interpretation* $\mathcal{I}$ (sometimes called a structure) in FOL is defined as triple:

$$\mathcal{I} = \langle \mathcal{I}_{domain}, \mathcal{I}_{predicate}, \mathcal{I}_{function} \rangle, \tag{1}$$

where

- $\mathcal{I}_{domain}$ is any nonempty set of objects under consideration called the domain of the interpretation,
- $\mathcal{I}_{predicate}$ is a set of interpretation mappings over $\mathcal{I}_{domain}$,
- $\mathcal{I}_{function}$ is a set of functions over $\mathcal{I}_{function}$.

Mappings from $\mathcal{I}_{predicate}$ assign meaning to the predicate symbols as follows: for every predicate symbol P of arity n, $\mathcal{I}[P] \in \mathcal{I}_{predicate}$ is an n-ary relation over $\mathcal{I}_{domain}$, that is $\mathcal{I}[P] \subseteq I_{domain} \times \ldots \times I_{domain}$.

Mappings from $\mathcal{I}_{function}$ assign meaning to the function symbols as follows: for every function symbol F of arity n, $\mathcal{I}[F] \in \mathcal{I}_{function}$ is an n-ary function over $\mathcal{I}_{domain}$, that is $\mathcal{I}[F] \in [\mathcal{I}_{domain} \times \ldots \times \mathcal{I}_{domain} \rightarrow \mathcal{I}_{domain}]$.

Given an interpretation $\mathcal{I}$, we can check which sentences of a FOL theory $\mathcal{D}$ are true and which are false according to this interpretation. If a sentence $\phi \in \mathcal{D}$ is true given $\mathcal{I}$, then we write it formally as $\mathcal{I} \models_m \phi$. Moreover, if $\mathcal{I}$ satisfies all sentences in $\mathcal{D}$, then it is called a *model* for theory $\mathcal{D}$ and formally it is denoted as $\mathcal{I} \models_m \mathcal{D}$.

3.2   Theorem Proving and Model Finding

There are three fundamental questions that are associated with FOL theories:

1. Is a given theory consistent?
2. What is a model for a consistent theory?
3. What are logical consequences (implications) of a consistent theory?

A FOL theory $\mathcal{D}$ is *consistent* (or satisfiable), iff there exists at least one model of this theory. The question on the consistency of $\mathcal{D}$ can be answered using *theorem proving* [11] that employs automatic reasoning (the resolution method) to construct a proof for $\mathcal{D}$. However, theorem proving techniques provide only a binary answer to the consistency question and no model is directly returned, even if it exists (i.e., when the answer is positive). In order to answer the question about a model for a consistent theory, one needs to use *model finding* techniques that can be considered as a special case of solving the constraint satisfaction problem [20], where possible interpretations are generated until a model is found.

The question about logical consequences is translated into checking if a FOL theory $\mathcal{D}$ entails sentence ϕ (or ϕ is a logical consequence of $\mathcal{D}$). Formally, we say $\mathcal{D}$ *entails* ϕ, written as $\mathcal{D} \models \phi$, iff, for every interpretation $\mathcal{I}$ such that $\mathcal{I} \models_m \mathcal{D}$, we have $\mathcal{I} \models_m \phi$. In other words, we say $\mathcal{D}$ entails ϕ (or ϕ can be deduced from $\mathcal{D}$), if ϕ is satisfied by all models for $\mathcal{D}$.

The entailment $\mathcal{D} \models \phi$ can be translated into checking whether a new theory $\mathcal{D} \cup \{\neg\phi\}$ is not consistent. This means that theorem proving techniques can equivalently be used to check for logical entailments of a theory $\mathcal{D}$.

Table 1. Defined predicates

Predicate	Description
$node(x)$	x is a node in AG
$action(x)$	x is an action node in AG
$decision(x)$	x is a decision node in AG
$executed(x)$	Action node x is executed
$value(x, v)$	Value v is associated with decision node x
$dosage(x, n)$	Action node x is characterized by medication dosage n
$directPrec(x, y)$	Node x directly precedes node y (there is an edge from x to y)
$prec(x, y)$	Node x precedes node y (there is a path from x to y)
$disease(d)$	d is a disease to be managed
$diagnosed(d)$	The patient has been diagnosed with disease d

4   Methodology

Using FOL in a framework for the mitigation of concurrently applied CPGs relies on four key components that are listed below and described in the following sections:

1. A vocabulary used to construct the FOL theory describing a particular mitigation problem (further referred to as to *combined mitigation theory*),
2. A combined mitigation theory composed of individual theories that describe various aspects of the mitigation problem,
3. A set of operators that encode the secondary knowledge needed to identify and address adverse interactions associated with the combined mitigation theory,
4. A mitigation algorithm that controls the application of operators to the combined mitigation theory.

4.1   Vocabulary

Following our previous work, we assume a CPG is represented as an *actionable graph* (AG) [19]. An AG is a directed graph composed of three types of nodes *context*, *action*, and *decision*, and arcs that represent transitions between nodes. A context node defines an entry point and indicates the disease associated with the CPG, an action node indicates a clinical action that needs to be executed, and a decision node indicates a selection from several alternative choices and allows for conditional branching.

The vocabulary of our FOL-based approach is composed of constants (denoted with upper case letters), variables (denoted with lower case letters) and predicates. The predicates used in the mitigation problem are listed in Table 1. We note there is no predicate corresponding to a context node, as information embedded in this node is provided by the predicate $disease(d)$.

4.2   Combined Mitigation Theory

We use the vocabulary to construct a combined mitigation theory. Formally, this combined theory $\mathcal{D}_{comb}$ is defined as a triple:

$$\mathcal{D}_{comb} = \langle \mathcal{D}_{common}, \mathcal{D}_{cpg}, \mathcal{D}_{pi} \rangle, \tag{2}$$

where:

- $\mathcal{D}_{common}$ is a theory that axiomatizes the universal characteristics of CPGs as part of the FOL representation. It is the common (shared and reusable) component of all mitigation theories and it contains the following axioms (for brevity we limit the list to the most relevant ones):
  - $\forall x, y \; directPrec(x, y) \Rightarrow prec(x, y)$ – association between precedence and direct precedence,
  - $\forall x, y, z \; prec(x, y) \wedge prec(y, z) \Rightarrow prec(x, z)$ – transitivity of precedence,
  - $\forall x, y, \; prec(x, y) \wedge prec(y, x) \Rightarrow x = y$ – antisymmetry of precedence,
  - $\forall x \; node(x) \Rightarrow (action(x) \wedge \neg decision(x)) \vee (\neg action(x) \wedge decision(x))$ – ensures that a node cannot be simultaneously an action and decision node,
  - $\forall x, n \; dosage(x, n) \Rightarrow action(x)$ – ensures that only an action node can be characterized with medication dosage,
  - $\forall x, v \; value(x, v) \Rightarrow decision(x)$ – ensures that only a decision node can be characterized by a value,
  - $\forall d \; diagnosed(d) \Rightarrow disease(d)$ – ensures that the diagnosed disease is the same as the disease to be managed.
- $\mathcal{D}_{cpg}$ is a union of theories, each theory representing a single AG (and thus the underlying CPG) that are being applied to a comorbid patient:

$$\mathcal{D}_{cpg} = \mathcal{D}_{cpg}^{d_1} \cup \mathcal{D}_{cpg}^{d_2} \cup \ldots \cup \mathcal{D}_{cpg}^{d_k}, \tag{3}$$

  where $\mathcal{D}_{cpg}^{d_i}$ is the theory that describes the AG associated with disease d_i by enlisting all nodes and paths, giving information about precedence between nodes and providing information on dosages associated with selected action nodes. Because of axioms in $\mathcal{D}_{common}$ it is sufficient to define only direct precedence between nodes ($directPrec$ predicate) – precedence between nodes represented with the $prec$ predicate is derived automatically,
- $\mathcal{D}_{pi}$ is the theory that describes available patient information. It contains sentences representing patient data, including results of tests and examinations, and indicating already prescribed therapies and procedures.

4.3   Interaction and Revision Operators

Interaction and revision operators were introduced in our previous research [19]. Here we reformulate them to account for the FOL-based representation and to enhance their capabilities (e.g., a revision operator may specify multiple operations – details provided below). An interaction operator IO^k encodes knowledge about indirect adverse interactions (usually drug-drug or drug-disease) and formally it is defined as:

$$IO^k = \langle \alpha^k \rangle, \tag{4}$$

where α^k is a sentence (constructed with the vocabulary described in Sect. 4.1) describing a specific indirect interaction. Checking whether IO^k is applicable to $\mathcal{D}_{comb}$ (or in other words, if the interaction represented by IO^k occurs in $\mathcal{D}_{comb}$) is an entailment problem $\mathcal{D}_{comb} \models \alpha^k$.

A revision operator encodes knowledge about the revisions that need to be introduced to the theory $\mathcal{D}_{cpg}$ in order to address encountered interactions (both direct and indirect). In layman terms, it describes changes that need to be introduced to concurrently applied CPGs. Formally, a revision operator RO^k is defined as:

$$RO^k = \langle \beta^k, Op^k \rangle, \tag{5}$$

where β^k is a logical sentence that defines the applicability of the operator to the theory $\mathcal{D}_{cpg}$, and Op^k describes the revisions introduced by RO^k. In particular, Op^k is a set of n pairs of formulas $\langle \phi_i^k, \psi_i^k \rangle$ ($i = 1 \ldots n$) that define single operations within the operator. As already stated, these operations are applied only to $\mathcal{D}_{cpg}$, so other components of $\mathcal{D}_{comb}$ are protected from unwanted revisions. For example, $\mathcal{D}_{pi}$ is never modified thus patient information is never inadvertently changed. The pairs of formulas are interpreted as follows ($\emptyset$ indicates an empty formula):

- $\langle \phi_i^k, \emptyset \rangle$ means that ϕ_i^k is removed from any sentence in $\mathcal{D}_{cpg}$ where it appears,
- $\langle \emptyset, \psi_i^k \rangle$ means that ψ_i^k is added as a new sentence to $\mathcal{D}_{cpg}$,
- $\langle \phi_i^k, \psi_i^k \rangle$ means that ϕ_i^k is replaced by ψ_i^k in any sentence in $\mathcal{D}_{cpg}$ where it appears.

It is possible to use unbounded variables in ϕ_i^k and ψ_i^k and these are interpreted as "wildcards" that are bound to a constant specific to a patient encounter when revisions are being introduced. For example, one can define an operation that increases the dosage of a medication by a given amount. Moreover, checking the applicability of RO^k to $\mathcal{D}_{comb}$ is analogous to checking the applicability of IO^k and translates into the entailment problem $\mathcal{D}_{comb} \models \beta^k$. In case of direct interactions this entailment problem is simplified – details are given in the next section.

4.4   Mitigation Algorithm

The algorithm consists of two phases and it is outlined in Fig. 1. The first phase involves mitigating direct adverse interactions. Their identification translates into checking the consistency of the $\mathcal{D}_{comb}$ theory (note that in order to check for consistency and entailment we need to create a temporary theory that is a union of all three components in $\mathcal{D}_{comb}$). If the theory is consistent, then it indicates there are no direct interactions and the algorithm passes to the second phase. Otherwise, the theory $\mathcal{D}_{comb}$ (specifically its $\mathcal{D}_{cpg}$ component) needs to be revised using applicable revision operators.

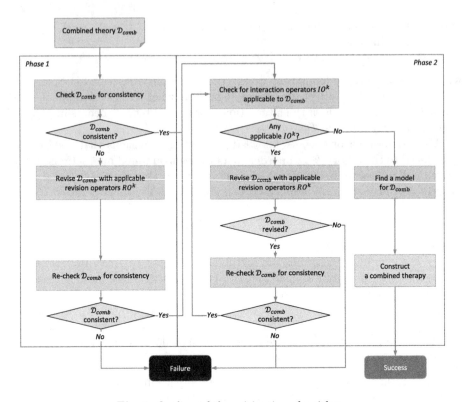

Fig. 1. Outline of the mitigation algorithm.

Since $\mathcal{D}_{comb}$ is inconsistent, entailment cannot be used to find applicable revision operators, as entailment problems can only be formulated over a consistent theory. Instead, we use the following procedure. First, we identify actions shared across individual theories (i.e., theories representing single CPGs) in $\mathcal{D}_{comb}$. Then, for each shared action x_s we check whether execution of this action and its negation are entailed by individual theories (i.e., $\mathcal{D}_{cpg}^{d_i} \models executed(x_s)$ and $\mathcal{D}_{cpg}^{d_j} \models \neg executed(x_s)$). Such entailments indicate inconsistency caused by x_s. Finally, we identify applicable RO^k by solving a simplified entailment problem: $executed(x_s) \models \beta^k$. The algorithm may stop here, reporting a failure to indicate that $\mathcal{D}_{comb}$ is still inconsistent, if it has failed to address the encountered direct interaction.

The second phase identifies and addresses indirect adverse interactions. It starts by identifying applicable interaction operators (for an operator IO^k this translates to checking the entailment $\mathcal{D}_{comb} \models \alpha^k$). If there is no applicable operator, then this means that there are no indirect interactions or they have been already addressed, and the algorithm finds a model for $\mathcal{D}_{comb}$. This model is equivalent to a solution in the CLP-based mitigation framework, and using its $\mathcal{I}_{predicate}$ component it is possible to construct a combined therapy for a patient.

This combined therapy highlights the clinical actions to be taken (*executed* and *dosage* predicates) along with the order in which they should be carried out (*prec* predicates), and includes the assumptions made about the patient's state (*value* predicates). Note that the combined therapy contains only these predicates that have not been provided as part of $\mathcal{D}_{pi}$, thus it is focused on future (suggested) actions and possible (assumed) patient state.

On the other hand, if direct interactions exist (there is at least one IO^k applicable to $\mathcal{D}_{comb}$), the algorithm attempts to revise $\mathcal{D}_{comb}$ using applicable revision operators, where checking applicability of an operator RO^k is formulated as an entailment problem ($\mathcal{D}_{comb} \models \beta^k$). In our previous research we assumed that an interaction had to be addressed by a single applicable revision operator. In this framework we relax this assumption and allow for more complex adverse interactions that may need to be mitigated by multiple revision operators. There is an additional explicit check if $\mathcal{D}_{comb}$ has been revised to avoid indefinite loops if there is no applicable RO^k. If the revised $\mathcal{D}_{comb}$ is consistent, then the algorithm checks again for an applicable IO^k, otherwise it fails. This loop is repeated until there are no more applicable interaction operators.

The implementation of the mitigation algorithm involves a number of software tools that were developed for FOL theories. In this research we are using Prover9 [19] to check consistency of all theories and to execute the entailment required for the identification and use of the operators. Moreover, we are using a model finding technique implemented in Mace4 [6] that returns a model on top of a theory that has been verified as a consistent one. The performance of Prover9 was verified on a set of benchmark FOL problems and compared to other solvers in [10]. The results show it was among two best performing solvers and for most of the considered problems the proofs were generated in seconds when running on a personal computer. The running times we observed in our tests were comparable or even shorter, thus they are negligible with regards to the patient management process. Moreover, the mitigation algorithm and its implementation are not bound to Prover9 and Mace4, thus they can be easily replaced by more efficient solvers, if performance becomes an issue.

5   Illustrative Example

In this section we illustrate our proposed FOL-based mitigation framework using the simple clinical case also used in [19]. The purpose of using the same example is to show how the methodology proposed here extends our earlier research. According to this example, a patient, who is treated for a duodenal ulcer (DU), experiences an episode of transient ischemic attack (TIA). AGs used in this example are derived from the guidelines published by the National Institute for Health and Clinical Excellence, UK (NICE) [9] and they have been simplified to include only the relevant action and decision nodes.

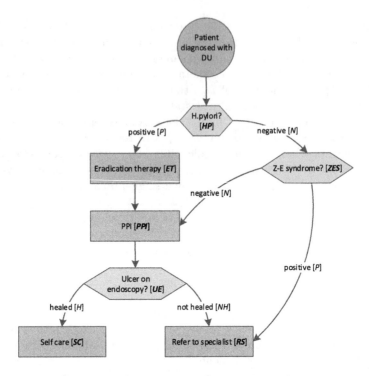

Fig. 2. Actionable graph for DU (AG_{DU}).

5.1 Actionable Graphs

Figures 2 and 3 present AGs for DU and TIA simplified guidelines respectively. In these figures the context nodes are indicated with circles, decision nodes are indicated with diamonds, and action nodes with rectangles. The figures also label constants associated with specific nodes and constants corresponding to alternative choices – they are given in square brackets after node and choice descriptions. For example, the HP constant is associated with the "H.pylori" decision node (checking for the presence of helicobacter pylori). There are two alternative choices at this decision node positive and negative. They are represented as P and N constants respectively.

5.2 Theories

The AGs are converted into the respective theories, $\mathcal{D}_{cpg}^{DU}$ for DU and $\mathcal{D}_{cpg}^{TIA}$ for TIA, illustrated in Figs. 4 and 5. As can be seen, this representation captures precedence relationships and attaches semantics to each node. All paths in the corresponding AG are described using a single sentence (a disjunction of conjunctions, where each conjunction corresponds to a single path). Each path contains formulas with the negated *executed* predicate to indicate these actions are not executed for a given path.

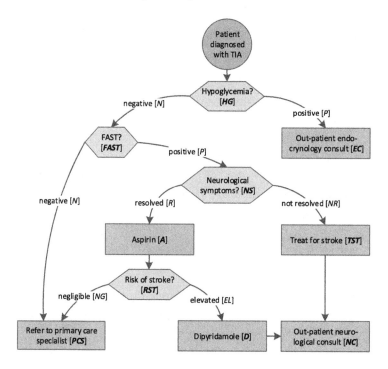

Fig. 3. Actionable graph for TIA (AG_{TIA}).

$disease(DU)$.
$node(HP)$. $node(ET)$. $node(ZES)$. $node(PPI)$. $node(UE)$. $node(SC)$. $node(RS)$.
$directPrec(HP, ET)$. $directPrec(HP, ZES)$. $directPrec(ET, PPI)$. $directPrec(ZES, PPI)$.
$directPrec(PPI, UE)$. $directPrec(UE, SC)$. $directPrec(UE, RS)$. $directPrec(ZES, RS)$.
$decision(HP)$. $decision(ZES)$. $decision(UE)$.
$action(ET)$. $action(PPI)$. $action(SC)$. $action(RS)$.
$(value(HP, P) \wedge executed(ET) \wedge executed(PPI) \wedge value(UE, H) \wedge executed(SC)$
$\quad \wedge \neg executed(RS))$
$\vee (value(HP, P) \wedge executed(ET) \wedge executed(PPI) \wedge value(UE, NH) \wedge executed(RS)$
$\quad \wedge \neg executed(SC))$
$\vee (value(HP, N) \wedge value(ZES, N) \wedge executed(PPI) \wedge value(UE, H) \wedge executed(SC) \wedge$
$\quad \neg executed(ET) \wedge \neg executed(RS))$
$\vee (value(HP, N) \wedge value(ZES, N) \wedge executed(PPI) \wedge value(UE, NH) \wedge executed(RS)$
$\quad \wedge \neg executed(ET) \wedge \neg executed(SC))$
$\vee (value(HP, N) \wedge value(ZES, P) \wedge executed(RS) \wedge$
$\quad \neg executed(ET) \wedge \neg executed(PPI) \wedge \neg executed(SC))$.

Fig. 4. The D_{cpg}^{DU} theory representing the CPG for DU.

5.3   Operators

Interaction and revision operators associated with clinical scenarios discussed below are given in Fig. 6 (for clarity only most relevant operations within revision operators are presented). Their interpretation is as follows:

$disease(TIA).$
$node(HG).$ $node(FAST).$ $node(EC).$ $node(NS).$ $node(A).$ $node(TST).$ $node(RST).$
$node(PCS).$ $node(D).$ $node(NC).$
$directPrec(HG, FAST).$ $directPrec(HG, EC).$ $directPrec(FAST, PCS).$
$directPrec(FAST, NS).$ $directPrec(NS, A).$ $directPrec(NS, TST).$ $directPrec(A, RST).$
$directPrec(RST, PCS).$ $directPrec(RST, D).$ $directPrec(D, NC).$ $directPrec(TST, NC).$
$decision(HG).$ $decision(FAST).$ $decision(NS).$ $decision(RST).$
$action(EC).$ $action(A).$ $action(TST).$ $action(PCS).$ $action(D).$ $action(NC).$
$dosage(A, 300).$ $dosage(D, 75).$
$(value(HG, N) \wedge value(FAST, N) \wedge executed(PCS)$
$\qquad \wedge \neg executed(EC) \wedge \neg executed(A) \wedge \neg executed(TST) \wedge \neg executed(D)$
$\qquad \wedge \neg executed(NC))$
$\vee\ (value(HG, N) \wedge value(FAST, P) \wedge value(NS, R) \wedge executed(A)$
$\qquad \wedge value(RST, NG) \wedge executed(PCS)$
$\qquad \wedge \neg executed(EC) \wedge \neg executed(TST) \wedge \neg executed(D) \wedge \neg executed(NC))$
$\vee\ (value(HG, N) \wedge value(FAST, P) \wedge value(NS, R) \wedge executed(A)$
$\qquad \wedge value(RST, EL) \wedge executed(D) \wedge executed(NC)$
$\qquad \wedge \neg executed(EC) \wedge \neg executed(TST) \wedge \neg executed(PCS))$
$\vee\ (value(HG, N) \wedge value(FAST, P) \wedge value(NS, NR) \wedge executed(TST) \wedge executed(NC)$
$\qquad \wedge \neg executed(EC) \wedge \neg executed(A) \wedge \neg executed(PCS) \wedge \neg executed(D))$
$\vee\ (value(HG, P) \wedge executed(EC)$
$\qquad \wedge \neg executed(A)) \wedge \neg executed(TST) \wedge \neg executed(PCS) \wedge \neg executed(D)$
$\qquad \wedge \neg executed(NC)).$

Fig. 5. The D_{cpg}^{TIA} theory representing the CPG for TIA.

Interaction operators:
$IO^1 = \left\langle \alpha^1 \right\rangle$
$\qquad \alpha^1 = diagnosed(DU) \wedge executed(A) \wedge \neg executed(PPI)$

Revision operators:
$RO^1 = \left\langle \beta^1, Op^1 \right\rangle$
$\qquad \beta^1 = diagnosed(DU) \wedge executed(A) \wedge \neg executed(PPI) \wedge \neg executed(D)$
$\qquad Op^1 = \{\langle executed(A), executed(CL)\rangle\}$
$RO^2 = \left\langle \beta^2, Op^2 \right\rangle$
$\qquad \beta^2 = diagnosed(DU) \wedge executed(A) \wedge \neg executed(PPI) \wedge executed(D)$
$\qquad Op^2 = \{\langle \neg executed(PPI), executed(PPI)\rangle, \langle dosage(A, x), dosage(A, x - 50)\rangle\}$

Fig. 6. Interaction and revision operators.

- IO^1 represents a drug-disease interaction (the increased risk of bleeding) that occurs when a DU patient is given aspirin (A) without a proton-pump inhibitor (PPI).
- RO^1 is applicable to a patient diagnosed with DU who has been prescribed aspirin (A) without a proton-pump inhibitor (PPI), and has not been prescribed dipyridamole (D). In such case, the patient is taken off of aspirin and prescribed clopidogrel (CL).
- RO^2 is applicable to a patient diagnosed with DU who has been prescribed aspirin (A) without a proton-pump inhibitor (PPI), and also has been prescribed dipyridamole (D). In such case, the patient is prescribed a proton-pump inhibitor (PPI) and dosage of aspirin (A) is reduced by 50 milligrams (mg).

5.4 Scenario 1: No Adverse Interactions

In this scenario we assume a patient suffering from DU who has tested positive for H.pylori (HP) and is undergoing eradication therapy (ET), on presentation to the emergency department with TIA symptoms has tested negative for hypoglycemia (HG) and the result of FAST test (FAST) is negative. The theory $\mathcal{D}_{pi}$ describing this patient is given in Fig. 7.

$diagnosed(DU)$. $value(HP, P)$. $executed(ET)$.
$diagnosed(TIA)$. $value(HG, N)$. $value(FAST, N)$.

Fig. 7. The $\mathcal{D}_{pi}$ describing the patient information in Scenario 1.

We create a theory $\mathcal{D}_{comb}$ to describe this specific patient encounter, where $\mathcal{D}_{cpg}$ are the union of $\mathcal{D}_{cpg}^{DU}$ and $\mathcal{D}_{cpg}^{TIA}$ discussed in Sect. 5.2.

The mitigation algorithm begins by applying theorem proving technique and checking if $\mathcal{D}_{comb}$ is consistent. Since the theory is consistent, the algorithm infers that no direct interactions exist. At this stage the mitigation algorithm proceeds to the second phase and checks for the existence of an indirect interaction. It starts with IO^1 by formulating the entailment problem $\mathcal{D}_{comb} \models \alpha^1$. Because α^1 is not entailed by $\mathcal{D}_{comb}$ (i.e., there exists at least one model, where α^1 is not satisfied), there are no indirect interactions present in the theory and the mitigation algorithm uses model finding techniques to find a model for the theory $\mathcal{D}_{comb}$. One such model is found and used to create a combined therapy given in Fig. 8 (for brevity we omitted the *prec* predicates).

$executed(PPI)$. $value(UE, H)$. $executed(SC)$. $executed(PCS)$.

Fig. 8. Combined therapy created for Scenario 1.

According to the combined therapy the patient should be prescribed a proton-pump inhibitor ($executed(PPI)$) and since the result of the endoscopy (UE) is not known (neither $value(UE, H)$ nor $value(UE, NH)$ is included in $\mathcal{D}_{pi}$), the combined therapy assumes a healed ulcer ($value(UE, H)$) and suggests self-care ($executed(SC)$) for DU and a referral to a primary care specialist for TIA ($executed(PCS)$). Such a combined therapy is returned by the mitigation algorithm and presented to the physician along with the known patient state ($\mathcal{D}_{pi}$). The physician evaluates the therapy by checking the appropriateness of assumptions made, such as the assumption of a healed ulcer in this particular scenario. If she deems some of these assumptions to be inappropriate, new patient information needs to be collected and the mitigation algorithm needs to be invoked again to generate a new combined therapy.

5.5   Scenario 2: Adverse Interactions Present

In this scenario we consider a patient suffering from DU, who has tested negative for H.pylori (HP) and positive for Zollinger-Ellison syndrome (ZES), and who on presentation to the emergency department with TIA symptoms has tested negative for hypoglycemia (HG), passed FAST test, has had neurological symptoms (NS) resolved, and for whom the risk of stroke (RST) has been evaluated as elevated. The theory $\mathcal{D}_{pi}$ describing this patient is given in Fig. 9.

$diagnosed(DU)$. $value(HP, N)$. $value(ZES, P)$.
$diagnosed(TIA)$. $value(HG, N)$. $value(FAST, P)$. $value(NS, R)$. $value(RST, EL)$.

Fig. 9. The $\mathcal{D}_{pi}$ describing the patient information in Scenario 2.

Similarly to the previous scenario, $\mathcal{D}_{comb}$ is consistent and as such no direct interactions exist. To check for the existence of an indirect interaction we consider IO^1 and formulate the entailment problem $\mathcal{D}_{comb} \models \alpha^1$. This time α^1 is entailed by $\mathcal{D}_{comb}$ (it is satisfied by each model of $\mathcal{D}_{comb}$) indicating that an indirect interaction exists.

Following the steps of the mitigation algorithm, we resolve an indirect interaction by selecting a relevant revision operator to revise $\mathcal{D}_{cpg}$. A relevant operator is found by iterating over available revision operators and formulating the entailment problem $\mathcal{D}_{cpg} \models \beta^k$ for each revision operator RO^k. In this scenario, for RO^1 β^1 is not entailed by $\mathcal{D}_{comb}$ as there exists at least one model that does not satisfy β^1. This indicates that RO^1 is not a relevant revision operator. Next, the algorithm considers RO^2 and formulates the entailment problem $\mathcal{D}_{comb} \models \beta^2$. Now β^2 is entailed by $\mathcal{D}_{comb}$ and RO^2 is considered a relevant revision operator.

---

executed(PPI). **executed(RS)**.
executed(A). **dosage(A, 250)**. **executed(D)**. **dosage(D, 75)**. executed(NC).

Fig. 10. Combined therapy created for Scenario 2 (underlined entries have been introduced by the revision operator).

The algorithm revises $\mathcal{D}_{comb}$ by modifying $\mathcal{D}_{cpg}$ according to the operations Op^2 defined in RO^2. These operations introduce a proton pump inhibitor (in fact $\neg executed\,(PPI)$ is replaced by $executed(PPI)$ to avoid direct interaction) and reduce the dosage of aspirin by 50 mg to 250 mg (replacing $dosage(A, 300)$ with $dosage(A, 250)$). After making these revisions, the mitigation algorithm checks if the revised $\mathcal{D}_{comb}$ is consistent. Since it is, the algorithm finds a model for the revised $\mathcal{D}_{comb}$ that includes the modified $\mathcal{D}_{cpg}$. This model is used to derive the combined therapy given in Fig. 10 (again the $prec$ predicates are excluded for brevity).

According to the combined therapy, the patient is prescribed PPI (*executed* (*PPI*)) and referred to a specialist for DU (*executed*(*RS*)). Also the therapy prescribes aspirin (*executed*(*A*)) with the dosage adjusted to 250 mg (*dosage*(*A*, 250)), prescribes dipyridamole (*executed*(*D*)) with the dosage set to 75 mg (*dosage*(*D*, 75)), and schedules an outpatient neurological consult for TIA (executed(NC)). As in the previous scenario, such combined therapy is presented for evaluation to the physician who may invoke the algorithm again once additional patient information becomes available.

6   Conclusions

We believe that FOL allows for a more flexible representation by including predicates to represent properties of domain objects, temporal relationships, and flexibly quantified sentences. In this paper we presented how using FOL theories allows us to augment the expressiveness of representation in order to capture intrinsic characteristics of the CPGs and combined therapies, and thus provides for a more complete mitigation framework. Using a simple clinical example we demonstrated the semantic interpretability of the models and combined therapies. In our earlier CLP-based framework we had to manually interpret the solutions, distinguishing between action and decision steps, and constructing temporal relationships to impose order in which steps should be taken. The new framework discussed here addresses all these shortcomings.

Presented new framework allows us to deal with such "hard" issues associated with CPGs as, for example, loops. This improved expressiveness comes at the cost of limited comprehensibility by non-experts. However, considering that we envisage the proposed framework to be embedded within a larger clinical decision support system that will present results of mitigation in a user-friendly way, a modeling complexity should not be an issue because actual model will not be seen/presented to a clinician. Only development of the operators will require direct involvement of a clinician, and this process will be guided by a knowledge transfer specialist.

For future research, we are working on a different representation of paths in $\mathcal{D}_{cpg}^{d_i}$, so disjunctions of conjunctions can be avoided, and on more sophisticated search methods employed by the mitigation algorithm to identify suitable revision operators. Considering that the ultimate goal of our research is to develop a generalized framework of mitigation, we are also studying different clinical situations involving comorbid patients to extract the full set of properties of CPGs that hold across mitigation scenarios.

Acknowledgment. The last two authors were supported by grants from the Natural Sciences and Engineering Research Council of Canada (Collaborative Health Research Program) and Telfer School of Management Research Support Program. This research was conducted when Dr. Tan was a postdoctoral fellow with MET Research Group at the University of Ottawa.

References

1. Duftschmid, G., Miksch, S.: Knowledge-based verification of clinical guidelines by detection of anomalies. Artif. Intell. Med. **22**(1), 23–41 (2001)
2. Fox, J., Glasspool, D., Patkar, V., Austin, M., Black, L., South, M., Robertson, D., Vincent, C.: Delivering clinical decision support services: there is nothing as practical as a good theory. J. Biomed. Inform. **43**, 831–843 (2010)
3. Isern, D., Moreno, A., Pedone, G., Sánchez, D., Varga, L.Z.: Home care personalisation with individual intervention plans. In: Riaño, D. (ed.) K4HelP 2008. LNCS (LNAI), vol. 5626, pp. 134–151. Springer, Heidelberg (2009)
4. Jafarpour, B., Abidi, S.S.R.: Merging disease-specific clinical guidelines to handle comorbidities in a clinical decision support setting. In: Peek, N., Marín Morales, R., Peleg, M. (eds.) AIME 2013. LNCS, vol. 7885, pp. 28–32. Springer, Heidelberg (2013)
5. López-Vallverdú, J.A., Riaño, D., Collado, A.: Rule-Based Combination of comorbid treatments for chronic diseases applied to hypertension, diabetes mellitus and heart failure. In: Lenz, R., Miksch, S., Peleg, M., Reichert, M., Riaño, D., ten Teije, A. (eds.) ProHealth 2012 and KR4HC 2012. LNCS (LNAI), vol. 7738, pp. 30–41. Springer, Heidelberg (2013)
6. McCune, W.: Prover9 and Mace4 (2005). http://www.cs.unm.edu/mccune/prover9
7. Michalowski, M., Wilk, S., Lin, D., Michalowski, W., Tan, X., Mohapatra, S.: Procedural approach to mitigating concurrently applied clinical practice guidelines. In: Proceedings of the First Workshop on Expanding the Boundaries of Health Informatics Using Artificial Intelligence (HIAI13) (2013)
8. Michalowski, M., Wilk, S., Michalowski, W., Lin, D., Farion, K., Mohapatra, S.: Using constraint logic programming to implement iterative actions and numerical measures during mitigation of concurrently applied clinical practice guidelines. In: Peek, N., Marín Morales, R., Peleg, M. (eds.) AIME 2013. LNCS, vol. 7885, pp. 17–22. Springer, Heidelberg (2013)
9. National Institute for Health and Clinical Excellence (NICE): NICE pathways (2014). http://pathways.nice.org.uk/
10. Otten, J.: leanCoP 2.0 and ileanCoP 1.2: high performance lean theorem proving in classical and intuitionistic logic (system descriptions). In: Armando, A., Baumgartner, P., Dowek, G. (eds.) IJCAR 2008. LNCS (LNAI), vol. 5195, pp. 283–291. Springer, Heidelberg (2008)
11. Pavlov, V., Schukin, A., Cherkasova, T.: Exploring automated reasoning in first-order logic: tools, techniques and application areas. In: Klinov, P., Mouromtsev, D. (eds.) KESW 2013. CCIS, vol. 394, pp. 102–116. Springer, Heidelberg (2013)
12. Peleg, M.: Computer-interpretable clinical guidelines: a methodological review. J. Biomed. Inform. **46**(4), 744–763 (2013)
13. Peleg, M., Tu, S.W., Leonardi, G., Quaglini, S., Russo, P., Palladini, G., Merlini, G.: Reasoning with effects of clinical guideline actions using OWL: al amyloidosis as a case study. In: Riaño, D., ten Teije, A., Miksch, S. (eds.) KR4HC 2011. LNCS (LNAI), vol. 6924, pp. 65–79. Springer, Heidelberg (2012)
14. Perez, B., Porres, I.: Authoring and verification of clinical guidelines: a model driven approach. J. Biomed. Inform. **43**(4), 520–536 (2010)
15. Riaño, D., Real, F., Lopez-Vallverdu, J.A., Campana, F., Ercolani, S., Mecocci, P., Annicchiarico, R., Caltagirone, C.: An ontology-based personalization of healthcare knowledge to support clinical decisions for chronically ill patients. J. Biomed. Inform. **45**(3), 429–446 (2012)

16. Rosenfeld, R., Shiffman, R.: Clinical practice guideline development manual: a quality-driven approach for translating evidence into action. Otolaryngol. Head Neck Surg. **140**(6), 1–43 (2009)
17. Sittig, D., Wright, A., Osheroff, J., Middleton, B., Teich, J., Ash, J., Campbell, E., Bates, D.: Grand challenges in clinical decision support. J. Biomed. Inform. **41**, 387–392 (2008)
18. ten Teije, A., Marcos, M., Balser, M., van Croonenborg, J., Duelli, C., van Harmelen, F., Lucas, P., Miksch, S., Reif, W., Rosenbrand, K., Seyfang, A.: Improving medical protocols by formal methods. Artif. Intell. Med. **36**(3), 193–209 (2006)
19. Wilk, S., Michalowski, W., Michalowski, M., Farion, K., Hing, M., Mohapatra, S.: Automatic mitigation of adverse interactions in pairs of clinical practice guidelines using constraint logic programming. J. Biomed. Inform. **46**(2), 341–353 (2013)
20. Zhang, H., Zhang, J.: MACE4 and SEM: a comparison of finite model generators. In: Bonacina, M.P., Stickel, M.E. (eds.) Automated Reasoning and Mathematics. LNCS, vol. 7788, pp. 101–130. Springer, Heidelberg (2013)

Conformance Analysis of the Execution of Clinical Guidelines with Basic Medical Knowledge and Clinical Terminology

Matteo Spiotta[1,2], Alessio Bottrighi[1], Laura Giordano[1],
and Daniele Theseider Dupré[1(✉)]

[1] DISIT, Sezione di Informatica,
Università del Piemonte Orientale, Alessandria, Italy
{alessio,dtd}@di.unipmn.it
[2] Dipartimento di Informatica, Università di Torino, Turin, Italy

Abstract. Clinical Guidelines (CGs) are developed for specifying the "best" clinical procedures for specific clinical circumstances. However, a CG is executed on a specific patient, with her peculiarities, and in a specific context, with its limitations and constraints. Physicians have to use Basic Medical Knowledge (BMK) in order to adapt the general CG to each specific case, even if the interplay between CGs and the BMK can be very complex, and the BMK should rely on medical terminological knowledge. In this paper, we focus on *a posteriori* analysis of conformance, intended as the adherence of an observed execution trace to CG and BMK knowledge. A CG description in the GLARE language is mapped to Answer Set Programming (ASP); the BMK and conformance rules are also represented in ASP. The BMK relies on the SNOMED CT terminology and additional (post-coordinated) concepts. Conformance analysis is performed in Answer Set Programming and identifies non-adherence situations to the CG and/or BMK, pointing out, in particular, discrepancies from one knowledge source that could be justified by another source, and discrepancies that cannot be justified.

1 Introduction

A Clinical Guideline (CG) is "a systematically developed statement to assist practitioner and patient decisions about appropriate health care for specific clinical circumstances" [1]. The CGs are developed in order to capture medical evidence and to put it into practice, and deal with general classes of patients, since the CG developers (typically expert committees) cannot define all possible executions of a CG on any possible specific patient in any possible clinical condition. CG developers make some implicit assumptions:

1. the CG is applied to an *ideal patient*, i.e., patients have just the single disease considered in the CG (thus excluding the concurrent application of more than one CG), and are statistically relevant (they model the typical patient affected by the given disease), not presenting rare peculiarities or side-effects;

This research is partially supported by Compagnia di San Paolo.

S. Miksch et al. (Eds.): KR4HC 2014, LNAI 8903, pp. 62–77, 2014.
DOI: 10.1007/978-3-319-13281-5_5

2. the CG is applied in an *ideal context*, i.e., in the context of execution, all necessary resources are available;
3. *ideal physicians* are executing the CG, i.e., physicians whose knowledge always allow them to properly apply the CGs to specific patients.

On the other hand, when a CG is applied to a specific patient, the patient and/or the context may not be ideal. The physicians indeed exploit Basic Medical Knowledge (BMK) to adapt the CG to the specific case at hand. The interplay between these two types of knowledge can be very complex, e.g., actions recommended by a CG could be prohibited by the BMK, or a CG could force some actions despite the BMK discourages them. Thus the physicians' judgment is very important in order to correctly execute a given CG in a specific case, as observed by the Infectious Diseases Society of America in its *Guide to Development of Practice Guidelines* [2]: "Practice guidelines, however, are never a substitute for clinical judgment. Clinical discretion is of the utmost importance in the application of a guideline to individual patients, because no guideline can ever be specific enough to be applied in all situations."

The issue of studying the interplay between the knowledge in CGs and BMK is relatively new in the literature. Several approaches have focused either on CGs or BMK in isolation, or have considered the BMK only as a source of information, such as definitions of clinical terms and abstractions [3]. Only recently some approaches (e.g., [4,5]) have considered that CGs cannot be interpreted and executed in "isolation", since CGs correspond to just a part of the medical knowledge that physicians have to take into account when treating patients. In this paper, we explore the interaction between CGs and BMK from the viewpoint of conformance analysis, intended as the adherence of an observed CG execution trace to both types of knowledge. Observe that both CG knowledge and BMK can be defeated (for a more detailed discussion see [4]), and it is, in general, the physician's responsibility to assess whether a trace can be deemed as conformant.

Our goal is to support the physicians in the conformance analysis task, providing them as much information as possible to make this task easier. The approach is based on GLARE ([6] and Sect. 2) to represent CGs, and on SNOMED CT ([7] and Sect. 3) for medical terminology; our general framework is described in Sect. 4 and its representation in Answer Set Programming in Sect. 5. In particular, we provide a set of rules defining, on the one hand, discrepancies from one source of knowledge that are, at least potentially, justified by another source; on the other hand, discrepancies that are not justified.

The BMK uses terms from SNOMED CT, and additional *post-coordinated* concepts, i.e., in the meta-terminology of medical ontologies, concepts defined or constrained in terms of the ones provided in advance. One such concept C can be used in a BMK rule to state, for example, that execution of an action which is not the CG currently being executed, or the fact that an action prescribed by the CG is not executed, is (potentially) justified if the patient, other than the problem being dealt with by the CG, has a problem in the class C.

2   The GLARE Representation Formalism

In this section, we highlight some of the main features of the GLARE representation formalism (a detailed description is provided in [6]). GLARE distinguishes between *atomic* and *composite* actions. Atomic actions are elementary steps in a CG, in the sense that they do not need a further de-composition into sub-actions to be executed. Composite actions are instead composed by other (atomic or composite) actions. GLARE provides four different types of atomic actions:

- *work actions*, i.e., actions to be executed at a given point of the CG;
- *decision actions*, used to model the selection among alternative paths in a CG. GLARE provides *diagnostic* decisions, used to make explicit the identification of the disease the patient is suffering from, among a set of possible diseases, compatible with her findings. Such a decision is based on patient's parameters. GLARE also provides *therapeutic* decisions, used to represent the choice between therapeutic paths in a CG, based on a pre-defined set of parameters: effectiveness, cost, side effects, compliance and duration;
- *query actions* model requests of information (typically patients' parameters), that can be obtained from the outside world (e.g. physicians, databases, patients visits or interviews). CG execution cannot proceed until such information has been obtained;
- *conclusion actions* represent the explicit output of a decision process.

Actions in a CG are connected through control relations. Such relations establish which actions might be executed next, in which order. GLARE introduces four different types of control relations: *sequence, concurrency, alternative* and *repetition*. The sequence relation explicitly establishes which is the next action to be executed; the alternative relation describes which alternative paths stem from a decision action, the concurrency relation between two actions states that they can be executed in any order, or also in parallel and the repetition relation, states that an action has to be repeated several times (i.e. the number of repetitions can be fixed a priori, or, alternatively, it can be asserted that the action must be repeated until a certain exit condition becomes true).

3   SNOMED CT

The Systematized Nomenclature of Medicine Clinical Terms (SNOMED CT) is a standardized healthcare terminology. It is developed and distributed by the International Health Terminology Standards Development Organization (IHTSDO). SNOMED CT was created with the aim of improving data quality and patient safety, facilitating semantic interoperability by capturing clinical data in a standardized, unambiguous and granular manner. It is used in more than 50 countries around the world, as the foundation for electronic health records and other applications [8]. SNOMED CT is distributed in its official release format RF2 with a parser to generate an OWL 2 EL version of the terminological knowledge. The number of concepts, descriptions, and relationships varies with every release.

SNOMED CT contains more than 300,000 concepts and consists of several independent hierarchies ranging from Disease, Drug, Living organism, Procedure, to more general concepts as Physical Object and Physical Force.

ELK [9] is a Description Logic reasoner developed to provide high performance reasoning support for OWL 2 EL, whose underlying logic is the low-complexity description logic $\mathcal{EL}^{++}$; see, e.g., [10] for a discussion on the expressiveness needed for the medical domain. In [11], ELK is evaluated to be the fastest reasoner in loading and classifying SNOMED CT as well as other ontologies.

4   Conformance Analysis Framework

A main goal of the framework presented in this paper is to exploit reusability of knowledge, in several ways:

- A model of the CG in Answer Set Programming (ASP, [12]) is derived automatically from the description of the CG in GLARE, and can be used for conformance analysis, as in this paper, i.e., analyzing if and how a single execution deviates from the CG, as well as for verifying properties of the CG, that should hold for all executions, e.g., using the approach in [13] as model checker in the loosely coupled framework in [14].
- A common repository of Basic Medical Knowledge (BMK) can be used, in the framework in this paper, with models of different CGs.
- The terminology, based on SNOMED CT, provides the link for triggering BMK rules for a specific CG and its execution on a specific patient.

Figure 1 presents the general framework. The main entities, to be input to an ASP solver, are ASP representations of the log, the CG model, BMK rules and the set of compliance annotation rules. BMK rules use subsumption of concepts in the terminology that make it possible to interpret the current situation as a case of application of the rule; in the current framework, subsumptions that may be relevant for a given log are queried in advance to ELK. The framework evaluates discrepancies of the log (actual execution) wrt executions suggested by the CG, considering the possible "variations" suggested by the BMK.

The log contains the data recorded during guideline execution. It includes data specific to the individual patient, such as medical records (from the Electronic Patient Record, EPR) and the actions performed on the patient; it also includes data related to the context (e.g., hospital) in which the CG is performed, such as availability of equipment and personnel.

The ASP model of the CG encodes all the admitted treatment paths provided by the CG. Tools such as GLARE provide a formal representation of CGs, which can be translated to ASP. In this framework, information on when an action is executed is used both to verify whether it is justified by the CG, and to justify execution of subsequent actions in the CG. Both the control flow perspective and the data perspective of the GLARE CG specification is encoded in the CG ASP model. In the current version, quantitative time constraints present in GLARE are not supported.

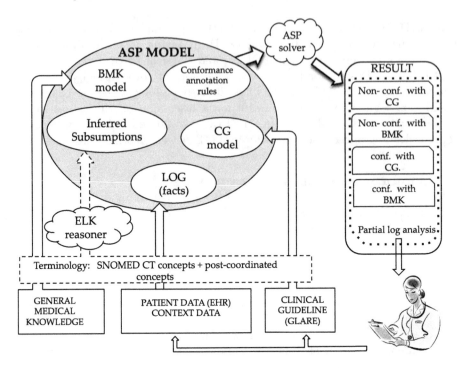

Fig. 1. General framework

To better evaluate the interplay of BMK and CG we take into account the action execution model in Fig. 2, similar to the one in [4]. At a given point in the execution of a CG on a specific patient, the control flow of the CG or rules in the BMK indicate that a given action has to be executed (is a candidate). A candidate action is discarded if its preconditions (modeled in the CG) are false; or it may be discarded because of conditions that are not explicitly modeled in the CG, but are, hopefully, modeled in the BMK as reasons for discarding it. Decision and conclusion actions are instantaneous. Work actions and query actions, once started, can either be completed or aborted. An action is aborted if a failure occurs during its execution, or it may be aborted because some condition arises; again, we expect that some of such reasons for aborting are modeled in the BMK.

Once an action of the CG is discarded or aborted, in general we cannot infer the correct way to continue the execution of the CG. In some cases the physician would continue the execution skipping the uncompleted action (e.g., for an action having minor impact on the treatment), in other cases she would restart the execution from some point further away (e.g., a previous decision point or the end of the partial plan), or the entire CG should be interrupted (e.g., in case the action is essential for the treatment). We do not assume that this information is modeled, therefore we suggest that the analyst should point out where in the CG and in the log the analysis can be restarted.

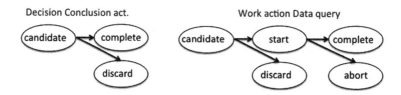

Fig. 2. Action model

The annotation compliance rules are the keystone of the entire framework. They define the output of the analysis, and are triggered by discrepancies, starting from the actions recorded in the log and the expected actions derived from the CG and BMK. Two different classes of discrepancies are provided:

- Discrepancies of the log with a knowledge source (KS; either the CG or a BMK rule) which are "supported" by another source.
- Discrepancies of the log with a KS that are not supported by another one.

While the second class represents incorrect behavior (wrt the considered KSs), the first one represents a case of (at least, potential) conflict between knowledge sources. Which one should prevail cannot be stated in general [4], and providing knowledge for stating this for all cases is, in general, too costly. Therefore we provide the information in the log, which can be filtered further by the analyst.

We assume completeness and correctness of the Log. Completeness with respect to actions means that for all actions taken, the following is recorded:

- start, discard, abort, complete and failure reason (human and/or technical problem which caused incorrect completion of an action);
- the outcome of completed decision actions.

Completeness with respect to (patient or context) data means that the log contains record of data which have driven the control flow (CF) and data which could force the physician to change the normal execution applying BMK rules. Correctness means that only verified information is recorded, no conflicting data can be stored (e.g., an action is first discarded and then completed).

We expect (see [4]) that the BMK provides pieces of knowledge such as:

- Actions of a given type, or specific actions, are contraindicated for patients in a given temporary or permanent condition; e.g. an invasive exam (suitable to get more information on the problem treated by the CG) is contraindicated for patients also suffering from a problem in a given class C;
- the execution of a CG may (have to) be suspended if a more urgent problem (e.g., a life threat) arises, and the latter one should be treated. Whether the execution actually *has* to be suspended depends, in general, on whether the current actions being executed are compatible with the treatment of the more urgent problem. Specific knowledge in this respect may be available or not. We intend that the other problem (e.g., a heart failure) is not part of

the class of problems dealt with by the CG. The source of knowledge for its treatment should, in principle, come from another CG; however, in this paper we do not address the problem of interaction of multiple CGs and we assume to have available, when analyzing logs for the execution of a CG, the set of possible treatments for other problems.

- Actions of a given type (e.g., routine exams) can be performed even if not part of the CG.

5 ASP Representation and Conformance Rules

In this section we describe the ASP representation including the one for the Log, the CG model, the BMK model, their relation with SNOMED CT, and the annotation rules.

5.1 Log Representation

In the ASP representation of the Log, context and patient data, action states and decision outcomes are encoded as follows:

- `holds(var(name,value),timeStamp)` represents the fact (from the EPR) that a patient or context datum `name` has value `value` at time `timeStamp`;
- `holds(problem,timeStamp)` represents the fact (from the EPR) that `problem` holds for the patient at time `timeStamp`;
- `action(actID,actState,timeStamp)` represents the fact that for action `actID` there is a transition to state `actState` (discard, started, aborted, completed) at time `timeStamp`;
- `decision(actID,actIDoutcome,timeStamp)` represents the fact that at time `timeStamp`, the result of the decision action `actID`, performed by the physician, is to perform action `actIDoutcome`.

We reconstruct the timeline for the framework with the predicate *next*:

```
next(S,SN):-state(S),state(SN),SN>S, not stateinbetween(S,SN).
stateinbetween(S,S2):-state(S),state(S2),state(S3),S<S3,S3<S2.
```

A predicate *state(S)* is true for all timestamps S; `next(S,SN)` is true for all the pairs of timestamps with no states in between. The rules below propagate data values up to the next change:

```
holds(var(N,V),SN):- holds(var(N,V),S), next(S,SN),
                      not holds(var(N,V1),SN), V!=V1.
```

The occurrence of a situation described by a term in the terminology (i.e., SNOMED CT extended with post-coordinated concepts) should be matched with information describing the situation at a given timestamp.

In medical reasoning it is not obvious how information that constitutes a problem to be treated should be separated from other information relative to the patient and context; the latter may be relevant or not for solving the problem, but we cannot expect to describe it together with the problem in a single medical term. More generally, part of the information on the patient should be aggregated into a set of problems which need treatment. Such a description has a dynamics: e.g., new information on a problem may become available, or the problem itself may change (e.g. it may become worse, or improve with treatment, or change from acute to chronic); or, more generally, the aggregation might change (a single problem should be split into two problems, or vice versa). However, modeling such evolution is not the purpose of this work. What we need is:

- conformance reasoning, which we intend to represent in ASP;
- terminological inference, which should classify, in the terminological knowledge base, a problem the patient has, or an action occurring in the CG or in a BMK rule; to this purpose, we use ELK, which is the obvious choice for SNOMED CT, and, as far as post-coordinated concepts are concerned, covers a significant subset of $\mathcal{EL}^{++}$ which, like the basic $\mathcal{EL}$, has low complexity, in particular, subsumption in $\mathcal{EL}^{++}$ is polynomial [15].

This is obtained as follows:

- a problem the patient has at a given snapshot t is supposed to be represented (as in [8]) as an atomic concept B occurring in the terminological knowledge base (in case it is a non-atomic concept C, a new name B is introduced and $B \equiv C$ is added to the terminological knowledge base);
- a constant b is used to represent B in ASP;
- holds(b,t) is used to state that problem b holds for the patient at time t;
- as we shall see in Sect. 5.3, BMK rules contain atoms of the form is_a(u,u'), where u,u' are either ASP constants corresponding to atomic concepts, or ASP variables; for ground instances is_a(b,c), the subsumption $B \sqsubseteq C$ is checked in ELK[1];
- persistence of the problem description is given by:

    holds(C,SN):- holds(C,S), next(S,SN), not -holds(C,SN).

- an explicit statement -holds(b,t') (where "-" represents explicit negation) is included (to block persistence) for the time t' when b is known to no longer be the description of a problem the patient has. This information is supposed to be given in the EPR when the problem description (in case new information has become available) or the problem itself has changed. In that case a statement holds(b',t') should also be provided for the new concept b' describing the current situation. Notice that this is correct, in particular, for the case where there is no evidence that the problem has changed, but new information has been acquired. In fact, a BMK rule may state that a discrepancy from a CG prescription is potentially justified at some time t

---

[1] This can be seen as an extension of ASP where, in the grounding of ASP rules, variables in such is_a atoms are instantiated in all possible ways with atomic concepts occurring in the ASP model; the semantics of the grounded program can be taken to be a special case of the weak answer set semantics in [16] where DL queries are restricted to be concept inclusions only.

if there is a problem which is a case of some problem class c, i.e., it would contain the condition: holds(P,S),isa(P,c). Information on the problem that only becomes available at time t' > t, should not be used to infer that the problem is a case of c in order to justify an action (or the absence of an action) at time t. This does not occur, because holds(b,t), holds(b',t'), and -holds(b,t') would be in the ASP representation of the log, where isa(b',c) can be inferred from terminological knowledge while isa(b,c) cannot.

5.2 CG Model

The CG model is not reported in full detail. The main CG component is the control flow (CF), we encode it in ASP similarly to the approach in [13]. The CF model defines candidate(A,S) for actions A and states S. There are atomic actions and composed actions. Predicates end(Type,A,S) and start(Type,A,S) (where Type is either group, plan or atomic) are defined to reconstruct the execution interval of composite actions from the ones of atomic actions, which are registered in the log. The definition of *end* relates the end of atomic actions to the end of composite actions and control structures; e.g., a set of actions in a group is considered ended in S only if all the sub-processes are ended in S.

Every candidate action *a* (atomic/composite) can be executed, and once it ends, it enables its successors (in the control flow) *a1* in the *next* time state by means of the predicate candidate(A,SN):

(a) candidate(A1,SN):-succ(A,A1),not excp(A1,S),end(_,A,S),next(S,SN).

(b) candidate(A1,SN):-decision(A,A1,S),end(action,A,S),next(S,SN).

(c) candidate(A1,SN):-end(_,A,S),next(S,SN),reExecute(A,S).

In rule (a), A1 is candidate in SN if A ended in S and A1 is the *successor* of A in the flow. The predicate excp(A,S), blocks execution after actions that terminated with errors or for other reasons (e.g. a completed data query without data) should not lead to the next action in the flow. Rule (b) corresponds to *decisions*: the outcome of the decision task, as registered in the log, enables the proper successor action. Rule (c) encodes *repetition*. All actions (atomic/composite), if specified by the CG, can be re-executed: reExecute(ID,state) is true if the action ends and the exit condition on data is false. Other CG specifications mapped in ASP are the list of data requested by a data query action, parameters to evaluate therapeutic decision, exit conditions for repetitions and preconditions of action.

5.3 BMK Rules and Clinical Terminology

The BMK model consists of a set of rules which prescribe or allow the introduction or cancellation of an action, based on conditions on the patient and contextual data. Such *conditions* are defined in other rules, also making use of the terminology. BMK rules have the following forms:

prescribe(id,A,normal/urgent,S):- *condition(S)*.

allow(id,A,S):- *condition(S)*.

prescribeCanc(id,A,S):- *condition(S)*.

allowCanc(id,A,S):- *condition(S)*.

The *id* is used to point out in the analysis the set of rules that has generated or justified a discrepancy. Multiple instances of *prescribe/allow* with the same id and different actions encode the request to execute one of a set of possible alternative actions; (*normal/urgent*) encodes the urgency to execute the action: in the *normal* case, there is no constraint on the order of execution wrt other actions, while, in the *urgent* case, it must be the first action to be executed once the condition is true. The difference between *prescribe* and *allow* is that:

– for *prescribe*, a discrepancy is reported both in case the action is executed (as it was not an action in the CG) and in case it is not executed (it is a discrepancy wrt the prescription in this rule, possibly due to the fact that the CG overrides BMK in this case)
– for *allow*, a discrepancy is reported only when the action is executed

and similarly for *prescribeCanc* and *allowCanc*. In fact, the four predicates are related to action events as follows, to define `candidate`, `discard` and `abort` which are used in the annotation rules to point out discrepancies:

```
candidate(A,S,ID):-prescribe(ID,A,normal,S),not running(A,S).
candidate(A,S,ID):-prescribe(ID,A,urgent,S),not running(A,S).
urgent(ID,A,S):-prescribe(ID,A,urgent,S),not running(A,S).
candidate(A,S,ID):-allow(ID,A,S),action(A,started,S).
discard(A,S,ID):-prescribeCanc(ID,A,S),candidate(A,S).
abort(A,S,ID):-prescribeCanc(ID,A,S),running(A,S).
discard(A,S,ID):-allowCanc(ID,A,S),action(A,discarded,S),candidate(A,S).
abort(A,S,ID):-allowCanc(ID,A,S),running(A,S),action(A,aborted,S).
```

The `conditions` in rules also make use of concepts defined in terminological knowledge. In particular, we use atoms of the form: `is_a(u,u')`, where `u,u'` are either ASP constants corresponding to atomic concepts, or ASP variables.

For all pairs `c,d` of constants, which occur in the log or BMK rules, and correspond to atomic concepts, before performing conformance analysis, ELK is queried to check whether $C \sqsubseteq D$, where C and D are the atomic concepts corresponding to `c` and `d`. In that case, `is_a(c,d)` is added to the ASP representation.

In the following we provide the representation for some of the rules in [4].

BMK: Calcemia and glycemia measurements are routinely performed in all patients admitted to the internal medicine ward of Italian hospitals, regardless of the disease.

SNOMED CT contains the concept name *blood calcium measurement* to represent calcemia measurement, and the concept name *blood glucose measurement* which subsumes 42 kind of glycemia tests. We add a concept *routine action* including such classes:

blood calcium measurement $\sqcup$ *blood glucose measurement* $\sqcup$ ... $\sqsubseteq$ *routine action*

and the rule:

```
allow(r1,A,S):-holds(var(admitted_Int_med,true),S),is_a(A,routine_act).
```

where `routine_act` corresponds to the concept *routine action*.

BMK: Contrast media administration for coronary angiography may cause a further final deterioration of the renal functions in patients affected by unstable advanced predialytic renal failure. Assuming that the latter is suitably defined, using the terms already available in SNOMED CT, as a concept corresponding to the ASP constant `adv_predial_renal_failure`, the rule can be represented as:

```
prescribeCanc(r2,A,S):- holds(D,S),is_a(D,adv_predial_renal_failure).
```

BMK: The execution of any CG may be suspended, if a problem threatening the patients life suddenly arises. Such a problem has to be treated first. One such problem is acute heart failure; an immediate response for it could be a Diuretic Therapy.

SNOMED CT provides a severity property for diseases; although there is no pre-coordinated concept using it, we assume that for diseases that are considered to be life threatening for the purpose of the above rule, their severity is provided (e.g., acute heart failure is stated to have a life-threatening severity), the concept *Life Threat* is added with the following constraint:

$$Life\,Threat \equiv Disease \sqcap \exists Severity.Life\,ThreateningSeverity$$

The following BMK rule models the fact that if there is a life threat D, then an action Act which is a special case of a treatment T, suitable for a superclass D1 of D, is justified:

```
prescribe(r3,Act,urgent,S):-holds(D,S), is_a(D,lifeThreat)
          treatment(D1,T),is_a(D,D1),is_a(Act,T)
```

and in the same situation an action which is not a (special case of) treatment for (a superclass of) D should be cancelled:

```
prescribeCanc(r3,T,S):-holds(D,S), is_a(D,lifeThreat),
          running(T,S),not is_a(T,T1):treatment(D1,T1):is_a(D1,D).
```

The `treatment` relation is modeled explicitly in ASP:

```
treatment(heartFailure,diureticTherapy).
treatment(heartFailure,betaBlockerTherapy).
treatment(heartFailure,inotropeTherapy) [...]
```

to mean that all diuretic therapies, beta blocker therapies, ..., are (in principle) suitable in case of heart failure. Of course, in case more specific information is available (i.e., that a type of therapy is only suitable for some specific class of heart failure), it should be provided. However, the BMK rule above is quite general: it is not intended to prescribe a specific appropriate treatment for a specific case (neither a CG is supposed to do so), but to provide a general justification for a deviation from the execution of a CG.

Notice moreover that properties in SNOMED CT are intended in $\mathcal{EL}$ as existential restrictions. If the property of *DiureticTherapy*, that consists in being a treatment for *HeartFailure*, were added as:

$$DiureticTherapy \sqsubseteq \exists IsTreatmentFor.HeartFailure,$$

it would only mean that for any *DiureticTherapy* there is some (individual) *HeartFailure* for which it is a treatment. Moreover, for any superclass C of *Heart-Failure*, $DiureticTherapy \sqsubseteq \exists IsTreatmentFor.C$ can be inferred, and of course we do not want to interpret this as "*DiureticTherapy* is a treatment for C".

5.4   Conformance Annotation Rules

In a state t, relatively to action a, the following discrepancies, potentially justified by a knowledge source (KS, either the CG or a BMK rule), are defined:

A1 **A discrepancy with a KS s, justified by a BMK rule r**, if a is recorded as discarded in t, rule r prescribes discarding a, and s suggests a as candidate.

A2 **A discrepancy with a BMK rule r, justified by a KS s**, if a is recorded as started in t, rule r prescribes discarding a, and s suggests a as candidate.

A3 **A discrepancy with a KS s, justified by BMK rule r**, if a is recorded as aborted in t, rule r prescribes aborting a and, until t, action a was running as suggested by s.

A4 **A discrepancy with a BMK rule r justified by the KS s**, if a is recorded as completed in t, rule r prescribes aborting a and, until t, action a was running as suggested by s.

A5 **A discrepancy with a BMK rule r justified by the KS s**, if in a state in t a rule r prescribes with urgency one or more actions and a different action, prescribed by s, is recorded as started.

In a state t, relatively to action a, the following discrepancies not justified by other knowledge sources are output:

B1 **A discrepancy with the KS s**, if a is recorded as discarded in t, s suggests a as candidate, no BMK rule r justifies discarding a and preconditions of a are satisfied at t.

B2 **A discrepancy with the KS s**, if a is recorded as started in t, s suggests a as candidate and preconditions of a are falsified at t.

B3 **A discrepancy with all KSs**, if a is recorded as started in t, there is no source s which suggests a as candidate.

B4 **A discrepancy with the KS s**, if a is recorded as aborted, no BMK rule r justify aborting a, no failure is recorded for a and, until t, action a was running as suggested by s.

B5 **A discrepancy with the CG**, if a was candidate by the CG at t and, after t, a is not recorded as started nor discarded.

B6 **A discrepancy with a BMK rule r**, if in an interval $[t_0, t]$ a rule r suggests a, and possibly alternative actions, as candidates; the actions are not candidate at $t+1$, and at $t+1$ no action suggested by r is executed or discarded.

The encoding of the above rules in ASP is relatively straightforward. E.g., for A1 we have the two clauses below; the first one is for discrepancies with respect to the CG, the second one for a discrepancy wrt a BMK rule, as recorded in the first argument of `discrepancy`:

```
discrepancy(cg,ID,A,S):-action(A,discarded,S),discard(A,S,ID),
            not precondFalse(A,S),candidate(A,S).
discrepancy(ID2,ID,A,S):-action(A,discarded,S),discard(A,S,ID),
            not precondFalse(A,S),candidate(A,S,ID2).
```

An ASP solver such as Clingo [17] computes an answer set of the overall ASP model (see Fig. 1); the set of instances of the *discrepancy* predicate in the answer set contains the information necessary to produce a user-friendly result.

6   Framework Execution Example

Let us consider an example of execution of a fragment of CG for acute myocardial infarction associated to a BMK containing the rules presented in Sect. 5.3. The fragment of CG (Fig. 3) consists of three activities in sequence, Electrocardiographic study (ECG), Echocardiographic study (ES) and Coronary Angiography (CA).

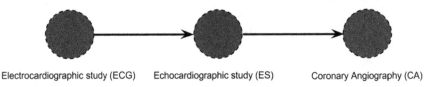

Electrocardiographic study (ECG)   Echocardiographic study (ES)   Coronary Angiography (CA)

Fig. 3. Fragment of CG for acute myocardial infarction

Consider now the partial log, shown in Fig. 4, of a specific execution of the CG. The log contains trace of actions that have been executed (started and completed): ECG, Glucose measurement blood test strip (BMTS) and ES; trace of the discarded action CA; and patient data: the patient was admitted to the internal medicine ward, the patient had an acute heart failure.

In this example the execution of ECG and ES is compliant with the model of the CG, but discarding CA is not, as the action has no preconditions which can fail. From the BMK perspective, executing BMTS and discarding CA is correct while the lack of a treatment for the heart failure is a violation of the expected behavior. The first rule introduced in Sect. 5.3 (r1), triggered by the admission in the internal medicine ward, allows the execution of any action subsumed by the (post-coordinated) concept "routine action". By the definition of this concept given before, the execution of BMTS is allowed since the action is subsumed by "glucose blood measurement" in SNOMED-CT. From time 17 the acute heart failure diagnosis triggers rule r3 in Sect. 5.3. This rule prescribes the cancellation of any action which is not a treatment for the life threatening problem, causing the annotation of the discrepancy A1 at time 19. Rule r3 also prescribes the execution with urgency of a reparative treatment, but no action is recorded as started, and the discrepancy B6 is reported at the end of the log.

7   Related Work and Conclusions

We presented a framework for analyzing conformance of execution traces for patient treatment with Clinical Guidelines relying on Basic Medical Knowledge and Clinical Terminology.

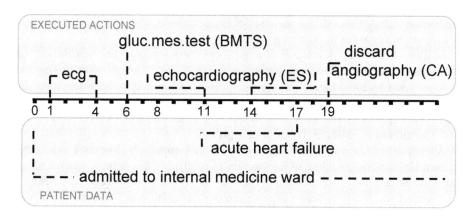

Fig. 4. Execution trace

The approach, as presented in the paper, is specific to healthcare processes, but a similar one can be used for comparing actual execution traces with process models in other organizations, i.e., for *business* processes; also in other contexts, in fact, there might be "ideal" process models, which make sense as a reference, but do not define all conceivable process adaptations in all situations.

Conformance analysis work in the process model area, e.g. [18–20], is mainly devoted to measuring the adherence of a model with execution traces, in order to refine a model, rather than to analyze, as in our approach, the correctness of an execution with respect to a model.

Our approach builds on the work in [4], which is mainly devoted to studying the interaction between CGs and BMK from the viewpoint of the conformance problem. In this paper, we proposed a general framework architecture, which allow us to integrate existing ontologies (SNOMED CT, in particular) as knowledge sources and to exploit terminological inference in conformance analysis. Moreover, in [4] the authors identify only non-adherence situations to the CG and/or BMK, while we propose a finer classification where we point out possible justifications, when one knowledge source "supports" a situation of non-adherence to another source.

The issue of compliance with clinical guidelines is discussed in [21] taking into account a wide range of reasons for non-adherence to guidelines, from "human factors" regarding both patients and physicians, who do not necessarily accept guidelines especially because they tend to be too rigid, to reasons that are considered in this paper, e.g., patient characteristics that make the guideline inappropriate for her. The author points out that even in a system that supports execution of guidelines, analyzing non-compliance at execution time might be inappropriate because treating patients may be more urgent than documenting the actions being performed, or because relevant data may not yet be stored in the system; patient discharge might be a more appropriate time when physicians can document non-compliance. In the present paper, we propose using annotation rules in an off-line analysis of logs; however, they could also be used to support annotation at discharge time.

Müller et al. [22] developed the AGENTWORK system for adaptation of (healthcare) workflows to handle exceptional situations; Event/Condition/Action rules are used to model such situations, given that explicitly modeling them in the workflow would greatly reduce its readability. Our approach is not devoted to provide support at run time, and in our case rules allow or suggest deviations from the guideline, without being prescriptive.

As regards CGs and medical knowledge, the approach does not take into account the general problem of interaction of multiple CGs, where general medical knowledge should of course play a role. A recent approach in this respect is presented in [23]; it is based on an ontology of intentions (goals that actions should achieve, e.g., decreasing blood pressure), drugs (whose administration can achieve the intentions) and interactions of such intentions and drugs. The approach also relies on SNOMED-CT. Such a model of interactions can of course be used to justify discrepancies from a CG execution, if not already used to support decision at action execution time for patients affected by multiple diseases.

References

1. Field, M.J., Lohr, K.N. (eds.): Guidelines for Clinical Practice: From Development to Use. National Academy Press, Institute of Medicine, Washington, D.C. (1992)
2. Kish, M.A.: Guide to development of practice guidelines. Clin. Infect. Dis. **32**(6), 851–854 (2001)
3. Ten Teije, A., Miksch, S., Lucas, P. (eds.): Computer-Based Medical Guidelines and Protocols: A Primer and Current Trends. Studies in Health Technology and Informatics, vol. 139. IOS Press, Amsterdam (2008)
4. Bottrighi, A., Chesani, F., Mello, P., Montali, M., Montani, S., Terenziani, P.: Conformance checking of executed clinical guidelines in presence of basic medical knowledge. In: Daniel, F., Barkaoui, K., Dustdar, S. (eds.) BPM Workshops 2011, Part II. LNBIP, vol. 100, pp. 200–211. Springer, Heidelberg (2012)
5. Brandhorst, C.J., Sent, D., Stegwee, R.A., van Dijk, B.M.A.G.: Medintel: decision support for general practitioners: a case study. In: Adlassnig, K.-P., Blobel, B., Mantas, J., Masic, I. (eds.) MIE, Studies in Health Technology and Informatics, vol. 150, pp. 688–692. IOS Press, Amsterdam (2009)
6. Terenziani, P., Molino, G., Torchio, M.: A modular approach for representing and executing clinical guidelines. Artif. Intell. Med. **23**(3), 249–276 (2001)
7. International Health Terminology Standards Development Organization: SNOMED CT. http://www.ihtsdo.org/snomed-ct/
8. Lee, D., Cornet, R., Lau, F., de Keizer, N.: A survey of SNOMED CT implementations. J. Biomed. Inform. **46**(1), 87–96 (2013)
9. ELK. https://code.google.com/p/elk-reasoner/
10. Rector, A.L.: Medical informatics. In: Baader, F., Calvanese, D., McGuinness, L., Nardi, D., Patel-Schneider, P.F. (eds.) Description Logic Handbook (2007)
11. Kazakov, Y., Krötzsch, M., Simancik, F.: ELK reasoner: architecture and evaluation. In: Horrocks, I., Yatskevich, M., Jiménez-Ruiz, E. (eds.) Proceeding of International Workshop on OWL Reasoner Evaluation (ORE-2012), CEUR 858 (2012)

12. Gelfond, M.: Answer Sets. Handbook of Knowledge Representation, chapter 7. Elsevier, New York (2007)
13. Giordano, L., Martelli, A., Spiotta, M., Theseider Dupré, D.: Business process verification with constraint temporal answer set programming. Theory Pract. Logic Program. **13**(4–5), 563–578 (2013)
14. Bottrighi, A., Giordano, L., Molino, G., Montani, S., Terenziani, P., Torchio, M.: Adopting model checking techniques for clinical guidelines verification. Artif. Intell. Med. **48**(1), 1–19 (2010)
15. Baader, F., Brandt, S., Lutz, C.: Pushing the $\mathcal{EL}$ envelope. In: IJCAI, pp. 364–369 (2005)
16. Eiter, T., Lanni, G., Lukasiewicz, T., Schindlauer, R., Tompits, H.: Combining answer set programming with description logics for the semantic web. Artif. Intell. **172**(12–13), 1495–1539 (2008)
17. Gebser, M., Kaminski, R., Kaufmann, B., Ostrowski, M., Schaub, T., Schneider, M.: Potassco: the Potsdam answer set solving collection. AI Commun. **24**(2), 105–124 (2011)
18. Adriansyah, A., van Dongen, B.F., van der Aalst, W.M.P.: Towards robust conformance checking. In: Muehlen, M., Su, J. (eds.) BPM 2010 Workshops. LNBIP, vol. 66, pp. 122–133. Springer, Heidelberg (2011)
19. Rozinat, A., van der Aalst, W.M.P.: Conformance checking of processes based on monitoring real behavior. Inf. Syst. **33**(1), 64–95 (2008)
20. Munoz-Gama, J., Carmona, J.: Enhancing precision in process conformance: stability, confidence and severity. In: Proceeding of CIDM, pp. 184–191 (2011)
21. Quaglini, S.: Compliance with clinical practice guidelines. In: Ten Teije, P.L.A., Miksch, S. (eds.) Computer-based Medical Guidelines and Protocols: A Primer and Current Trends. IOS Press, Amsterdam (2008)
22. Müller, R., Greiner, U., Rahm, E.: AgentWork: a workflow system supporting rule-based workflow adaptation. Data Knowl. Eng. **51**(2), 223–256 (2004)
23. Piovesan, L., Molino, G., Terenziani, P.: An ontological knowledge and multiple abstraction level decision support system in healthcare. Decis. Anal. **1**(8), 1–24 (2014)

Semantic Representation of Evidence-Based Clinical Guidelines

Zhisheng Huang[1](✉), Annette ten Teije[1](✉), Frank van Harmelen[1],
and Salah Aït-Mokhtar[2]

[1] Department of Computer Science, VU University Amsterdam, Amsterdam,
The Netherlands
{huang,annette,Frank.van.Harmelen}@cs.vu.nl
[2] Xerox Research Centre Europe, Meylan, France
Salah.Ait-Mokhtar@xrce.xerox.com

Abstract. Evidence-based Clinical Guidelines (EbCGs) are document
or recommendation which have been created using the best clinical research findings of the highest value to aid in the delivery of optimum clinical care to patients. In this paper, we propose a lightweight formalism
of evidence-based clinical guidelines by introducing the Semantic Web
Technology for it. With the help of the tools which have been developed
in the Semantic Web and Natural Language Processing (NLP), the generation of the formulations of evidence-based clinical guidelines become
much easy. We will discuss several usecases of the semantic representation of EbCGs, and argue that it is potentially useful for the applications
of the semantic web technology on the medical domain.

1 Introduction

Clinical guidelines (CGs) are recommendations on the appropriate treatment
and care of people with specific diseases and conditions. Evidence-based Clinical
Guidelines are that the document or recommendation has been created using an
unbiased and transparent process of systematically reviewing, appraising, and
using the best clinical research findings of the highest value to aid in the delivery
of optimum clinical care to patients. Clinical guidelines have been proved to be
valuable for clinicians, nurses, and other healthcare professionals in their work.
Of course, clinical guidelines would not replace the medical knowledge and skills
of healthcare professionals.

Computerized Clinical Guidelines, alternatively called Computer-Interpretable Guidelines (CIGs), implement the guidelines in computer-based decision
support systems. Computerized clinical guidelines are expected to improve the
acceptance and application of guidelines in daily practice for healthcare professionals, because their actions and observations can be monitored by a semi-
automatic way with the support of a computer-based decision support system.
When the decision support system has detected that a guideline is not followed,
an advice would be generated by the system [4]. Various computerized clinical
guidelines as well as decision support systems that incorporate these guidelines

S. Miksch et al. (Eds.): KR4HC 2014, LNAI 8903, pp. 78–94, 2014.
DOI: 10.1007/978-3-319-13281-5_6

have been developed. Those main standards of computerized clinical guidelines or medical decision support languages are: the Arden Syntax[1], PROforma [6,7], Asbru [14], EON [16], GLIF [12,13][2].

In this paper, a main concern is the semantic interoperability, which is usually achieved by mapping concepts in the specification of guidelines to standard terminologies and domain ontologies. Both EON and GLIF emphasize its integration with medical terminologies and domain ontologies. Neither PROforma and nor Asbru is developed for the integration of medical terminologies or domain ontologies.

In this paper, we propose a semantic representation of evidence-based clinical guidelines as a lightweight formalism of EbCGs. Those evidence-based guidelines are represented by using the RDF/RDFS/OWL standards, which have been widely used in the Semantic Web Technology. We have used XMedlan, an NLP tool [1], to generate the semantic data of clinical guidelines. The proposed formalism is designed to serve for the task of the guideline update in the European 7th framework project EURECA [3][3].

Compared with existing other formalisms of Computer-Interpretable Guidelines, which usually require a lot of manual processing for the generation of the formulation, this lightweight formalism of evidence-based clinical guidelines has the advantage that they can be generated quite easy by using the tools that have been developed in the NLP and Semantic Web. We will argue that this semantic representation of evidence-based clinical guidelines have some novel features, and can be used for various application scenarios in the medical domain.

The main contribution of this paper is:

1. propose a framework of semantic representation of evidence-based clinical guidelines,
2. show how to use an NLP tool to generate semantic data of clinical guidelines,
3. present several use cases of the lightweight formalism of evidence-based clinical guidelines for the semantic operability.

This paper is organized as follows: Sect. 2 introduces the general ideas of evidence-based clinical guidelines. In Sect. 3 we propose a semantic representation of evidence-based clinical guidelines by using the semantic web technology. Section 4 describes the NLP tools that have been used to convert the textual clinical guidelines into semantic data. Section 5 discusses several use cases of the semantic representation of evidence-based clinical guidelines. Section 6 discusses the related work, future work, and make the conclusions.

2 Evidence Based Clinical Guidelines

As we have discussed above, Evidence-based Clinical Guidelines are a series of recommendations on clinical care, supported by the best available evidence in

---

[1] http://www.hl7.org/special/Committees/arden/index.cfm
[2] http://web.squ.edu.om/med-Lib/med/net/e-pathways-net/Docs/GLIF3_TECH_SPEC.pdf
[3] http://eurecaproject.eu

the clinical literature. In evidence-based clinical guidelines, the answers to the fundamental questions are based on published scientific research. The articles selected were evaluated by an expert in methodology for their research quality, and graded in proportion to evidence using the classification system described in [11]. In [11], the following classification of research results are proposed on level of evidence.

- A1. Research on the effects of diagnostics on clinical outcomes in a prospectively monitored, well-defined patient group, with a predefined policy based on the test outcomes to be investigated, or decision analysis research into the effects of diagnostics on clinical outcomes based on results of a study of A2-level and sufficient consideration is given to the interdependency of diagnostic tests.
- A2. Research relative to a reference test, where criteria for the test to be investigated and for a reference test are predefined, with a good description of the test and the clinical population to be investigated; this must involve a large enough series of consecutive patients; predefined upper limits must be used, and the results of the test and the "gold standard" must be assessed independently. Interdependence is normally a feature of situations involving multiple diagnostic tests, and their analysis must be adjusted accordingly, for example using logistic regression.
- B. Comparison with a reference test, description of the test and population researched, but without the other features mentioned in level A.
- C. Non-comparative trials
- D. Opinions of experts, such as guideline development group members.

Furthermore, the conclusions in the guidelines, alternatively called *guideline items*, are annotated with an evidence level. Based on the medical literature, one or more relevant conclusions are made for each section. The most important literature is listed according to the level of evidential strength, allowing conclusions to be drawn based on the level of evidence. All the medical literature included in the conclusion is described in the bibliography. The classification of conclusions are based on literature analysis. The following evidence levels are proposed in [11].

- Level 1. Based on 1 systematic review (A1) or at least 2 independent A2 reviews.
- Level 2. Based on at least 2 independent B reviews
- Level 3. Based on 1 level A2 of B research, or any level C research
- Level 4. Opinions of experts, such as guideline development group members

Here are some examples of evidence-based clinical guidelines:

```
Level 1
Breast cancers detected through regular breast self-examination have no better
prognosis than breast cancers detected by other means.
A1 Ksters 2003, Elmore 2005, Weiss 2003, Nelson 2009.
```

Level 1
A self reported lump by the woman is positively associated with an actual mass
being present.
A2 Barlow 2002, Lumachi 2002, Aiello 2004.

Each guideline consists of an evidence level, a guideline statement, and their references with the classification of the research results (e.g. A1 or A1).

3   A Lightweight Formalism of Evidence-Based Clinical Guidelines

The advantage of Computer-Interpretable Guidelines is that they implement the guidelines in computer-based decision support systems. However, the generation of the formulations of the guidelines according to the existing formalisms requires a lot of manual processing. That leads to different formalisms of Computer-Interpretable Guidelines, which can be ranged from a high-level representation (i.e., more expressive and more logic-oriented), such as Asbru to a low-level representation such as the Arden Syntax. There may exist different requirements on evidence-based clinical guidelines from different perspectives or application scenarios. In this paper, we are concerned with the following requirements on evidence-based clinical guidelines:

- Structured Data: Existing clinical guidelines are usually available at the textual format (i.e., a pdf file or word document). They are not computer-Interpretable. We have to convert those textual data into the structured data. Structured data has the advantage of being easily entered, stored, queried and analyzed.
- Semantic Interoperability. Semantic interoperability is the ability of computer systems to exchange data with unambiguous, shared meaning. Semantic interoperability is therefore concerned not just with the packaging of data (syntax), but the simultaneous transmission of the meaning with the data (semantics). This is accomplished by adding data about the metadata, linking each data element to a controlled, shared vocabulary.[4]
- Reasoning Support: The formalism should be enriched with the knowledge technology, in particular, support for reasoning over the knowledge which have been contained in clinical guidelines.
- Generation Convenience: The generation of the formulation of clinical guidelines from the existing textual documents are usually time-consuming, because it requires a lot of manual processing. Although a natural language processing (NLP) tool is helpful to improve the efficiency of the generation, converting those information which have been obtained by using the NLP tool into a high-level formalism is still needed to be done by professional people.
- Evidence-oriented Representation: The formalism of evidence-based clinical guidelines should be convenient to represent different fine-grained levels of evidences.

---

[4] http://en.wikipedia.org/wiki/Semantic_interoperability

Considering the requirement above, we made the following design decision. There are different data models to structure a data. They can be just simply structured as a relational database, or to be an XML file. Consider the requirements on the semantic interoperability and reasoning support, we prefer using the RDF/RDFS/OWL data format, because they have been widely used as a solution to the semantic interoperability and reasoning. Although the existing OWL reasoning may not be powerful enough to cover all the aspects of clinical guidelines such as reasoning about actions, description of uncertainty, temporal and spatial processing, workflow processing, and others, we should make a trade-off between the expressibility of high-level representation and the convenience of generation. Thus, in this paper, we propose a RDF/OWL-based formalism for the semantic representation of evidence-based clinical guidelines. For the requirement on evidence-orientation, we design RDF-based terminologies (thus a lightweight ontology) to express clinical evidences, so that those concepts can be used to represent various evidence information in clinical guidelines.

The semantic representation of evidence-based clinical guidelines consists of the following sections:

- Heading. The heading section of the guidelines provide the basic description of the information such as the title, published time, version number, and provenance.
- Body. The body section of the guidelines provide the main description of guidelines and their evidences. The body section consists of a list of guideline items (i.e., an evidence-based guideline statement), which contains the evidence information and the RDF/OWL-representations of a single guideline statement.
  - Evidence description. It provides the formal description of the evidence (i.e., evidence level and its references which use the Dublin core format, the standard metadata to represent a publication.
  - Guideline description. It provides the RDF/OWL description of the guideline statement.

We have used the XMedlan NLP tool to generate the semantic statements of guideline description. In the next section, we will discuss the features of XMedlan and how to use this NLP tool to generate the RDF/OWL statements for clinical guidelines.

Here are the examples of the semantic representation of evidence-based clinical guidelines in the RDF Triples:

The heading:

```
PREFIX xsd: <http://www.w3.org/2001/XMLSchema#>
PREFIX dc: <http://purl.org/dc/1.1#>
PREFIX rdf: <http://www.w3.org/1999/02/22-rdf-syntax-ns#>
PREFIX owl: <http://www.w3.org/2002/07/owl#>
PREFIX rdfs: <http://www.w3.org/2000/01/rdf-schema#>
PREFIX sct: <http://wasp.cs.vu.nl/sct/sct#>
PREFIX sctid: <http://wasp.cs.vu.nl/sct/id#>
```

```
PREFIX ctec: <http://eurecaproject.eu/ctec/>
sctid:gl002-zsh140412 rdf:type sct:EvidenceBasedGuidelines.
sctid:gl002-zsh140412 dc:title "Dutch Breast Cancer Guideline".
sctid:gl002-zsh140412 dc:creator "NABON".
sctid:gl002-zsh140412 sct:publicationYear "2012".
```

For each guideline item, we have the following statements of the evidence description:

```
sctid:gl002-zsh140412 sct:hasConclusions sctid:gl002-zsh140412_1 .
sctid:gl002-zsh140412_1 rdf:type sct:GuidelineConclusions.
sctid:gl002-zsh140412_1 sct:about
        "Regular breast self-examination as a screening method".
sctid:gl002-zsh140412_1 sct:hasGuidelineItem  sctid:gl002-zsh140412_1_1 .
sctid:gl002-zsh140412_1_1 sct:hasEvidenceLevel "1"^^xsd:integer .
sctid:gl002-zsh140412_1_1 sct:hasReferences  sctid:gl002-zsh140412_1_1ref .
sctid:gl002-zsh140412_1_1ref sct:hasReference sctid:gl002-zsh140412_1_1ref1 .
sctid:gl002-zsh140412_1_1ref1 sct:hasReference sctid:gl002-zshref-Ksters2003 .
sctid:gl002-zsh140412_1_1ref1 sct:evidenceClassification "A2".
sctid:gl002-zsh140412_1_1ref sct:hasReference sctid:gl002-zsh140412_1_1ref2 .
sctid:gl002-zsh140412_1_1ref2 sct:hasReference sctid:gl002-zshref-Elmore2005 .
sctid:gl002-zsh140412_1_1ref2 sct:evidenceClassification "A2".
sctid:gl002-zsh140412_1_1ref sct:hasReference sctid:gl002-zsh140412_1_1ref3 .
sctid:gl002-zsh140412_1_1ref3 sct:hasReference sctid:gl002-zshref-Weiss2003 .
sctid:gl002-zsh140412_1_1ref3 sct:evidenceClassification "A2".
sctid:gl002-zsh140412_1_1ref sct:hasReference sctid:gl002-zsh140412_1_1ref4 .
sctid:gl002-zsh140412_1_1ref4 sct:hasReference sctid:gl002-zshref-Nelson2009 .
sctid:gl002-zsh140412_1_1ref4 sct:evidenceClassification "A2" .
sctid:gl002-zsh140412_1_1 sct:hasRelations _:e5 .
```

which describes the guideline items with their evidence levels and references.

The following RDF N-Triples relations are extracted from the guideline statement using the NLP tool:

```
_:e1  <http://eurecaproject.eu/ctec/isA>  <http://eurecaproject.eu/ctec/diagnosis> .
_:e1  <http://eurecaproject.eu/ctec/hasObject>  _:e2 .
_:e2  <http://eurecaproject.eu/ctec/hasTerm>  "cancers".
_:e2  <http://eurecaproject.eu/ctec/hasCUI> "C0006826".
_:e2  <http://eurecaproject.eu/ctec/isA>
            <http://eurecaproject.eu/ctec/disease_or_syndrome> .
_:e3  <http://eurecaproject.eu/ctec/isA>
            <http://eurecaproject.eu/ctec/diagnosis> .
_:e3  <http://eurecaproject.eu/ctec/hasObject>  _:e4 .
_:e4  <http://eurecaproject.eu/ctec/hasTerm>  "cancers".
_:e4  <http://eurecaproject.eu/ctec/hasCUI> "C0006826".
_:e4  <http://eurecaproject.eu/ctec/isA>
            <http://eurecaproject.eu/ctec/disease_or_syndrome> .
_:e5  <http://eurecaproject.eu/ctec/hasFragment> _:e1 .
_:e5  <http://eurecaproject.eu/ctec/hasFragment> _:e3 .
_:e6  <http://eurecaproject.eu/ctec/hasTerm> "Breast".
_:e6  <http://eurecaproject.eu/ctec/hasCUI> "C0006141|C1268990".
_:e5  <http://eurecaproject.eu/ctec/hasFragment> _:e6 .
_:e5  <http://eurecaproject.eu/ctec/isA>  <http://eurecaproject.eu/ctec/EC> .
```

```
_:e5 <http://eurecaproject.eu/ctec/hasText> "Breast cancers detected through
regular breast self-examination have no better prognosis than breast cancers
detected by other means." .
```

which states the guideline statement (i.e., the text of the guideline) and the relation extractions from the statement. They provide the detailed RDF description of the guideline statement and their annotation with the concepts in UMLS, a well-known meta-thesaurus of medical terms developed by the National Library of Medicine [10] and offering mappings to most of widely used medical terminologies such as SNOMED-CT, NCI, LOINC, etc.

4   NLP Tool

XMedlan is the Xerox linguistic-based module of the relation extraction system of the EURECA project [1]. The main characteristic of this component is that it uses a linguistic parser [2] to perform rich linguistic analysis of the input text. Figure 1 depicts the processing steps of the NLP extraction: after an optional structure analysis of the input text document, the linguistic parser annotates each sentence with rich linguistic features and structures, which then serve as a the basis of the extraction of relations and attributes in the form of triples.

4.1   Linguistic Analysis

First, the text is tokenized into a sequence of tokens, each token is looked up in a lexicon and assigned all its possible morpho-syntactic categories and features, and possibly additional semantic features. Ambiguous tokens (with more than one possible syntactic category) are disambiguated with a part-of-speech (POS) tagger leveraging the left and right contexts of the tokens. A medical concept identifier recognizes mentions of medical concepts in the sequence of tokens, and annotates them with their UMLS unique concept identifiers (CUIs) and semantic types (Anatomical_Structure, Clinical_Drug, Disease_or_Syndrome, etc.). Other types of mentions, not specific to the medical domain, are also recognized: time expressions and measures. During the syntactic parsing phase, sub-sequences of tokens and concept mentions are grouped into syntactic constituents, called chunks, by the parser: Noun Phrases, Verb Phrases, etc. Most importantly, tokens and concepts mentions are linked with syntactic dependency relations, e.g. subject, direct object, noun modifier, etc. Finally, the linguistic parser performs a local and partial semantic analysis of the input sentence and produces semantic annotations. Examples of such semantic annotations include negation on concepts, and the structural representation of measures with the following relations: hasValue, hasMin, hasMax and hasUnit.

4.2   Extraction of Relations and Attributes

All the annotations produced by the linguistic analyzer are exploited by the relation extraction engine to identify relations and attributes of concepts and

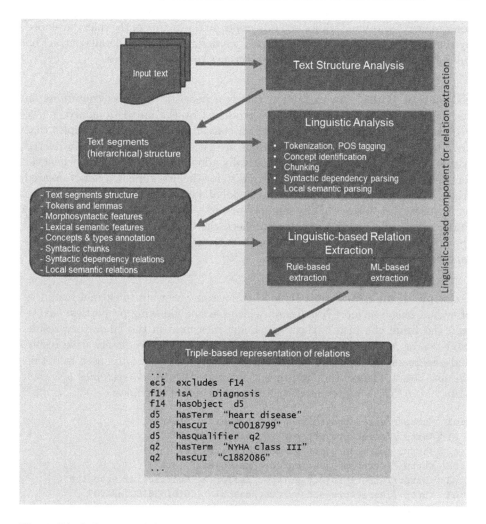

Fig. 1. Block diagram of the architecture of the Xerox linguistic-based relation extraction component

entities in the input text. These relations and attributes are expressed as triples, i.e. typed binary relations in the form ⟨*Subject, Property, Object* ⟩, and can be serialized in the RDF N-Triples format.

The extraction engine has a rule-based and a machine learning sub-component. Currently we use only the former, as the implementation of the latter is not yet finalized. The rule-based sub-component is a rule interpreter implemented on top of a Prolog engine. It takes an (ordered) set of extraction rules and applies each of them to each sentence of the input text. The rules are not exclusive, several of them can succeed on the same input sentence and yield additional, and possibly inconsistent, triples: in its current state, the tool does not check the semantic consistency of extracted triples and fully relies on the quality of the rules developed by the user. In the following paragraphs, we describe in more details extraction rules and the way they apply on input sentence to produce triples.

Extraction Rules. An extraction rule is a heuristic that has *conditions* on the linguistic features and structures produced by the linguistic analyzer (see previous sub-section), and *actions*, which consist in the creation of triples that are added to the context if the conditions are satisfied. Note that UMLS-related triples (hasTerm, hasCUI) are automatically added by the rule engine whenever a node that is a UMLS concept is referred to for the first time in a newly created triple. The scope of the rule conditions is global, i.e. a rule can express conditions on linguistic annotations of any sentence or text segment in the input document. Furthermore, the conditions can also check the existence of triples created by the previous successful execution of rules on the current sentence, or on previous sentences within the same document.

Example of an Extraction Rule. Let's assume we want to extract instances of a class *Laboratory_or_Test_Result*, which has the following properties: *hasObject*, the value of which is the thing being measured in the laboratory result, *hasValue* or *hasMaxValue* or *hasMinValue*, which give the quantitative result, and *hasProcedure*, the value of which is the laboratory procedure used to obtain the test result. Hence, the following input text *"Ventricular ectopics less than 4/min on EKG"* is represented with the following set of triples:

```
_:e1   <http://eurecaproject.eu/ctec/hasUnit>   "/min".
_:e1   <http://eurecaproject.eu/ctec/hasQuant> "4".
_:e2   <http://eurecaproject.eu/ctec/hasMaxValue>   _:e1 .
_:e2   <http://eurecaproject.eu/ctec/hasObject>   _:e3 .
_:e3   <http://eurecaproject.eu/ctec/hasTerm> "Ventricular ectopics".
_:e3   <http://eurecaproject.eu/ctec/hasCUI> "C0151636|C0488470".
_:e2   <http://eurecaproject.eu/ctec/isA>   <http://eurecaproject.eu/ctec/
                                            laboratory_or_test_result> .
_:e2   <http://eurecaproject.eu/ctec/hasProcedure>   _:e4 .
_:e4   <http://eurecaproject.eu/ctec/hasTerm> "EKG".
_:e4   <http://eurecaproject.eu/ctec/hasCUI> "C1623258" .
```

and the (simplified) rule example below would trigger the creation of 3 triples representing an instance of Laboratory_or_Test_Result, *fact1*, with the *hasObject* and *hasProcedure* properties populated:

```
RULE Conditions
  - Node1, a concept of type Clinical_Attribute
  - Node2, of type Quantitative_Value
  - Node3, a concept of type Laboratory_Procedure or Diagnostic_Procedure
  - A syntactic dependency relation between Node1 and Node2
  - A syntactic dependency relation between Node1 and Node3
```

```
RULE Actions:
    fact1  isA  Laboratory_or_Test_Result
    fact1  hasObject  Node1
    fact1  hasProcedure  Node3
```

Application of Extraction Rules. An extraction rule applies successfully on an input sentence if all its conditions are satisfied. When a condition is evaluated, its free variables are instantiated with nodes from the input sentence and/or current set of triples. For instance, in the rule example above, the first condition is satisfied as many times as there are medical terms of type Clinical_Attribute in the input sentence, and variable *Node1* is successively assigned values that corresponds to those terms. For each possible value of *Node1*, the second condition is evaluated and similarly, variable *Node2* will successively be assigned to the terms of type *Quantitative_Value*, if any. When the fourth condition is considered (existence of a syntactic dependency relation between *Node1* and *Node2*), variables *Node1* and *Node2* are not free and the condition evaluates to true at most once, including if there are multiple dependency relations between the two nodes. In other words, the whole conditions of a rule are satisfied (and its actions are run) **for each distinct set** of variable instantiations that make every individual condition evaluate to true. And for each distinct set of variable instantiations satisfying the conditions, the rule actions are run, i.e. each triple in the rule actions is created.

Rule Order. A rule condition can consist in requiring the existence of a triple produced by a previous rule that applied successfully on current input. This means rules apply sequentially and their order is important: extraction rules for simple semantic classes come first. Simple semantic classes are classes with literal property values or property value constraints that strongly discriminate them within the conceptual schema, which allows for the expression of discriminative rule conditions, leading to unambiguous or weakly ambiguous instantiations from input sentences. An example of a simple class is *Quantitative_Value*, having *hasQuantity* and *hasUnit* properties with literal values: whenever an input text contains a numerical value and a measurement unit linked with a syntactic dependency, these two "concept" occurrences can unambiguously instantiate the object of the aforementioned properties, yielding an instance node of class *Quantitative_Value*, with two triples. The instance node can then be used in the next extraction rules as the object of a property of a more complex semantic class (e.g. *Laboratory_or_Test_Result*, in the rule example above).

Development of Extraction Rules. The starting point for creating rules is the definition of the semantic representation of the information we want to extract in a use case, i.e. the ontology or conceptual schema that we want to "populate" from text content: a set of classes and their properties. The properties are relation or attribute types that link instances of the classes. For example, for the extraction of eligibility criteria in clinical trials [1], we defined classes such as *Diagnosis, Laboratory_or_test_result, Age, Gender, Treatment*, etc. The *Diagnosis* class has two main properties: *hasObject*, the value of which is the disease being diagnosed, and *hasProcedure*, the value of which is the diagnostic procedure employed in the diagnosis. Each extraction rule is dedicated to the extraction of one or more relation types defined in the conceptual schema of the use case for which the rule set is created. Hence, the rules are highly dependent on the domain (medical), and even dependent on the use case: the proportion of rules that can be reused for another use case is determined by the proportion of classes and properties that are common to the conceptual schemas of the two use cases: as an example, class *Diagnosis* can be relevant both in clinical trial use cases and for the structuring of clinical guidelines.

In the current version, we are using the initial set of rules developed for the extraction of clinical trial eligibility criteria (CTEC) [1]. We plan to enrich this initial rule set and adapt it to the extraction of relations specific to the semantic representation of evidence-based clinical guidelines.

5   Implementation and Feasibility

5.1   Implementation

We have implemented a tool to generate the semantic representation of evidence-based clinical guidelines. We select the Dutch breast cancer guidelines version 2.0, which has been published in 2012, as test data. The transformation consists of the following processing:

- XML document generation. We create an XML document which contains the conclusions of the guidelines which have been marked with the evidence. Since the existing draft of the guidelines are in the pdf textual format, we have developed a tool which can extract the conclusions from a clinical guideline if those conclusions are stated with a textual pattern shown in the example above. Of course, we can also generate the XML document manually by copying and pasting the corresponding documents.
- Evidence statement generation. We use the XSLT tool to convert the XML document into a set of RDF statements which corresponding with the evidence description.
- Guideline statement generation. We use the NLP tool to generate the RDF statements for each guideline statement.

We are implementing a component of evidence-based clinical guidelines in the SemanticCT system, a semantics-enable system for clinical trials[5] [8]. The goals of SemanticCT are not only to achieve interoperability by semantic integration of heterogeneous data in clinical trials, but also to facilitate automatic reasoning and data processing services for decision support systems in various settings of clinical trials. SemanticCT is built on the top of the LarKC (Large Knowledge Collider) platform[6], a platform for scalable semantic data processing [5,17].

---

[5] http://wasp.cs.vu.nl/sct/
[6] http://www.larkc.eu

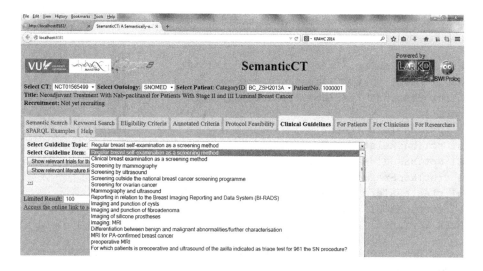

Fig. 2. The guideline component in SemanticCT

The SemanticCT management component manages the SPARQL endpoint which is built as a SemanticCT workflow which consists of a generic data processing and reasoning plugin in the LarKC platform. That generic data processing and reasoning plug-in provides the basic reasoning service over large scale semantic data, like RDF/RDFS/OWL data.

SemanticCT provides the interface of semantic search, so that a user can post SPARQL queries to obtain the results. For the users who have no any background knowledge of the Semantic Web, they can use the graphical interface to use the system for the services. A screenshot of the interface of the guideline component in SemanticCT is shown in Fig. 2.

5.2 Feasibility

Different from the existing expressive formalisms of Computer-Interpretable Guidelines such as Asbru, the lightweight formalism of the evidence-based clinical guidelines may not be efficient to be used directly for the workflow processing in clinical decision making systems. In this paper, our main concern is the semantic interoperability.

The guideline statements of the semantic representation of guidelines have been annotated with the well-known medical terminologies/ontologies such as UMLS. Although the mappings among various terminologies are usually not easy, the annotations with the same ontology like that has been done in the XMedlan provides the way to connect different data resources with the same concept annotation. It also provides the possibility for querying a SPARQL endpoint on a triple store.

Below we give a number of example queries based on our lightweight formalisation of evidence-based clinical guidelines. The first example is a SPARQL query to list a set of concepts which have been used in the annotation of the guideline statement.

```
PREFIX sct: <http://wasp.cs.vu.nl/sct/sct#>
PREFIX ctec: <http://eurecaproject.eu/ctec/>
select distinct ?id ?text ?conceptid ?term
where {
?s ctec:hasText ?text.
?s1 sct:hasRelations ?s.
?s1 sct:hasGuidelineItemID ?id.
?s ctec:hasFragment ?e1.
?e1 ctec:hasTerm ?term.
?e1 ctec:hasCUI ?conceptid.}
ORDER BY ?id
```

Another example of the SPARQL query is to list two guideline statements which have been annotated with the same concept:

```
PREFIX ...
select distinct ?id1 ?text1 ?id2 ?text2
where {
?s ctec:hasText ?text1.
?s1 sct:hasRelations ?s.
?s1 sct:hasGuidelineItemID ?id1.
?s ctec:hasFragment ?e1.
?e1 ctec:hasTerm ?term.
?e1 ctec:hasCUI ?conceptid.
?e2 ctec:hasCUI ?conceptid.
?e2 ctec:hasTerm ?term.
?s2 ctec:hasText ?text2.
?s2 ctec:hasFragment ?e2.
?s3 sct:hasRelations ?s2.
?s3 sct:hasGuidelineItemID ?id2.
FILTER (!(?e1=?e2)).}
ORDER BY ?id
```

We are also interested in the semantic operability from different data sources. For example, the following query can be used to check the connection between evidence-based guidelines and clinical trials.

```
PREFIX ...
select distinct ?guidelineid ?guidelinetext ?term ?trialid
where {
?s ctec:hasText ?guidelinetext.
?s1 sct:hasRelations ?s.
?s1 sct:hasGuidelineItemID ?guidelineid.
?s ctec:hasFragment ?e1.
```

```
?e1 ctec:hasTerm ?term.
?e1 ctec:hasCUI ?conceptid.
?e2 ctec:hasCUI ?conceptid.
FILTER (!(?e1=?e2)).
?e1 ctec:hasTerm ?term.
?e3 ctec:hasObject ?e2.
?s2 ctec:hasFragment ?e3.
?s2 sct:NCTID ?trialid.}
```

One of the answers of this query is that the guideline with guidelineid l002-zsh140412_4_1, with the guidelinetext "Adding MRI to mammography for the screening of high-risk women results in a higher sensitivity for breast cancer" is connected to the trial with trialID NCT00112749 by the term "screening".

The last example shows that we search for the information of the evidence level over guidelines, like this:

```
select distinct ?conceptid ?guidelineid ?guidelinetext ?evidenceLevel
where {
?e1 ctec:hasTerm "flat epithelial atypia".
?e1 ctec:hasCUI ?conceptid.
?e2 ctec:hasObject ?e1.
?s ctec:includes ?e2.
?s ctec:hasText ?guidelinetext.
?s1 sct:hasRelations ?s.
?s1 sct:hasGuidelineItemID ?guidelineid.
?s1 sct:evidenceLevel ?evidenceLevel.
FILTER (?evidenceLevel <= 2)
}
```

Those example queries show the feasibility of reasoning based on the proposed lightweight formalization of evidence-based guidelines. The results encourage us to perform real experiments in collaboration with medical experts in the near future.

6   Discussion and Conclusions

6.1   Future Work

The advantage of the NLP tool is that it provides not only the concept annotation, but also relation statements with the RDF NTriple format. That would be quite convenient for us to check the similarity over fine-grained structures over two statements. One of the application scenarios of those semantic similarity and relevance checking is the guideline update, a task in the EURECA project.

Guideline update concerns how to transfer new research findings into existing clinical guidelines (e.g. the national breast cancer guidelines). These research findings can be stronger evidence or even new evidence for update of existing guidelines. It can have an effect on the care decision making based on the guideline.

Those new research findings can be collected from the latest publications, like those papers in PubMed, reports from clinical trials, or other available sources.

As one of the future work of this paper, we are going to develop a method to incorporate those new research results are linked to the interface of clinical guidelines on the SemanticCT system and the EURECA platform for the users (i.e., Guideline developers). With the help of the semantic representation of evidence-based clinical guidelines, we are going to create a model to check the relevance of new research results to the chosen clinical guidelines and demonstrate that the increased level of evidences brings substantial benefits to the clinical decision support applications.

6.2 Related Work

There has been a large body of work on providing formal representations of medical guidelines, using a wide variety of representation languages, such as the Arden Syntax, PROforma [6,7], Asbru [14], EON [16] and GLIF [12,13].

These earlier approach differ from the work presented in this paper in two important ways: the "semantic weight" of the representation, and the degree of automation of the modelling process (and these two are in fact coupled), as follows:

Most of the existing modelling languages are "semantically heavyweight": they try to capture as much as possible of content of the clinical guideline, including control structure, applicability conditions, intentions, etc. As a consequence, these languages are very rich, with many features and high expressivity.

Consequently, the process of modelling guidelines in these languages is inevitably a manual task. As example, we take the pioneering work on the Digital Electronic Guideline Library (DeGeL) [15]. It facilitates gradual conversion of clinical guidelines from text to a formal representation in a chosen guideline ontology. The architecture supports use cases like guideline classification, semantic markup, context-sensitive search, browsing, run-time application, and retrospective quality assessment. Similar observations could be made for toolkits that support Asbru, ProForma, etc.

In contrast, in our case we are using NLP techniques that result in a light weight formalisation in the form of annotations. This means that we do not capture the full semantics of the guideline, but as we have shown in the previous section, this lightweight semantics is still sufficient to support a number of relevant and non-trivial use cases (and in fact, use cases which are not immediately supported by using the existing languages and environments).

The main difference is perhaps that our representation is specifically geared towards catching the evidence levels of guideline recommendations, an aspect that is missing from some of the older guideline representation languages.

GEM cutter is an XML guideline editor which is developed for GEM (the Guideline Elements Model), an XML-based guideline document model [9]. It can also serve as a tool for the generation of the XML data for evidence-based clinical guidelines. However, the XML data are just intermediate results of the semantic representation of guidelines. The target in our approach is to obtain the semantic data so that they can be loaded into a triple store.

6.3 Conclusions

In this paper, we have proposed a framework of semantic representation of evidence-based clinical guidelines by using the Semantic Web standards, such as RDF/RDFS/OWL. We have reported how to use the XMedlan NLP tool to generate semantic data of evidence-based clinical guidelines. We have shown several example queries of the lightweight formalism of evidence-based clinical guidelines on the semantic operability. The relation extraction of the guideline statements provides an approach for semantic similarity and relevance checking between guideline statements and the statements in PubMed, which can be used for the use case of guideline update in the future.

Acknowledgments. This work is partially supported by the European Commission under the 7th framework programme EURECA Project (FP7-ICT-2011-7, Grant 288048).

References

1. Aït-Mokhtar, S., Bruijn, B.D., Hagège, C., Rupi, P.: Initial prototype for relation identification between concepts, D3.2. Technical report, EURECA Project (2013)
2. Aït-Mokhtar, S., Chanod, J.-P., Roux, C.: Robustness beyond shallowness: incremental deep parsing. Nat. Lang. Eng. **8**(2), 121–144 (2002)
3. Claerhout, B., De Schepper K., et al.: Initial EURECA architecture, D2.2. Technical report, EURECA Project (2013)
4. de Clercq, P., Blom, J., Korsten, H., Hasman, A.: Approaches for creating computer-interpretable guidelines that facilitate decision support. Artif. Intell. Med. **31**, 1–27 (2004)
5. Fensel, D., van Harmelen, F., Andersson, B., Brennan, P., Cunningham, H., Della Valle, E., Fischer, F., Huang, Z., Kiryakov, A., Lee, T., School, L., Tresp, V., Wesner, S., Witbrock, M., Zhong, N.: Towards LarKC: a platform for web-scale reasoning. In: Proceedings of the IEEE International Conference on Semantic Computing (ICSC2008). IEEE Computer Society Press, CA, USA (2008)
6. Fox, J., Johns, N., Lyons, C., Rahmanzadeh, A., Thomson, R., Wilson, P.: Proforma: a general technology for clinical decision support systems. Comput. Methods Programs Biomed. **54**, 59–67 (1997)
7. Fox, J., Johns, N., Rahmanzadeh, A., Thomson, R.: Proforma, approaches for creating computer-interpretable guidelines that facilitate decision support. In: Proceedings of Medical Informatics Europe, Amsterdam (1996)
8. Huang, Z., ten Teije, A., van Harmelen, F.: SemanticCT: a semantically-enabled system for clinical trials. In: Riaño, D., Lenz, R., Miksch, S., Peleg, M., Reichert, M., ten Teije, A. (eds.) KGC 2013 and ProHealth 2013. LNCS, vol. 8268, pp. 11–25. Springer, Heidelberg (2013)
9. Karras, B., Nath, S., Shiffman, R.: A preliminary evaluation of guideline content markup using GEM - an XML guideline elements model. In: Proceedings of AMIA Annual Symposium (2000)

10. Lindberg, D., Humphreys, B., McCray, A.: The unified medical language system. Methods Inf. Med. **32**(4), 281–291 (1993)
11. NABON.: Breast cancer, dutch guideline, version 2.0. Technical report, Integraal kankercentrum Netherland, Nationaal Borstkanker Overleg Nederland (2012)
12. Peleg, M., Boxwala, A., Ogunyemi, O., et al.: GLIF3: The evolution of a guideline representation format. In: Proceedings of AMIA Annual Fall Symposium, pp. 645–649 (2000)
13. Peleg, M., Boxwala, A., Tu, S., Ogunyemi, O., Zeng, Q., Wang, D.: Guideline interchange format 3.4. Technical report (2001)
14. Shahar, Y., Miksch, S., Johnson, P.: The asgaard project: a task specific framework for the application and critiquing of time oriented clinical guidelines. Artif. Intell. Med. **14**, 29–51 (1998)
15. Shahar, Y., Young, O., Shalom, E., Mayaffit, A., Moskovitch, R., Hessing, A., Galperin, M.: DEGEL: a hybrid, multiple-ontology framework for specification and retrieval of clinical guidelines. In: Dojat, M., Keravnou, E., Barahona, P. (eds.) AIME 2003. LNCS (LNAI), vol. 2780, pp. 122–131. Springer, Heidelberg (2003)
16. Tu, S., Musen, M.: A flexible approach to guideline modeling. In: Proceeding of 1999 AMIA Symposium, pp. 420–424 (1999)
17. Witbrock, M., Fortuna, B., Bradesko, L., Kerrigan, M., Bishop, B., van Harmelen, F., ten Teije, A., Oren, E., Momtchev, V., Tenschert, A., Cheptsov, A., Roller, S., Gallizo, G.: D5.3.1 - requirements analysis and report on lessons learned during prototyping. LarKC project deliverable, June 2009

META-GLARE: A Meta-System for Defining Your Own CIG System: Architecture and Acquisition

Paolo Terenziani[1], Alessio Bottrighi[1(✉)], Irene Lovotti[1],
and Stefania Rubrichi[1,2]

[1] Computer Science Institute, DISIT, University of Piemonte Orientale,
Alessandria, Italy
{paolo.terenziani,alessio.bottrighi,stefania.
rubrichi}@unipmn.it
[2] Laboratory for Biomedical Informatics "Mario Stefanelli", Dipartimento
di Ingegneria Industriale e dell'Informazione, University of Pavia, Pavia, Italy

Abstract. Clinical practice guidelines (CPGs) play an important role in medical practice, and computerized support to CPGs is now one of the most central areas of research in Artificial Intelligence in medicine. In recent years, many groups have developed different computer-assisted management systems of Computer Interpretable Guidelines (CIGs). From one side, there are several commonalities between different approaches; from the other side, each approach has its own peculiarities and is geared towards the treatment of specific phenomena. In our work, we propose a form of generalization: instead of defining "yet another CIG system", we propose a META-GLARE, a "meta"-system (or, in other words, a shell) to define new CIG systems. From one side, we try to capture the commonalities, by providing (i) a general tool for the acquisition, consultation and execution of hierarchical directed graphs (representing the control flow of actions in CIGs), parameterized over the types of nodes and of arcs constituting it, and (ii) a library of different elementary components of guidelines nodes (actions) and arcs, in which each type definition involves the specification of how objects of this type can be acquired, consulted and executed. From the other side, we provide generality and flexibility, by allowing free aggregations of such elementary components to define new primitive node and arc types. In this paper, we first propose META-GLARE general architecture and then, for the sake of brevity, we will focus only on the acquisition issue.

Keywords: Formalization of medical processes and knowledge-based healthcare models · Computer interpretable guideline (CIG) · Meta CIG system · System architecture · CIG acquisition

1 Introduction

Clinical practice guidelines (CPGs) represent the current understanding of the best clinical practice. In recent years the importance and the use of CPGs are increasing in order to improve the quality and to reduce the cost of health care. ICT technology can further enhance the impact of CPGs. Thus, in the last twenty years, many different

© Springer International Publishing Switzerland 2014
S. Miksch et al. (Eds.): KR4HC 2014, LNAI 8903, pp. 95–110, 2014.
DOI: 10.1007/978-3-319-13281-5_7

systems and projects have therefore been developed in order to manage computer interpretable CPGs (CIG for short; see, e.g., the collections [1–3]). A comparison among some existing systems is described in [4]. Such analysis concerns six approaches: Asbru [5], EON [6], GLIF [7, 8], GUIDE [9], PRODIGY [10], and PROforma [11]. An excellent survey including many different approaches has recently been proposed by Peleg [12].

Surveys and comparisons demonstrate that (i) from one side, there are several commonalities between the different systems, since most of them are general and domain-independent but (ii) there are also important distinguishing features, often due to the fact that, since so many challenging tasks have to be faced, each system mainly focuses of some of them. Indeed, many of such systems are mostly research tools that evolve and expand to cover an increasing number of phenomena/tasks. This is, for instance, the history of GLARE (Guideline Acquisition, Representation, and Execution), the prototypical system we have been building since 1996 in cooperation with ASU San Giovanni Battista in Turin, one of the major hospitals in Italy. Though GLARE's basic formalism, and its acquisition and execution modules (henceforth: GLARE's "*kernel*") were defined in the early years [13], many extensions have been added later on, to address new phenomena and/or to provide new facilities to user-physicians. While some extensions have lead to new modules, loosely interacting with the kernel of GLARE (e.g., the verification module, to check CIGs' properties [13], or the decision support module, providing decision-theoretic cost/benefit analysis [14], other additions have involved an extension of the representation formalism (and thus of the acquisition module), and, in some cases, also of the execution module itself (this is the case, e.g., of the treatment of temporal constraints [15], or the treatment of exceptions [16]). Unfortunately, the more the system kernel was increasing, the more modifications to it were difficult, sometimes leading us to the choice (for fast proto-typing purposes) to develop specific sub-versions of the system, to address a new phenomenon in isolation. Thus, we have first decided to work a new, engineered and easily extendable version of GLARE's kernel. However, while trying to design a highly structured and modular code, we have abstracted so much from the actual system to lead to the definition of a meta-system (called META-GLARE), or, in other words, a shell that allows one to easily build his own CIG system (comprehensive of representation formalism, acquisition, consultation and execution tools). The core idea of our meta-approach is

(i)   To define an open library of elementary components (e.g., textual attribute, Boolean condition, Score-based decision), each of which was equipped with methods for acquiring, consulting and executing them.

(ii) To provide system-designers with an easy way of aggregating such components to define node and arc types (constituting the representation formalism of a new system).

(iii) To devise general and basic tools for the acquisition, consultation and execution of CIGs, represented by hierarchical directed graphs which are parametric over the node and arc types (in the sense that the definition of node and arc types are an input for such tools).

(iv) To couple each part of a system (e.g., elementary components, node definitions, system definition) with a declarative description of its main features and composition (automatically built during the system acquisition).

In such a way, we achieve several advantages:

- Using META-GLARE, one can easily define her/his own system, basically by defining the nodes and arcs types as an aggregation of components from the library. No other effort (e.g., building acquisition or execution modules) is needed.
- The extension of a system can be easily achieved by adding new node/arc types, or adding components to already existing types (with no programming effort at all; notice that the treatment of *versioning* is outside the goals of the current paper).
- User programming is needed only in case a new component has to be added in the component library. However, the addition is modular and minimal: the programmer has just to focus on the added component, and to provide the code for acquiring, consulting, and (if needed) execute it (while the "general" acquisition, consultation and execution engines have not to be modified).
- Each system, node/arc type, and component is equipped with a declarative description of its main features and components, thus making each system clear and easy to understand and modify.

To better understand the underlying META-GLARE logic, please consider that the basic idea is the same of YACC (Yet Another Compiler of Compilers [17]), which can be considered a meta-compiler. In particular, META-GLARE takes in input any CIG formalism and provides as output a CIG system for such formalism just as YACC takes in input any context free language (expressed through a formal grammar) and provides as output a compiler for it.

In the rest of the paper, we discuss our approach, with specific focus on acquisition. In Sect. 2, we analyse some commonalities and differences between CIG formalisms, as the basis for the definition of our "meta"-system. We then describe the general architecture of META-GLARE. In Sect. 3, we discuss the acquisition of a new system, with specific emphasis on the general formalism that META-GLARE provides to define attribute types, node/arc types, and CIG systems. In Sect. 4, we discuss the acquisition of a CIG, using one of the defined systems. Finally, Sect. 5 contains discussions, conclusions, and future work.

Before starting the technical content, we just stress that, in this paper, we deal with what we regard as the "kernel" of CIG systems: the definition of a representation formalism, and of tools for acquiring, consulting and executing guidelines. In particular, we will focus on acquisition, and, as regards CIG acquisition, we will only consider non-automatic acquisition (i.e., acquisition directly performed by a team of expert physicians and knowledge engineers – and not automatic acquisition from text). We are aware that several other facilities should be added (e.g., verification or decision-making facilities, and so on). We have already provided many of such facilities in GLARE. Investigating whether and to what extent such facilities can be generalized and thus provided also in META-GLARE is a challenging research task that we will address in our long-term future work.

2 META-GLARE Architecture

The possibility of building a meta-system is grounded from one side on the ability of identifying and isolating the commonalities between the different systems, at a high level of abstraction, and, on the opposite side, on the capacity of providing proper tools to generate and "personalize" a new system, with the minimum possible (computational) effort.

Therefore, before providing the architecture of META-GLARE, we point out, at a high level of abstraction, what are the commonalities it takes into account, and what kind of "personalizations" it supports.

2.1 Commonalities Between Representation Formalisms

All CIG systems are characterized by the adoption of a specific formalism to represent guidelines, and their acquisition, consultation and execution tools are strictly geared towards the specific formalism. For instance, different types of nodes (*actions*) have been proposed by different approaches, and their acquisition (and consultation, and execution) tool specify exactly how to acquire (consult, execute) each type. However, to build a meta-system, representation and interpretation (we use "interpretation" as a cover term for acquisition, consultation and execution) must be decoupled. The idea is simple: since our meta-interpreter must be general enough to interpret different formalisms, it must be based on the commonalities between them, and it must "parameterize" over their differences. It is thus important to analyse the "high-level" commonalities between different CIG representation systems, and where differences lie. Proceeding in a "top-down" analysis, "high-level" commonalities concern the notions of (1) graph, (2) nodes and arcs types (3) attribute types.

(1) Graphs. Though there are several exceptions (such as, e.g., systems based on Arden Syntax [18]), many CIG systems represent guidelines as **hierarchical directed graphs**. **Different types of nodes and arcs** are used. Graphs are often hierarchical, in that non-atomic types of nodes are allowed, representing, in turn, a hierarchical directed graph. In several approaches, there are also "meaning" **constraints** regulating the possible **relationships between node types and arc types**. For instance, in GLARE, multiple arcs can only exit from specific types of nodes, i.e., decision nodes.

(2) Node and Arc types. Quite different types of nodes and arcs have been provided in the literature. The main commonality is that each **type** (of node and of arc) is defined as **a set of attributes**.

(3) Attribute types. There is a huge variety of such attributes, ranging from purely textual attributes (e.g., the textual description of the action performed) to complex attributes such as those used to embody (score-based or boolean) conditions and/or decisions. For the sake of convenience, it is worth distinguishing between two categories of attributes: **control** attributes (i.e., those attributes that, in some way, affect the execution of a node/arc; e.g., decision attributes) and **non-control** ones (e.g., textual attributes).

2.2   Towards a "Meta" Interpreter of CIG Formalisms

Given the analysis above, our meta-interpreter

(i)   deals with **hierarchical directed graphs,** and
(ii) abstracts from the types of nodes and arcs, and the constraints between them, and the types of attributes.

Thus, our interpreter (guideline acquisition, consultation and execution tools) only assumes that a guideline is a hierarchical directed graph, and is ***parameterized*** on the features in (ii). How is thus possible to actually make it effective? There is only one solution: enforcing strict ***compositionality*** throughout the meta-system. Indeed, one of the central ideas of our approach is that the interpretation of each node/arc type is obtained through the sequenced interpretation of the attributed composing it. This means that, practically, each attribute type (e.g., textual attribute, Boolean condition attribute, etc.) must consists of the methods to acquire, consult, and execute it. Thus, for instance, guideline acquisition consists in the acquisition of a directed hierarchical graph, which in turn adopts the methods in each attribute type definition to acquire the specific attributes of the involved nodes/arcs (see Sect. 4 for more details; notably, the same compositional method also applies to consultation and execution).

2.3   CIG System Acquisition vs Guideline Acquisition

Before moving to the general architecture of META-GLARE, a remark is important. Two different kinds of acquisition are provided by our meta-system:

(1)   the system acquisition tool, which assist the system-designer in the definition of its own CIG system, and
(2)   the guideline acquisition tool, which assist a team of physicians and/or knowledge engineers in the acquisition of a specific CIG (e.g., the ischemic stroke guideline) using a specific system (already acquired, see point 1).

Of course, the two acquisitions are very different. The first one is used just in case a system designer wants to define a new system, of his own. Once a system has been acquired, it can be used "forever", to acquire (and consult, and execute) many different clinical guidelines.

2.4   The General Architecture

In Fig. 1, we show the general architecture of META-GLARE. Oval nodes represent data structures, and rectangles represent computational modules.

The DEFINITION_EDITOR module supports system-designers in the definition of a new system. It consists in four sub-components: ATTRIBUTE_TYPE_DEF, NODE/ ARC_DEF, CONSTRAINT_DEF, and SYSTEM_DEF. ATTRIBUTE_TYPE_DEF allows the introduction of a new attribute type (e.g., "fuzzy-logic decision"), giving in output an XML representation in the ATTRIBUTE_LIBRARY, which also include (pointers to) the methods to acquire, consult and (in the case of control attribute)

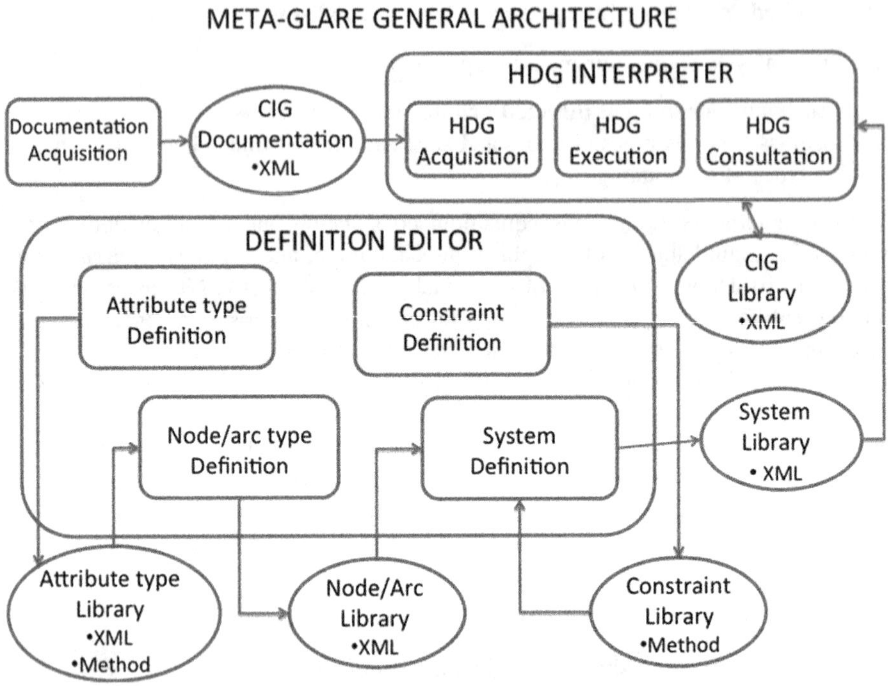

META-GLARE GENERAL ARCHITECTURE

Fig. 1. The architecture of META-GLARE

execute it. NODE/ARC_TYPE_DEF supports the definition of new types of nodes and arcs. Such types are simply defined as ordered lists of typed attributes, where the type of each attribute must be included into the ATTRIBUTE_TYPE_LIBRARY. An XML representation is provided as output (in the NODE/ARC_LIBRARY). Finally, SYSTEM_DEF supports the definition of a new system, which includes two components: the set of types of nodes and arcs it adopts (taken from the NODE/ARC_LIBRARY) and a set of constraints regulating the relationships between such nodes/arcs (taken from the CONSTRAINT_LIBRARY). Once again, an XML representation is provided in output (in the SYSTEM_LIBRARY).

Globally, the SYSTEM_DEF module manages the definition of the system-dependent features of a new system. On the other hand, the HDG_INTERPRETER deals with the aspects which are system-independent (i.e., common to all the systems that can be generated by META-GLARE; notably, HDG is an acronym for Hierarchical Directed Graph). It consists of three sub-components: HDG_ACQUISITION, HDG_CONSULTATION, and HDG_EXECUTION. All of them are based on the compositionality criterion discussed in Sect. 2.2. In the paper, we focus on the HDG_ACQUISITION module only (in Sect. 3). Finally, the CIG_DOCUMENTA-TION_ACQ is used in order to acquire the "documentation" information concerning a specific CIG (e.g., who are the authors, when the guideline has been first produced, the data of its last update, the documentation on which it is based, and so on). We think that the treatment of such a documentation can be regarded as independent of the specific system. The CIG_DOCUMENTATION_ACQ produces an XML file which is an input of HDG_ACQUISITION, which adds it to the description of the specific guidelines. The acquisition and representation of such metadata is largely based on GLIF3's approach [8], and is not discussed in the rest of this paper.

META-GLARE and its modules are developed as *Java Applets* [19] (thus *methods* in Fig. 1 are implemented by *Java classes*). In this way, META-GLARE is a cross-platform application: it can be embedded into a web page and executed via web browsers without any installation phase. The libraries in Fig. 1 are implemented by databases stored in PostgreSQL [20], which is one of most popular free and open source database management systems.

3 System Definition, Acquisition and Representation

In META-GLARE, a system is defined through the definition of its formalism, i.e., of the types of its nodes (*actions*) and arcs, and of the constraints between them. Such a definition is explicitly represented by XML documents, stored the libraries shown in Fig. 1. The syntax of such XML documents is defined via XML schema [21]. In Sects. 3.1 and 3.2 we describe our representation of attribute types, node/arc types, constraints and systems, but for the sake of brevity we show only the XML schema of attribute types (see Fig. 2).

To facilitate the acquisition of a new system, or the extension of an existing one, a graphical interface is provided by the Definition Editor (Sect. 3.3).

3.1 Attribute Types

In our approach, attribute types are characterized by several features (*attributes*), which are specified according to the XML document showed in Fig. 2.

A XML tag, which describes an *attribute type*, has four attributes (lines 7–10 in Fig. 2); the first three attributes are necessary. They define its name (line 7; e.g. BooleanCondition), whether such an attribute is a composite attribute or a simple attribute (line 8; e.g. the attribute type BooleanDecision is a composite attribute based on the attribute BooleanCondition), whether the attributes have some constraints (line 9; e.g. a numeric attribute can be associated a range of admissible values). The fourth attribute is optional and defines whether the attributes is linked to an ontology (line 10). Note that at this definition level, we do not specify any particular ontology (e.g. SNOMED), but we specify a type of ontology, which can be selected from a predefined set of values (i.e. OntologyType has actually three allowed values: finding, drugs and action).

Moreover, every attribute type has a set of XML tags, which describes its declarative and procedural characteristics. The tag syntax (line 12 in Fig. 2) contains the syntax defining the possible values for the attribute, and is expressed in Backus-Naur Form [22]. The tag description (line 13) contains a textual description. "Procedural" tags are very important, since they define (pointers to) the methods that are used by the HDG_INTERPRETER to acquire, store, consult and execute any instance of

```
1  <xs:schema qualified" xmlns:xs="http://www.w3.org/2001/XMLSchema">
2    <xs:element name="attribute">
3      <xs:complexType>
4        <xs:sequence>
5          <xs:element name="type">
6            <xs:complexType>
7              <xs:attribute type="xs:string" name="name" use="required"/>
8              <xs:attribute type="xs:boolean" name="composite" use="required"/>
9              <xs:attribute type="xs:boolean" name="constraint" use="required"/>
10             <xs:attribute type="OntologyType" name="ontology" />
11             <xs:sequence>
12               <xs:element type="xs:string" name="syntax"/>
13               <xs:element type="xs:string" name="description"/>
14               <xs:element name="acquisition">
15                 <xs:complexType>
16                   <xs:simpleContent>
17                     <xs:extension base="xs:string">
18                       <xs:attribute type="xs:string" name="class_open"/>
19                       <xs:attribute type="xs:string" name="class_save"/>
20                     </xs:extension>
21                   </xs:simpleContent>
22                 </xs:complexType>
23               </xs:element>
24               <xs:element name="consultation">
25                 .....
26               </xs:element>
27               <xs:element name="execution">
28                 .....
29               </xs:element>
30             </xs:sequence>
31           </xs:complexType>
32         </xs:element>
33       </xs:sequence>
34     </xs:complexType>
35   </xs:element>
36 </xs:schema>
```

Fig. 2. The XML schema of attribute type.

such types. Notably, the XML definition of "procedural" attributes does not contain the Java code of the methods, but only symbolic pointers to them. Specifically, the tag acquisition (line 14) has two attributes, which are pointers to the methods to acquire (*class_open* at line 18 in Fig. 2) and to store (*class_save* at line 18 in Fig. 2) it.

For example, the tag acquisition of the attribute BooleanCondition is:

```
<acquisition
class_open="it.glare.visual.components.primitives.DialogCondition"
class_save="it.glare.model.primitives.PrimitiveCondition"/>
```

Moreover, there are other two tags (line 24 and line 27 in Fig. 2) that define (pointers to) the methods to consult and execute the attribute type. In our formalism, we support the fact that the consultation and the execution methods may be task and user dependent. For example, if the task is education, the execution may be different depending on whether the user is a teacher or a student. Thus, a consultation/execution method can be defined for every possible couple <task, user>. For the sake of brevity, their XML schema is not provided in Fig. 2.

In this phase of implementation we have already defined some typed attributes (and their classes for acquisition and memorisation): Integer, IntegerRanged, Double, DoubleRanged, Enumerate, String, BooleanCondition, BooleanDecision, ScoredDecision, DataEnquiry.

3.2 Arc/Node Types, Constraints and Systems

In our meta-formalism, any node/arc type is defined as an ordered list of typed attributes, that must be contained into the ATTRIBUTE_TYPE_LIBRARY. In particular, the description of nodes/arcs must also include a visualization attribute, to specify the icon to be used to represent such a node/arc in the graph. Moreover, the definition of node types must also include the specification of whether the node is atomic or composed (the actions can be further defined in terms of other actions via the has-part relation). The different attributes are distinguished among different categories. In particular, control attributes (e.g., "REPEAT", "GOTO") are those attributes that affect the execution of a CIG. Attributes are also distinguished depending on when they assume a specific value. As a matter of facts, in our approach, we consider four possibilities. (1) Some attribute has a "static" value (that is fixed once and for all for that type; e.g., the icon used for the visualization of a given type of node), or (2) their value can have to be fixed for each system (e.g., the reference ontologies), or (3) for each instantiation in a specific CIG (e.g., the name and description of an action node – called *CIG-valued* attributes henceforth), or (3) for each execution (e.g., the execution time of actions).

Node/arc definitions are recorded (as XML documents) in the NODE/ARC_LIBRARY (see Fig. 1).

Our representation of constraints is trivial: a constraint is described by a XML document, in which the user specifies its name and (the pointer to) the method to check it. Constraint definitions are recorded (as XML documents) in the CONSTRAINT_LIBRARY (see Fig. 1).

Finally, in our meta-formalism, the definition of a system consists in the definition of the components of its representation formalism: the set of types of nodes and arcs it adopts (which, in turn, are based on the attribute types in the ATTRIBUTE_TYPE_LIBRARY), and the set of constraints regulating the relationships between such nodes/arcs. System definitions are recorded (as XML documents) in the SYSTEM_LIBRARY (see Fig. 1).

3.3 Acquisition/Extension of a System and of Its Components: The Definition Editor

The Definition Editor (see Fig. 1) provides a user-friendly interface to acquire new attribute types, new node/arc types, new constraints, and new systems, automatically producing the corresponding XML documents and storing them into the appropriate libraries.

Indeed, several different possibilities are provided to the users of META-GLARE. As already discussed in the introductory section, a user might:

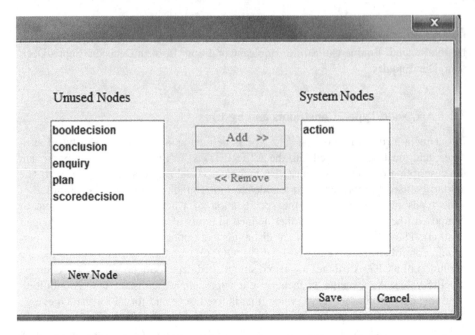

Fig. 3. The Definition Editor GUI for adding/removing nodes during the definition system phase

- extend an existing system by adding new node/arc types (see Fig. 3), or adding attributes to already existing node/arc types (with no programming effort at all)
- define a new system, basically by defining the nodes and arcs types using attributes from the ATTRIBUTE_TYPE_LIBRARY (with no programming effort at all).

As shown in Fig. 3, the Definition Editor GUI allows users to modify a system easily: the users should only select the node types which want to add/remove to a specific system in order to add/remove them from such system (the procedures for the management of arc types in a system and of attributes in any node/arc type are the same). Observe that user programming is needed only in case a new attribute types or new constraints have to be added in the libraries. However, the addition is modular and minimal: for instance, in the case of a new attribute type, the programmer has just to focus on the added type, and to provide the code for acquiring, consulting, and (if needed) execute it (while the HDG_INTERPRETER has not to be modified).

4 Acquisition of a CIG in a System

In this paper, we do not describe the whole HDG_INTERPRETER, but we just focus on acquisition (i.e., on the HDG_ACQUISITION module, see Fig. 1). The HDB_ ACQUISITION module aims at acquiring CIGs described as hierarchical directed graphs. It takes in input (from the SYSTEM_LIBRARY) the specification of the chosen system, and supports users in the acquisition of any CIG, expressed in the system's formalism.

Thus, in order to acquire a CIG, the user must first select one of the systems stored in SYSTEM_LIBRARY, whose description (stored in a XML document) will be provided in input to the HDG_ACQUISITION (see Fig. 1) module. Note that HDG_ACQUISITION module is parameterized over the system, and therefore over the node/arc types and constraint types it adopts. Moreover the CIG_DOCUMENTA-TION_ACQ module (which is, in our proposal, system independent; see Fig. 1) allows one to define the CIG documentation, which will be added to the description of the specific CIG.

Operationally speaking, our HDG_ACQUISITION module consists of two main components: (i) a component used in order to acquire the hierarchical directed graph representing the "control flow" of actions in the CIG, and (ii) the module used in order to acquire the "content" of each node and arc in the graph.

Acquisition of the "control flow". In the first module, we support acquisition through the insertion/deletion of node/arcs selected from bar menu of options. In Fig. 3 we show the GUI of HDG_ACQUISITION module. It consists of three main parts: (i) a bar menu, in the upper part of the figure, showing the icons associated with the node/arc types adopted by the system; (ii) the left part of the window representing the general structure of the CIG being acquired as a tree; (iii) the right part that allows users to draw a specific level of the hierarchical graph (users can move along the different levels by navigating the tree structure in the left part of the window).

Since the HDG_ACQUISITION module works on the basis of the system given in input, this GUI is parameterized on the system. As a matter of fact, it allows to acquire only the specific node/arc types provided in input and to manage them graphically using their specific definitions. In particular, the nodes/arcs icons in the bar menu are retrieved in the NODE/ARC_LIBRARY, considering only the nodes/arcs described in the system definition (in the SYSTEM_LIBRARY). In the specific case shown in Fig. 4, the selected system is composed by the following node types:

– Decision node (yellow rhombus): it represents decision based on well defined conditions;
– Data Enquiry node (green parallelogram): it allows to model the patient data acquisition task;
– Conclusion node (orange triangle): it is used to point out a specific patient' state (e.g. diagnosis) as result of a previous evaluation;
– Work Action node (blue circle): it models several types of clinical activity (e.g. visits, tests, therapy prescriptions);
– Plan node (red octagon): it is a composed nodes that represents a more complex process that will be expanded in a more detailed flow;

and by the following arc types:

– Sequence arc (continuous line): used to connect actions that are in sequence;
– Alternative arc (dotted line): used to connect a Decision node to the related alter-native actions;
– Concurrent arc (parallel lines): used to connect concurrent actions.

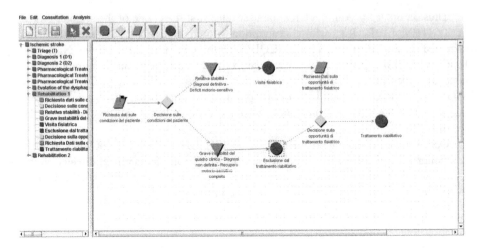

Fig. 4. A part of guideline for ischemic ictus acquired via the HDG_ACQUISITION module.

Starting from the selected system definition, the HDG acquisition module allows users to acquire a CIG drawing (using the JGraphX package [23]) a directed graph formed by the related nodes/arc types. In the case that the system adopts composed node types, the graph of the nodes/arcs composing it can be acquired by first selecting the composed node in the tree structure (in the left part of the window), and then drawing the graph in the right part of the window. In Fig. 4 a part of ischemic ictus guideline[1] is shown: the expansion of "Rehabilitation1" Plan node. This flow is meant to represent the choice of physiatric rehabilitation for patient with ischemic ictus. The graph starts with a Data Enquiry node, which models the task of patient's data acquisition. Then, a decision pass is represented for defining the diagnosis (i.e. the two Conclusion nodes) and accordingly the next work actions (i.e. physiatric visit, rehabilitation program exclusion). Just in case of physiatric visit, a further data acquisition is performed and afterward a final decision process allows physicians to decide about eligibility of the patient for the rehabilitation treatment.

Acquisition of the "content" of nodes and arcs. The HDG_ACQUISITION module is parameterized over node/arc types. However, as described in the previous section, each node and arc has a type (stored in the NODE/ARC_LIBRARY), which is described in terms of the list of typed attributes (defined in the ATTRIBUTE_TYPE_LIBRARY) constituting it. During CIG acquisition, the values of all "*CIG-valued*" attributes (see Sect. 3.2) of nodes and arcs must be acquired. This task can be easily achieved by the HDG_ACQUISITION module, operating in three steps. First, it looks at the node/arc type definition (in the NODE/ARC_LIBRARY) to retrieve the type of each attribute, and to see whether it has been categorized as "CIG-valued". Second, if the attribute is "CIG-valued", it access the ATTRIBUTE_TYPE__LIBRARY, to retrieve the (pointers

---

[1] The guideline for ischemic ictus has been developed by Azienda Ospedaliera S. Giovanni Battista in Turin, one of the largest hospitals in Italy.

to) the methods to acquire and store it. Third, the acquisition module simply executes such methods.

For example, if a node of a given type (e.g., a decision node) has an attribute of type "BooleanCondition", the HDG_ACQUISITION module retrieves from the XML describing such a type the pointer to the acquisition method (i.e. it.glare.visual.components.primitives.DialogCondition; see example in the Sect. 3), and invokes it to create the GUI in Fig. 5, to allow the user to acquire it. When the user has defined the boolean condition and decides to save it, the HDG_ACQUISITION module retrieves the pointer to memoritation method (i.e. it.glare.model.primitives.PrimitiveCondition), which defines the memorization object used to store a boolean condition, and saves (and stores) it appropriately.

Constraint checking. During the acquisition phase, the constraints on the graph must be checked (notice that such constraints are relative to each specific system, and are stored in the CONSTRAINT_LIBRARY). The HDG_ACQUISITION module first looks at the definition of the system, to retrieve the proper constraints (if any), and then accesses the CONSTRAINT_LIBRARY, to retrieve the (pointers to) the methods to execute them.

In our approach, the HDG_ACQUISITION module supports (for each constraint) two different modalities of constraint checking: *automatic* and *manual*. If the users acquiring a CIG select the manual modality for a given constraint, the check is performed only when the user will explicitly require it; otherwise the check is executed by the system whenever the CIG is updated (and saved).

Saving and storing a CIG. An XML representation of the acquired CIG is provided by HDG_ACQUISITION and then stored in the CIG_LIBRARY (see Fig. 1).

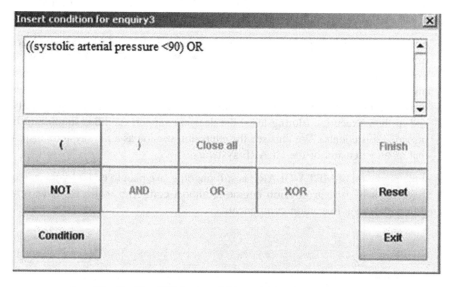

Fig. 5. The GUI for acquisition of a boolean condition

5 Conclusions and Future Work

In this paper, we propose a (partial) description of META-GLARE, an innovative approach to cope with CIGs. In short, instead of proposing "yet another system" to acquire, represent and execute CIGs, we propose a "meta-system", i.e., a shell to define (or modify) CIG systems. Roughly speaking, the input of META-GLARE is a description of a representation formalism for CIGs, and the output is a new system able to acquire, represent, consult and execute CIGs described using such a formalism. Indeed, the basic idea is not at all new in Computer Science: for instance, YACC (Yet Another Compiler of Compilers [17]) takes in input any context free language (expressed through a formal grammar), providing as output a compiler for it. However, to the best of our knowledge, the application of such an idea to the context of CIG is completely new. Such an application has mainly motivated by our goal of designing and implementing a flexible and powerful vehicle for research about CIG. In our opinion, META-GLARE provides two main types of advantages, both strictly related to the notion of *easy* and *fast prototyping*. Using META-GLARE

(1) the definition of a new system (based on a new representation formalism) is easy and quick;
(2) the extension of an existing system (through the modification of the representation formalism) is easy and quick[2].

In both cases, fast prototyping of the new (or extended) system is achieved: programming is needed just in case new attribute types or new constraints have to be added, and, even in such cases, only local programming is needed (in the sense that no modification of the HDG_INTERPRETER has to be done). We thus look META-GLARE as a valuable vehicle to address new CIG phenomena.

For instance, besides using META-GLARE to have a new and "engineered" version of GLARE's kernel, we are planning to use it

(i)   To extend GLARE formalism with new features (new attributes in the description of nodes), needed to cope with comorbidities
(ii) To implement a new system, geared towards education. The education task involves quite different solutions both in the representation of CIGs (for instance, it may be useful to add erroneous treatments and paths to test students' ability) and in their execution (during tests, the decision-support facilities should not be provided to students). We thus see the education version as a new system, instead that as an extension of the GLARE system.

The implementation of META-GLARE is still ongoing (we plan to end it by the end of this year). Actually, the acquisition engine is almost complete, while we have only started to address the execution components.

---

[2] The treatment of versioning is outside the goals of our present work. However, we are planning to face this issue in the future, also taking advantage of the formal approach we already devised [24].

Acknowledgements. The research described in this paper has been partially supported by Compagnia San Paolo, within the GINSENG project.

References

1. Gordon, C., Christensen, J.P. (eds.): Health Telematics for Clinical Guidelines and Protocols. IOS Press, Amsterdam (1995)
2. Fridsma, D.B. (Guest ed.): Special issue on workflow management and clinical guidelines. J. Am. Med. Inform. Assoc. **22**(1), 1–80 (2001)
3. ten Teije A., Miksch, S., Lucas, P. (eds.): Computer-Based Medical Guidelines and Protocols: A Primer and Current Trends. IOS Press, Amsterdam (2008)
4. Peleg, M., Tu, S., Bury, J., Ciccarese, P., Fox, J., Greenes, R.A., Hall, R., Johnson, P.D., Jones, N., Kumar, A., Miksch, S., Quaglini, S., Seyfang, A., Shortliffe, E.H., Stefanelli, M.: Comparing computer-interpretable guideline models: a case-study approach. J. Am. Med. Inform. Assoc. **10**(1), 52–68 (2003)
5. Miksch, S., Shahar Y., Johnson, P.: Asbru: a task-specific, intention-based, and time-oriented language for representing skeletal plans. In: Proceedings of 7th Workshop on Knowledge Engineering Methods and Languages, pp. 9–20 (1997)
6. Musen, M.A., Tu, S.W., Das, A.K., Shahar, Y.: EON: a component-based approach to automation of protocol-directed therapy. J. Am. Med. Inform. Assoc. **3**(6), 367–388 (1996)
7. Ohno-Machado, L., Gennari, J.H., Murphy, S., Jain, N.L., Tu, S.W., Oliver, D.E., et al.: The guideline interchange format: a model for representing guidelines. JAMIA **5**(4), 357–372 (1998)
8. Peleg, M., Boxawala, A.A., et al.: GLIF3: the evolution of a guideline representation format. In: Proceedings of AMIA'00, pp. 645–649 (2000)
9. Quaglini, S., Stefanelli, M., Cavallini, A., Miceli, G., Fassino, C., Mossa, C.: Guideline-based careflow systems. Artif. Intell. Med. **20**(1), 5–22 (2000)
10. Johnson, P.D., Tu, S.W., Booth, N., Sugden, B., Purves, I.N.: Using scenarios in chronic disease management guidelines for primary care. In: Proceedings of the AMIA Annual Fall Symposium 2000, pp. 389–393 (2000)
11. Fox, J., Johns, N., Rahmanzadeh, A., Thomson, R.: Disseminating medical knowledge: the PROforma approach. Artif. Intell. Med. **14**, 157–181 (1998)
12. Peleg, M.: Computer-interpretable clinical guidelines: a methodological review. J. Biomed. Inform. **46**(4), 744–763 (2013)
13. Terenziani, P., Molino, G., Torchio, M.: A modular approach for representing and executing clinical guidelines. Artif. Intell. Med. **23**(3), 249–276 (2001)
14. Anselma, L., Bottrighi, A., Molino, G., Montani, S., Terenziani, P., Torchio, M.: Supporting knowledge-based decision making in the medical context: the GLARE approach. IJKBO **1**(1), 42–60 (2011)
15. Anselma, L., Terenziani, P., Montani, S., Bottrighi, A.: Towards a comprehensive treatment of repetitions, periodicity and temporal constraints in clinical guidelines. Artif. Intell. Med. **38**(2), 171–195 (2006)
16. Leonardi, G., Bottrighi, A., Galliani, G., Terenziani, P., Messina, A., Della Corte, F.: Exceptions handling within GLARE clinical guideline framework. In: Proceedings of AMIA Annual Symposium 2012, pp. 512–521 (2012)
17. Johnson, S.C.: Yacc: Yet Another Compiler-Compiler, vol. 32. Bell Laboratories, Murray Hill (1975)

18. Hripcsak, G.: Writing Arden syntax medical logic modules. Comput. Biol. Med. **24**(5), 331–363 (1994)
19. http://docs.oracle.com/javase/tutorial/deployment/applet/index.html. Accessed 30 March 2014
20. http://www.postgresql.org. Accessed 30 March 2014
21. http://www.w3.org/standards/xml/schema. Accessed 4 April 2014
22. Naur, P. (ed.): Revised report on the algorithmic language ALGOL 60. Commun. ACM **3** (5), 299–314 (1960)
23. http://www.jgraph.com/. Accessed 2 April 2014
24. Anselma, L., Bottrighi, A., Montani, S., Terenziani, P.: Managing proposals and evaluations of updates to medical knowledge: theory and applications. J. Biomed. Inform. **46**(2), 363–376 (2013)

Assessment of Clinical Guideline Models Based on Metrics for Business Process Models

Mar Marcos[1]([✉]), Joaquín Torres-Sospedra[2], and Begoña Martínez-Salvador[1]

[1] Department of Computer Engineering and Science, Universitat Jaume I,
Av. de Vicent Sos Baynat s/n, 12071 Castellón, Spain
mar.marcos@uji.es
[2] Institute of New Imaging Technologies, Universitat Jaume I,
Av. de Vicent Sos Baynat s/n, 12071 Castellón, Spain

Abstract. The formalisation of clinical guidelines is a long and demanding task which usually involves both clinical and IT staff. Because of the features of guideline representation languages, a clear understanding of the final guideline model may prove complicated for clinicians. In this context, an assessment of the understandability of the guideline model becomes crucial. In the field of Business Process Modelling (BPM) there is research on structural metrics and their connection with the quality of process models, concretely with understandability and modifiability. In this paper we adapt the structural metrics that have been proposed in the field of BPM in terms of the features of a specific guideline representation language, which is PROforma. Additionally, we present some experiments consisting in the application of these adapted metrics to the assessment of guideline models described in PROforma. Although it has not been possible to draw meaningful conclusions on the overall quality of the models, our experiments have served to shed light on important aspects to be considered, such as the hierarchical decomposition of processes.

Keywords: Clinical guidelines · Formalisation of clinical guidelines · Evaluation of clinical guideline models

1 Introduction

The formalisation of clinical guidelines is a long and demanding task which usually requires the involvement of both clinical and IT staff. On one hand, clinical knowledge is required for a proper understanding of most of the contents of guideline texts. On the other hand, knowledge engineering skills are required to analyse the clinical procedures they contain and to describe them in terms of the guideline representation language of choice. This is because guideline languages are not always accessible for clinicians. To alleviate this problem, several

---

This work has been supported by Universitat Jaume I through the research project P1·1B2013-15.

works propose a gradual formalisation process. For instance, some authors use an intermediate XML representation intended for making explicit the connections between the guideline document and the formalised guideline model –the so-called *document-centric approaches* [1]. Even so, a clear understanding of the final guideline model may prove complicated for clinicians. In reality the opposite should be the case, clinicians should be able to analyse and understand the guideline model. In this context, an assessment of the understandability of guideline models becomes crucial.

In this regard, a related topic is that of quality of business process models, in the field of Business Process Modelling (BPM). It is a relatively new topic which has mainly focussed on structural metrics and their connection with the quality of process models, concretely with understandability and modifiability [2,3]. The emphasis on understandability stems from the observation that process models, as source code in a programming language, must be constantly re-interpreted by modellers [3]. Moreover there is evidence that process models usually have to be re-worked/re-designed. On the other hand, there exist obvious similarities between BPM languages and guideline languages regarding descriptions of processes, despite the specific features of the latter. Altogether this has prompted us to consider the utilisation of metrics for business process models in the assessment of clinical guideline models.

In this paper we examine the structural metrics that have been proposed in the field of BPM, and reinterpret them in terms of a particular guideline representation language, which is PROforma. In the adaptation we take into account some of the specific features of this guideline language. Additionally, we apply these adapted metrics to the assessment of guideline models described using the PROforma language.

2   Metrics for Business Process Models

Several studies have been published recently related to the quality of business processes, mostly focussed on process model aspects [2,4]. According to Mendling *et al.*, the lines of research related to the quality of business process models include [5]: (1) metrics and their relationship with the understandability and modifiability of process models; (2) research on modelling techniques and languages; and (3) pragmatic guidelines for process modelling. When examining an already finished process model, there is no possible control over the particular modelling language nor the modelling process itself. Hence our interest in the stream of research oriented towards metrics for process models.

A recent paper by Mendling summarises different metrics from the fields of network analysis, software engineering and BPM, and proposes a set of 15 metrics dealing with various aspects of the structure and state space of the process model [2]. These metrics, initially described in terms of the EPC (Event-driven Process Chain) language and validated with experiments using models in this language, have been adapted to the BPMN language and further validated by Sánchez *et al.* [4]. The metrics fall in the following categories: size, density, partitionability, connector interplay, cyclicity, and concurrency.

The concrete metrics are described in terms of the elements of the process model, which is regarded as a special type of graph $G = (N, A)$ with different types of nodes $N = T \cup S \cup J$, namely tasks, split connectors, and join connectors, and with control flow arcs connecting these nodes $A \subseteq N \times N$. The metrics are defined as follows:

- *size, S_N*: number of nodes in the graph
- *diameter, diam*: length of the longest path from a start node to an end node
- *density, Δ*: ratio of arcs to maximum number of arcs (number of arcs divided by the maximum number of arcs, given the number of nodes)

$$\Delta(G) = \frac{|A|}{|N| \cdot (|N| - 1)}$$

- *coefficient of connectivity, CNC*: ratio of arcs to nodes (number of arcs divided by the number of nodes)

$$CNC(G) = \frac{|A|}{|N|}$$

- *average degree of connectors, $\overline{d_C}$*: calculated from the degree of a connector $d(c)$, which is the number of arcs (both incoming and outgoing) of the connector

$$\overline{d_C(G)} = \frac{1}{|C|} \sum_{c \in C} d(c)$$

- *maximum degree of connectors, $\widehat{d_C}$*

$$\widehat{d_C(G)} = max\{d(c)|c \in C\}$$

- *separability, Π*: ratio of cut vertices to nodes, where a cut vertex is defined as a node that increases the number of connected components in the graph, if removed

$$\Pi(G) = \frac{|\{n \in N | n \text{ is a cut vertex}\}|}{|N| - 2}$$

- *sequentiality, Ξ*: ratio of arcs between non-connector nodes to total number of arcs

$$\Xi(G) = \frac{|A \cap (T \times T)|}{|A|}$$

- *structuredness, Φ*: one minus the number of nodes in the reduced process graph G' (see e.g. the algorithm by Sadiq and Orlowska [6]) divided by the number of nodes in the original process graph G

$$\Phi_N = 1 - \frac{S_N(G')}{S_N(G)}$$

- *depth*, Λ: maximum depth of all nodes, where the depth of a node $\lambda(c)$ is calculated as the minimum of the in-depth and out-depth of the node. The in-depth $\lambda_{in}(c)$ refers to the maximum number of split connectors that must be traversed in a path reaching the node minus the number of join connectors in the path. The out-depth $\lambda_{out}(c)$ is defined analogously with respect to the successor nodes

$$\Lambda(G) = max\{\lambda(c)|n \in N\}$$

- *connector mismatch*, MM: number of mismatches for each connector type, namely parallel (*and*), exclusive (*xor*), and inclusive (*or*). Matching occurs when each split connector corresponds to a join connector of the same type

$$MM(G) = MM_{and} + MM_{xor} + MM_{or}$$

- *connector heterogeneity*, CH: entropy over the different connector types, based on the relative frequency of each connector type $p(l) = |C_l|/|C|$

$$CH(G) = - \sum_{l \in \{and,xor,or\}} p(l) \cdot log_3(p(l))$$

- *control flow complexity*, CFC: sum of all split connectors weighted by the potential combinations of states after the split. These amount to 1 in the case of *and* splits, to the number of successor nodes $c\bullet$ in the case of *xor* splits, and to $2^{|c\bullet|} - 1$ in the case of *or* splits

$$CFC(G) = \sum_{c \in S_{and}} 1 + \sum_{c \in S_{xor}} |c_{xor}\bullet| + \sum_{c \in S_{or}} (2^{|c_{or}\bullet|} - 1)$$

- *cyclicity*, CYC: ratio of nodes in a cycle to total number of nodes

$$CYC(G) = \frac{|N_C|}{|N|}$$

- *token split*, TS: sum of output degrees of *and* splits and *or* splits minus one

$$TS(G) = \sum_{c \in S_{and} \cup S_{or}} (d_{out}(n) - 1)$$

The correlation between the above metrics and process model understandability is for the most part negative, i.e. the higher the score the lower the understandability is, resulting in an error-prone model. This is so except in the case of separability and sequentiality. If the sequentiality ratio of the model is high then it should be easy to understand. The same holds for a high separability ratio, e.g. if every intermediate node is a cut-vertex then the model is sequential. For the rest of metrics the correlation with understandability is negative. For instance if the process model contains a big number of nodes or if the density of arcs is high it should be more likely to contain errors, because the modeller would only have a partial view at a particular moment.

3   Adaptation to Clinical Guideline Models in PROforma

We are interested in the adaptation of the previous metrics in terms of guideline representation languages. As an illustration we have chosen PROforma [7], which is an established guideline language that can be regarded as a graph-oriented process language. In PROforma a process is modelled as a plan made up of one or more tasks. There are four basic types of tasks, namely, actions, enquiries, decisions and plans. Actions correspond to clinical procedures to be performed in the external environment. Enquiries are tasks that supply information from the external environment. Decisions are tasks that involve some kind of choice among candidates, based on arguments for and against these candidates. Finally, plans are used to group together a set of tasks to be performed to achieve a goal. The tasks within a plan are usually ordered via scheduling constraints and preconditions. If no constraints are given, a parallel execution of tasks is performed by default. Likewise, an implicit synchronisation of the end tasks takes place before the completion of the plan.

In the PROforma graphical notation processes are represented as directed graphs in which nodes represent tasks and arcs represent scheduling constraints. An arc indicates that the task at the head of the arc cannot start until the task at the tail of the arc (antecedent task) has completed [8]. A task can only be considered for activation when all its scheduling constraints have been met, i.e. when all its antecedent tasks have been completed or discarded. When this is fulfilled, the task will be activated if at least one of the antecedent tasks has completed, otherwise it will be discarded. The precondition of the task is checked when the scheduling constraints are met. Thus, the task becomes active if the precondition holds, otherwise the task is discarded.

The adaptation of the metrics has been made considering key differences of the PROforma process model graph. First and foremost, nodes correspond to tasks and arcs correspond to scheduling constraints. Second, in the absence of proper connectors, we consider that a task with more than one outgoing arc and/or more than one incoming arc plays the connector role –hereafter referred to as connector task. Third, we do not make any difference between connector tasks, since their actual behaviour (parallel, exclusive, or inclusive) is determined by the preconditions of subsequent tasks. Fourth, given that in general guidelines do not contain unstructured loops, we have ruled out the possibility of arbitrary cycles in the process model graph. As a matter of fact, graph cycles are signalled as potential problems by the PROforma editor. A final consideration is related to the implicit parallel split and/or join that take place within a plan, whenever there is more than one start task and/or more than one end task. Accordingly, we incorporate a number of dummy components (tasks and scheduling constraints) to the graph that account for these splits/joins.

Below we introduce a reinterpretation of the metrics for business process models in terms of the elements of the PROforma language. From the original list by Mendling we have omitted two metrics, concretely *connector heterogeneity* and *cyclicity*, because they are not relevant for PROforma (see above). The most significant differences are in the *connector mismatch* and *control flow complexity* metrics, which have been reformulated considering that there are no different types of connectors. In the case of *control flow complexity* we have chosen to view all connector tasks as *or* connectors, which is the worst case scenario.

- *size*: number of tasks in the graph
- *diameter*: length of the longest path from a start task to an end task
- *density*: ratio of scheduling constraints to maximum number of scheduling constraints
- *coefficient of connectivity*: ratio of scheduling constraints to tasks
- *average degree of connectors*: average number of scheduling constraints of connector tasks
- *maximum degree of connectors*: maximum number of scheduling constraints of connector tasks
- *separability*: ratio of cut vertices to tasks
- *sequentiality*: ratio of scheduling constraints between non-connector tasks to total number of scheduling constraints
- *structuredness*: one minus the number of tasks in the reduced process graph divided by the number of tasks in the original process graph
- *depth*: maximum depth of all tasks (see definition of *depth* in Sect. 2)
- *connector mismatch*: number of mismatches of connector tasks, i.e. number of split connector tasks that do not have a corresponding join connector task
- *control flow complexity*: sum of all split connector tasks weighted by the maximum possible combinations of states after the split, i.e. $2^{|c\bullet|} - 1$ (*or* connectors are considered the worst case scenario)
- *token split*: sum of output degrees of all split connector tasks

4   Application of Metrics for Clinical Guideline Models in PROforma

We have conducted a few experiments with the metrics described in the previous section. We have applied them to fragments of two different PROforma models of the same guideline, concretely the 2012 version of the National Comprehensive Cancer Network (NCCN) guideline for prostate cancer [9]. One of the models –which we refer to as *direct model*– was manually developed by a knowledge engineer directly in PROforma. The other model –which we refer to as *transformed model*– was obtained starting from an initial model described in the BPMN language [10], by means of a transformation algorithm that translated it to PROforma [11]. Our aim was to assess the quality of these two different models, and ultimately to determine the usefulness of the metrics we have derived from the ones for business process models.

The direct model describes the guideline processes hierarchically, using plans to decompose complex tasks up to the desired level of detail. By convention, the direct model includes an explicit enquiry prior to the utilisation of each data item. The plan decomposition of the transformed model is obviously determined by the design of the initial BPMN model, in combination with the mechanics of the transformation algorithm. It is worth noting that the transformed model contains no enquiries, since the BPMN model barely describes data. Although the transformed model is more complete than the direct one, the degree of detail of the two models varies across tasks. With respect to the size, the direct model includes a total of 244 tasks (of which 60 are plans, 102 are actions, 59 are enquiries, and 19 are decisions), and the transformed one includes 376 tasks (of which 131 are plans, 188 are actions, and 57 are decisions). This larger size is to a significant extent related to the mechanics of the transformation algorithm.

As an illustration, Table 1 compares the values of the metrics for the upper-level plan of the two models. The PROforma graphical notation of the plans is shown in Figs. 1 and 2. The table does not include the values of the *structuredness* metric, which has been deliberately left out because it requires the development of the notion of PROforma graph reduction. Here the metrics have been calculated considering the graph of the upper-level plan alone. In such a way the values can be wrongly interpreted because the plan of the transformed model, which is much larger, scores better than the one of the direct model in nearly all the metrics (except for the *density*, which is higher but not significant because the *sequentiality* value is 1). What occurs is that the upper-level plan of the transformed model hides most of the complexity in a nested plan grouping the tasks from `treatment decision`. Note that we have applied the metrics to the direct and transformed models as they are, with all their subplans, rather than flattening them to obtain a single-layer model containing all the connectors and tasks. The rationale for this is that in our view hierarchical decomposition is an important feature that must be considered.

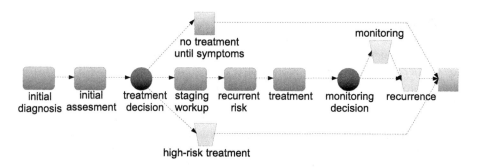

Fig. 1. PROforma graphical notation of the upper-level plan in the *direct model*. In this notation plans are depicted as rounded boxes, actions as squares, decisions as circles, and scheduling constraints as directed arcs. Note that the dummy elements that have been introduced to account for implicit splits/joins are marked with dashed lines.

Fig. 2. PROforma graphical notation of the upper-level plan in the *transformed model*.

Table 1. Metric values for the upper-level plan.

metric	direct model	transformed model
size	12	3
diameter	9	2
density	0.106	0.333
coefficient of connectivity	1.167	0.667
average degree of connectors	3.334	N/A
maximum degree of connectors	4	N/A
separability	0.2	1
sequentiality	0.214	1
depth	2	0
connector mismatch	0	0
control flow complexity	10	0
token split	3	0

Table 2 shows another comparison, with the values of the metrics for the prostatectomy plan of the two models. Unlike the previous plan, this plan does not use any nested subplan but rather includes directly all its constituent tasks (actions, enquiries, and/or decisions). In this case the values of the metrics are relatively homogeneous, which agrees with the assessment of the knowledge engineers who informally examined the models.

5   Discussion

We have conducted a few experiments on the application of process model metrics to hierarchical guideline models in PROforma. As can be observed in the first example (see Table 1), the application of the metrics to a plan graph in isolation can lead to misleading results when it contains subplans that decompose complex tasks. This suggests that some kind of aggregation may be required for the calculation of metrics of a plan graph, which uses the values of the metrics of the subplans. The aggregation of some of the metrics should be straightforward (e.g. *size*), but others may require a careful analysis (e.g. *separability*). Notwithstanding, such aggregated metric values should not be considered solely. Otherwise a single plan graph including all low-level tasks and scheduling constraints would score the same as a well-designed hierarchical plan with the same tasks, when clearly the latter would be more appropriate. A possibility would be to consider as well the averages of the metrics of all plan graphs. The issues of process model modularisation have been recognised in the BPM field [12], however there are no clear criteria for the consistent application of metrics to process models with hierarchical subprocesses.

Our experiments have led us to consider the definition of additional metrics for PROforma. Related to the hierarchical decomposition of plans, an aspect that

Table 2. Metric values for the `prostatectomy` plan.

metric	direct model	transformed model
size	28	23
diameter	18	16
density	0.044	0.051
coefficient of connectivity	1.179	1.130
average degree of connectors	3	3
maximum degree of connectors	4	4
separability	0.154	0.261
sequentiality	0.212	0.346
depth	2	1
connector mismatch	1	0
control flow complexity	18	13
token split	6	4

can be considered is the size (number of tasks) of plans. In general hierarchical decomposition improves understandability, however an overuse of plans (e.g. plans with a single task) may have the opposite effect. Another aspect related to hierarchical decomposition that can be analysed is the depth of plans. Additionally, decisions are one distinctive feature of PROforma that could be taken into account. According to our experience, the complexity of decision descriptions (at least candidates, arguments, and rules must be specified) has a negative impact on understandability, compared to alternative descriptions based on preconditions. Consequently, the ratio of decisions to total number of tasks could be considered as an additional metric.

6   Conclusions

In this paper we adapt the structural metrics that have been proposed in the field of BPM in terms of the features of a specific guideline representation language, which is PROforma. Our aim was to determine the usefulness of these adapted metrics for the assessment of guideline models. For this purpose we have conducted some experiments consisting in the application of the metrics to small fragments of two different PROforma models of the same guideline. Due to the way in which we have calculated the metric values, i.e. considering plan graphs in isolation, it has not been possible to draw meaningful conclusions on the overall quality of the models. However our experiments have served to shed light on important aspects to be considered when applying BPM structural metrics, particularly the hierarchical decomposition of processes.

As future work we plan to devise a proposal for the calculation of metrics which regards the aggregation of the metrics of a plan graph based on the ones of its subplans. Furthermore, we envisage to develop additional metrics that may be considered for guideline models. As mentioned before no clear criteria exist for the application of metrics to hierarchical process models, nor to process models with the specific features (other than graph-oriented) of guideline languages. We also plan to work on the *structuredness* metric, which has been left out in this study. Finally we intend to perform some validation study to check whether our set of metrics actually serves for the assessment of the quality of guideline models in PROforma.

References

1. Sonnenberg, F., Hagerty, C.: Computer-interpretable clinical practice guidelines. where are we and where are we going? In: IMIA Yearbook of Medical Informatics pp. 145–158 (2006)
2. Mendling, J.: Metrics for Business Process Models. In: Metrics for Business Process Models. Empirical Foundations of Verification, Error Prediction, and Guidelines for Correctness. LNBIP, vol. 6. Springer, Heidelberg (2008)
3. Sánchez González, L., García Rubio, F., Ruiz González, F., Piattini Velthuis, M.: Measurement in business processes: a systematic review. Bus. Process. Manage. J. **16**(1), 114–134 (2010)
4. Sánchez-González, L., García, F., Mendling, J., Ruiz, F.: Quality assessment of business process models based on thresholds. In: Meersman, R., Dillon, T.S., Herrero, P. (eds.) OTM 2010. LNCS, vol. 6426, pp. 78–95. Springer, Heidelberg (2010)
5. Mendling, J., Reijers, H., van der Aalst, W.: Seven process modeling guidelines (7PMG). Inf. Softw. Technol. **52**(2), 127–136 (2010)
6. Sadiq, W., Orlowska, M.E.: Applying graph reduction techniques for identifying structural conflicts in process models. In: Jarke, M., Oberweis, A. (eds.) CAiSE 1999. LNCS, vol. 1626, p. 195. Springer, Heidelberg (1999)
7. Fox, J., Johns, N., Rahmanzadeh, A.: Disseminating medical knowledge: the PROforma approach. Artif. Intell. Med. **14**(1–2), 157–182 (1998)
8. Interdisciplinary Research Collaboration in Cognitive Science & Systems Engineering: Tallis training. http://archive.cossac.org/tallis/index.html. Accessed April 2014
9. Mohler, J.L., Armstrong, A.J., Bahnson, R.R., Boston, B., Busby, J.E., D'Amico, A.V., Eastham, J.A., Enke, C.A., Farrington, T., Higano, C.S., Horwitz, E.M., Kantoff, P.W., Kawachi, M.H., Kuettel, M., Lee, R.J., MacVicar, G.R., Malcolm, A.W., Miller, D., Plimack, E.R., Pow-Sang, J.M., Roach 3rd, M., Rohren, E., Rosenfeld, S., Srinivas, S., Strope, S.A., Tward, J., Twardowski, P., Walsh, P.C., Ho, M., Shead, D.A.: Prostate cancer, version 3.2012: featured updates to the NCCN guidelines. J. Natl. Compr. Canc. Netw. **10**(9), 1081–1087 (2012)
10. OMG: Business Process Model and Notation (BPMN) Version 2.0. Technical report, OMG (2011)
11. Martínez-Salvador, B., Marcos, M., Sánchez, A.: An algorithm for guideline transformation: from BPMN to PROforma. In: Proceedings of the 6th Workshop on Knowledge Representation for Health Care (KR4HC 2014) (2014)
12. Reijers, H., Mendling, J., Dijkman, R.: Human and automatic modularizations of process models to enhance their comprehension. Inf. Syst. **36**(5), 881–897 (2011)

An Algorithm for Guideline Transformation: From BPMN to PROforma

Begoña Martínez-Salvador$^{(\boxtimes)}$, Mar Marcos, and Anderson Sánchez

Department of Computer Engineering and Science, Universitat Jaume I,
Av. de Vicent Sos Baynat s/n, 12071 Castellón, Spain
`begona.martinez@uji.es`

Abstract. In healthcare domain, business process modelling technologies are able to support clinical processes recommended in guidelines. It has been shown that BPMN is intuitively understood by all stakeholders, including domain experts. However, if we want to develop any computer system using clinical guidelines, we need them in an executable format. Thus, we need computer-interpretable guidelines. Although there are several formalisms tailored to capture medical processes, encoding a guideline in any of them is not as intuitive. We propose an automatic transformation from a guideline represented in BPMN to a computer-interpretable formalism, in this case, PROforma. To tackle this problem, we have studied the approaches that transform graph-oriented languages into block-oriented languages. We have adapted the solution to our specific-domain problem and to our target language, PROforma, which has features of both, graph and block-oriented paradigms.

Keywords: Guideline representation · Guideline transformation · Clinical processes · BPMN · PROforma

1 Introduction and Motivation

There is a widespread interest in Business Process Modelling (BPM) technologies in different domains. Among them, healthcare is one of the most promising and challenging. In healthcare, it is possible to build process-oriented solutions able to support not only organizational processes and but also clinical processes. In the future, BPM methods and technologies may contribute to enhance IT support for healthcare processes [13].

BPM can provide an abstract view on systems and allows to design them in an independent language. BPM can separate process logic from implementation. The Business Process Modelling Notation BPMN [11] is becoming more popular in clinical settings as recent literature shows [6,14,15]. Most of these works agree in emphasizing that BPMN is easy to use and to understand by all stakeholders. On the other hand, BPMN is formal enough to provide the basis for a

This work has been supported by Universitat Jaume I through the research project P1·1B2013-15.

S. Miksch et al. (Eds.): KR4HC 2014, LNAI 8903, pp. 121–132, 2014.
DOI: 10.1007/978-3-319-13281-5_9

later implementation. Due to the fact that the BPMN 2.0 specification provides some execution semantics in terms of BPEL, in general BPEL is mistaken as an executable expression of BPMN. In fact, the full equivalence of BPMN cannot be expressed in BPEL [3]. For this reason we do not regard BPMN as the target execution language, but rather as an initial representation that can be used as a basis for a later implementation.

Clinical guidelines are usually paper-based documents that contain the processes describing the activities to be performed regarding a particular disease in a specific clinical setting. A prerequisite for the implementation of any system based on or using clinical guidelines is to transform the textual guideline in a Computer-Interpretable Guideline (CIG) language. Formalisms for CIGs are tailored to capture the medical knowledge of guidelines. Most of them provide tools for authoring and graphically editing CIGs. However, encoding a guideline is a difficult and demanding task, usually done by a knowledge engineer.

In this work, given a BPMN representation of a clinical process, we propose to transform it to a representation in a CIG formalism. Thus, we aim for a transformation between BPMN and a CIG formalism in the context of clinical guidelines. We have chosen PROforma as CIG formalism.

BPMN can be understood intuitively by all stakeholders, even those who do not know about CIG formalisms, encoding or programming in general [6,14,15]. Thus, the use of BPMN can empower domain experts and put clinicians in the driver's seat of the clinical guideline modelling task. Another advantage is that the effort to model a clinical process in BPMN can be leveraged for the implementation of models in several CIG languages, provided that methods are developed to automatically translate from BPMN to these languages.

In the literature, there are several works which address the transformation from graph-oriented languages (such as BPMN, XPDL) to block-oriented languages (BPEL, HTN), [4,5,9,12]. Since our source code is a graph-oriented representation, we propose a semi-automatic transformation algorithm for clinical guidelines based on these approaches.

The rest of the paper is organized as follows. Section 2 explains the main features of BPMN models representing a clinical guideline. In Sect. 3 we summarize the existing transformation approaches between graph-oriented and block-oriented languages. Section 4 is devoted to the development of our approach. Conclusions and future work are discussed in Sect. 5.

2   Clinical Guidelines in BPMN

In this section we aim to explain the characteristics of our source model, based on our experience in modelling the clinical procedures contained in clinical guidelines. BPMN has plenty of modelling elements, although only 20 % of them are used [11]. For clinical guideline representation, we have used flow objects (activities and sub-processes, events and gateways), and sequence flows (in the category of connecting objects). Among the events, we have used the start event as entry point to the process and the end event as finishing point. Regarding gateways, we have AND-gateways for parallel flows, XOR-gateways for alternative paths in a process flow, and OR-gateways for alternative paths with the possibility of parallel flows. The representation is usually depicted as a business process diagram (BPD). Figure 1 shows a BPMN representation of clinical processes.

Clinical guidelines contain rather complex processes. Among the most important goals of BPM are communication and clarity. Therefore, complex multi-page diagrams are discouraged. Our experience in modelling clinical processes with BPMN shows that it is necessary to use sub-processes and ad-hoc sub-processes. A sub-process is an activity represented as a single node in the diagram, but whose internal details are modelled using its own BPD. This feature compels us to work with graphs that may contain sub-graphs and so on, recursively.

The BPD representing a clinical guideline is structured. A structured model is one in which every split gateway (e.g. split AND-gateway) has a matching join gateway of the same type (e.g. in this case, join AND-gateway), and in which all split-join pairs are properly nested [7]. Clinical guidelines are formulated in natural language, therefore non-structuredness is not an essential nor useful feature for clinical process models. In fact, this is an advantage rather than a limitation because structuredness is a desirable property in BPDs [7].

In BPDs, it is expected that at least one action is done in the paths between two gateways. However, in clinical guidelines is common to find actions to be done only for a sub-group of patients. For example, the guideline for the diagnosis and treatment of prostate cancer [10] recommends additional imaging (bone scan, tomography or MRI) for a subgroup of patients while no additional imaging is required for the rest. This example of recommendation fits in the schema of Fig. 2, in which a flow goes straight from the split node (A) to the join node (B).

Clinical guidelines may contain recommendations that can be considered as iterative processes. According to our experience, we have used loop tasks or loop sub-processes for this type of processes. Thus, in our domain-specific implementation we have not considered cycles in the BPDs.

3   Related Work: From Graph-Oriented to Block Oriented Languages

Research work on transformation between different process modelling languages propose generic strategies by distinguishing two major paradigms for BPM languages: graph-oriented languages (such as BPMN, EPCs, YAWL, XPDL) and block-oriented ones (such as BPEL and BPML) [9]. The literature presents several strategies for both-senses transformation, although not all of them are always applicable to the source model.

These strategies are referred to as element-preservation, element-minimization, structure-identification and structure-maximization strategies. They exploit the graph-oriented paradigm, so the first step is to read the BPD into a directed graph: tasks, gateways and events are the nodes, and sequence flows are the arcs. The element-preservation strategy maps all elements in the process graph to flow constructs, and arcs to links. One prerequisite is that input process graphs must be acyclic. With this strategy, the resulting model includes more elements than needed since joins and splits are translated to empty activities. The element-minimization strategy simplifies the code generated with the previous strategy by removing empty activities. Obviously, the input process graph must also be acyclic.

The idea of the structure-identification strategy is to identify "structured activities" in the process graph and apply the proper mappings. That is, to define relevant structures of the target model and to identify these structures in the input process graph. Each time a structure is identified in the source model, it is mapped to the target language and the process graph is reduced by substituting the identified structure according to some rules [9]. In this case, the source model must be structured and acyclic. The main advantage of this strategy is the readability of the resulting code.

Finally, the idea of the structure-maximization strategy is to apply the structure-identification rules as often as possible. And then, to translate the rest of the process graph using the element-preservation strategy. This strategy can work with unstructured process graphs with some types of cycles.

Götz et al. [5] and Ouyang et al. [12] use the structure-identification strategy for implementing solutions that transform BPMN to BPEL. González-Ferrer et al. [4] implement a similar approach for transforming from XPDL to HTP. All these approaches exploit the graph-oriented paradigm of the source language and the block-oriented paradigm of the target one. Our source language is also BPMN, therefore our aim is to apply a similar structure-identification strategy. In fact, our source processes are structured, so this is not a drawback. However, the main difference is that our target language, PROforma, is not strictly block-oriented but it also has some features of graph-oriented languages. Moreover, PROforma is not a BPM language so we are dealing with a language tailored for a different purpose, and thus, with different expressiveness.

In order to apply the structure-identification strategy, the structures of the target language must be studied. In the case of BPEL, these structures comprise sequence, flow, if, pick, while and repeatUntil [9,12]. Then, equivalent components to this structures are identified in the source graph. A component (or block) is a connected sub-graph without start or end events and with a single entry point and a single exit point, named source and sink, respectively. All the flows must enter and exit the component through these points. All the nodes in a component must have at least one incoming arc, except the source; and all the nodes must have at least one outgoing arc, except the sink. We assume that a component has at least two nodes.

The components identified are roughly sequences and parallel components. Parallel components divide the flow using gateways. Therefore, it is possible to have AND-parallel components, OR-parallel components and XOR-parallel components. González-Ferrer et al. [4] find the same types of blocks in the source model.

Component identification is a key step in the approach. However, few papers address this topic. We have studied two approaches: the Token Analysis

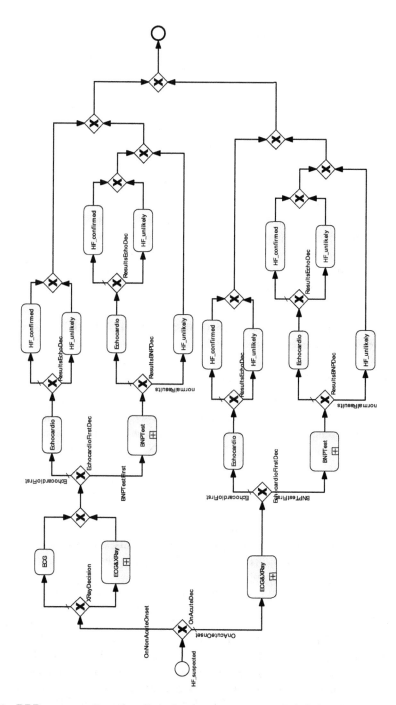

Fig. 1. BPD representing the clinical processes recommended for the diagnosis of chronic heart failure

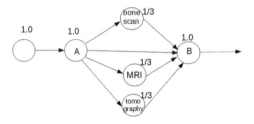

Fig. 2. Nodes A and B represent respectively a pair of split and join XOR-gateways, and there is an arc that connects them directly.

algorithm [5] and the Branch-water algorithm [1]. This last method transforms a process graph into Event-Condition-Action rules. In both algorithms, the first phase consists in traversing the graph and properly labelling its nodes. The labels are used to identify the components. The input process graph must be structured. In next section, we present how we have adapted the algorithms to our domain-specific problem.

4   Approach for the Transformation of BPMN to PROforma

4.1   Structure-Identification for PROforma

In order to apply the structure-identification strategy with PROforma as target language, we have studied the building blocks/structures of PROforma, comprising plans, decisions and actions. Plans group processes but also can represent parallel flows. Thus, it is necessary to identify AND-parallel blocks in the source model in order to map them to PROforma plans. PROforma decisions model the patterns if-then, pick one, and pick one or more. Thus, XOR and OR-parallel components must be identified in the graph model and mapped to the appropriate PROforma decision. We also need to map sequences which do not have an equivalent block in PROforma but require scheduling constraints between each pair of elements of the sequence. In a way, plans and decisions represent the block-oriented features of PROforma while sequences, or better scheduling constraints, represent the graph-oriented features.

Therefore, the blocks we need to find in the source model are sequences and parallel blocks (AND, OR and XOR). Any parallel block will be mapped to a PROforma plan. Then, every split OR/XOR gateway will be transformed into a PROforma decision inside the corresponding plan. Candidates and arguments must be specified in PROforma decisions. In order to define the candidates, we need the successor elements of the split gateway. To set the arguments, we will use the condition expression of the outgoing sequence flows of the split gateway.

Not only blocks are mapped to PROforma, but also single BPMN elements. Therefore, every BPMN sub-process is mapped to a PROforma plan. Thus, we will have the same level of process abstraction in both representations.

Any type of BPMN task is mapped to a PROforma action. We also set a mapping for the attributes related with iterations: `loopCondition` to `cycleUntil`, or `timeDuration` to `cycleInterval`. Remark that there are some BPMN elements that will not be mapped to any PROforma element, such as the start and end events, and all join gateways.

4.2   Component Identification

The implementation of the structure-identification strategy is based on the identification of components in the source graph. In our approach, since we deal with sub-processes, we will use a graph of graphs. In fact, each graph has two arrays of graphs: one for storing the graphs of its sub-processes, and another for storing the graphs of its ad-hoc sub-processes. This is because an ad-hoc sub-process may contain two or more sub-graphs. Therefore, for every ad-hoc sub-process we have an array of graphs. In the graph not only nodes and arcs are stored but also the types of gateways, conditions and so on.

Regarding the component identification algorithm, we have decided to adapt the branch-water algorithm [1] to our domain-specific model. This algorithm first labels all the nodes. For doing that, it assigns a value to the first node and propagates it through the graph. If the actual node divides the flow into n branches, its value is also divided into n and propagated to the nodes at the head of each subsequent arc. Conversely, given a node with several incoming arcs, its value is calculated as the addition of the labels of the nodes at the tail of the arcs.

Our domain-specific BPMN models usually have sub-graphs like the one in Fig. 2. It is easy to see that the previously described labelling algorithm does not work in those cases. In our implementation, we have defined the concept of *valid successor node*: Given a node representing a split gateway, a node at the head of any of its outgoing arcs is said to be a valid successor if it does not represent the corresponding join gateway. Therefore, the label of the nodes will be calculated considering the number of valid successor nodes, instead of the number of outgoing arcs. And reciprocally, we consider *valid predecessor nodes* for calculating the label of the join gateway. In Fig. 2 we have three valid successor/predecessor nodes according to these definitions.

In the branch-water algorithm, each time a component is identified, its type and its content are registered. Then, the component is replaced by a single node in the graph. The algorithm proceeds in this way until the graph is reduced to a trivial graph. Let us remark that the mapping to the target equivalent structure is not done in this step. During the graph reduction process an intermediate tree structure is generated, which will guide the further mapping to PROforma. Starting with the single node of the trivial graph, if we replace it by its content, and we proceed successively in this way until arriving to the original graph nodes, we will obtain a tree structure.

The original algorithm [1] always uses the minimum label to find the most inner component, either sequential or parallel. First, it searches for the first node of a sequence with that minimum label. When no further sequence is found, it proceeds to search for parallel blocks with the minimum label. Therefore, the graph is traversed several times.

Our algorithm implementation first traverses the graph once and identifies and replaces all sequences. Then, the algorithm iterates looking for the most inner parallel component. If found, it replaces it by a single node and finds out if a new sequence appears considering the new node. Thus, the graph is not traverse several times.

The procedure for identifying all sequences begins at the start node of the graph and follows a depth-first traversal. Nodes are marked to avoid repeating a search after join gateways. Since all sequences have been already identified and registered, the search of a parallel component by minimum label assures that we will find the most inner one. We use a data structure that points to the split gateway with the minimum label, without the need for traversing the graph.

Due to the use of sub-processes, all our procedures are recursive. Each time the graph reduction algorithm finds a node representing a sub-process, steps in to the graph or graphs corresponding to the sub-process.

Figure 3 shows an example of the execution of our algorithm. S and E are the start and end nodes, respectively. C, F, I and M are the nodes corresponding to gateways. First, all sequences are identified and replaced by component nodes, labelled with $Se1$ to $Se3$ in Fig. 3(b). Then, the innermost parallel component is found and replaced by a component node $PC1$ (Fig. 3(c)) and a new sequence block is identified, $Se4$ (Fig. 3(d)). These last two steps are repeated until the graph is reduced to the trivial graph (Fig. 3(f)).

4.3   The Mapping to PROforma

As we stated in previous subsection, the identification of components gives rise to a tree structure (see in Fig. 4 the tree for the example of Fig. 3). The mapping to PROforma is done following a top-down traversal of this tree, according to the mappings described in Subsect. 4.1. In fact, the transformation to PROforma is done in two traversals of the tree. In the first traversal, the mapping of every node is stored in the node itself. In the second traversal, the mappings are written to a file.

Thus, in the first traversal of the tree, each component node is mapped to a PROforma plan with the exception of sequences. There is no block in PROforma equivalent to sequences, however they need to be identified since it is necessary to set the value of the scheduling constraints of the corresponding PROforma tasks. These scheduling constraints are generated in the second traversal of the tree.

Split AND-gateways are not mapped to any PROforma element, since the mapping is done with the AND-parallel component. However, a split XOR/OR-gateway is mapped to a decision. Candidates are defined by the end nodes of the outgoing arcs of the gateway. These candidates will be plans or actions. The argument of each candidate is determined by the condition expression of the sequence flows.

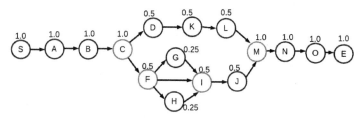

(a) Initial graph representing a process

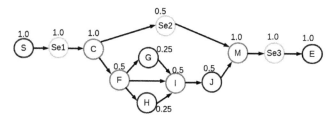

(b) Sequences have been identified and replaced

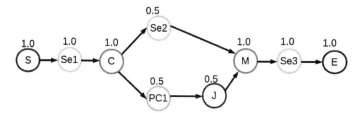

(c) The most inner parallel component is found and replaced

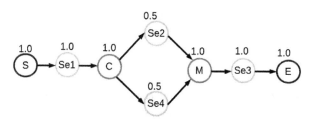

(d) A new sequence is identified

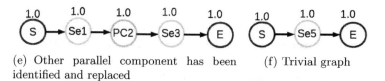

(e) Other parallel component has been identified and replaced

(f) Trivial graph

Fig. 3. Example of how the component identification algorithm works for a given graph

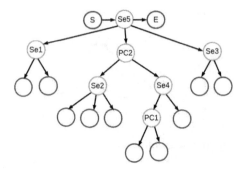

Fig. 4. Unfold of the trivial graph obtained for the example of Fig. 3

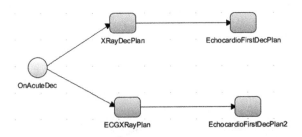

Fig. 5. Second level plan of the transformed PROforma model of Fig. 1

Regarding technology, the procedures have been implemented in Java and using the open-source Java JDOM API[1].

5   Conclusions and Future Work

We have tested our algorithms with several BPMN models of clinical procedures, with the aim to check that structures of interest have been properly identified in the source BPMN model, and that they have been adequately translated to PROforma. Some details of the BPMN model of Fig. 1 follow. It comprises 10 split and 10 join XOR-gateways, 2 sequential ad-hoc sub-processes, 2 sub-processes and 23 tasks. The algorithm identifies 14 parallel components and 8 sequences.

Furthermore, we have compared the transformed PROforma model to a PROforma model of the same clinical process developed from scratch, with the aim of testing that the two models are semantically equivalent. We have observed that both the number of plans and the depth of the transformed model are greater. The main reason is that XOR/OR-parallel components are always mapped to a

---

[1] http://www.jdom.org/docs/apidocs/org/jdom2/input/SAXBuilder.html (last access:13-06-13).

new plan enclosing a decision. For this reason, the top level plan of the transformed model contains a single task/plan, since the BPMN model starts with a split XOR-gateway (Fig. 1). The content of this plan is shown in Fig. 5 as an illustration.

Sequence flow conditions have been used in decisions to define the argument for a candidate but also to define the source data of the decision. However, condition expressions in BPMN can be just plain text. We have meticulously written the expressions, which allows us to parse them and extract the data and their type properly. This cannot be presupposed and therefore the transformed model will require a revision of data sources.

Our experiments show that a semi-automatic transformation from BPMN to PROforma in the context of clinical guidelines is possible. Only a manual revision of the data sources is required. We have implemented the structure-identification approach tailored to the domain of clinical processes. Moreover, the target language, PROforma, contains features of both block-oriented and graph-oriented languages.

The only transformation approaches we are aware of in the context of clinical guidelines are the works of González-Ferrer et al. [4] and Dominguez et al. [2]. The first one transforms from XPDL to HTN and the second one implements Java modules from UML state diagrams. Therefore, none of them specifically deals with CIGs formalisms, as we do in this work.

One of the advantages of our approach is that part of the implementation may be re-used to transform a source BPMN model to other CIG languages. The mapping to PROforma is postponed until the intermediate tree structure is built. Therefore, all the previous algorithms may be re-used when considering a different target language. On the other hand, the transformation algorithm may be adapted to deal with other graph-oriented languages different from BPMN.

In the experiments we have conducted to date, data specification has been considered a minor issue. Therefore, dealing with data is a main aspect to consider in future work. Another goal for future work is improving the approach in order to reduce the number of plans, and thus the depth of the transformed models. Related to this, we regard the assessment of the understandability of the transformed guideline model as a priority [8].

References

1. Bae, J., Bae, H., Kang, S.H., Kim, Y.: Automatic control of workflow processes using ECA rules. IEEE Trans. Knowl. Data Eng. **16**(8), 1010–1023 (2004). http://ieeexplore.ieee.org/xpls/abs_all.jsp?arnumber=1318584
2. Domínguez, E., Pérez, B., Zapata, M.: Towards a traceable clinical guidelines application. A model-driven approach. Methods Inf. Med. **49**(6), 571–580 (2010)
3. Dugan, L., Palmer, N.: BPMN 2.0 Handbook, chap. Making a BPMN 2.0 Model Executable, p. 71:92. Future Strategies Inc. in association with the Workflow Management Coalition (2012)
4. González-Ferrer, A., Fdez-Olivares, J., Castillo, L.: From business process models to hierarchical task network planning domains. Knowl. Eng. Rev. **28**(2), 175–193 (2013)

5. Götz, M., Roser, S., Lautenbacher, F., Bauer, B.: Token analysis of graph-oriented process models. In: Enterprise Distributed Object Computing Conference Workshops, 2009. EDOCW 2009. 13th. pp. 15–24. IEEE, IE (2009). http://ieeexplore. ieee.org/xpls/abs_all.jsp?arnumber=5332020

6. Hashemian, N., Abidi, S.S.R.: Modeling clinical workflows using business process modeling notation. In: 25th International Symposium on Computer-Based Medical Systems (CBMS), 2012, pp. 1–4. IEEE (2012). http://ieeexplore.ieee.org/xpls/abs_ all.jsp?arnumber=6266322

7. Kiepuszewski, B., ter Hofstede, A.H.M., Bussler, C.J.: On structured workflow modelling. In: Wangler, B., Bergman, L.D. (eds.) CAiSE 2000. LNCS, vol. 1789, pp. 431–445. Springer, Heidelberg (2000)

8. Marcos, M., Torres-Sospedra, J., Martínez-Salvador, B.: Assessment of clinical guideline model based on metrics for business process models. In: Workshop on Knowledge Representation for Health Care (KR4HC) (2014)

9. Mendling, J., Lassen, K.B., Zdun, U.: On the transformation of control flow between block-oriented and graph-oriented process modelling languages. Int. J. Bus. Process Integr. Manage. 3(2), 96–108 (2008). http://inderscience.metapress.com/index/8644JG867545H066.pdf

10. Mohler, J., Amstrong, A., Bahnson, R., Boston, B., Busby, J., D'Amico, A., Eastham, J., Enke, C., Farrington, T., Higano, C., Horwitz, E., Kantoff, P., Kawachi, M., Kuette, l.M., Lee, R., MacVicar, G., Malcolm, A., Miller, D., Plimack, E., Pow-Sang, J., Roach, M.r., Rohren, E., Rosenfeld, S., Srinivas, S., Strope, S., Tward, J., Twardowski, P., Walsh, P., Ho, M., Sheadm, D.: Prostate cancer, Version 3.2012: featured updates to the NCCN guidelines. J. Natl Compr. Cancer. Netw. 10(9), 1081–1087 (2012)

11. OMG: Busines Process Model and Notation (BPMN) Version 2.0. OMG Specification, Object Management Group (2011). http://www.omg.org/spec/ BPMN/2.0

12. Ouyang, C., Dumas, M., Aalst, W.M., Hofstede, A.H.T., Mendling, J.: From business process models to process-oriented software systems. ACM Trans. Softw. Eng. Methodol. (TOSEM) 19(1), 2 (2009). http://dl.acm.org/citation.cfm?id=1555395

13. Reichert, M.: What BPM technology can do for healthcare process support. In: Peleg, M., Lavrač, N., Combi, C. (eds.) AIME 2011. LNCS, vol. 6747, pp. 2–13. Springer, Heidelberg (2011)

14. Rojo, M.G., Rolón, E., Calahorra, L., García, F., Sánchez, R.P., Ruiz, F., Ballester, N., Armenteros, M., Rodríguez, T., Espartero, R.M., et al.: Implementation of the business process modelling notation (BPMN) in the modelling of anatomic pathology processes. Diag. Pathol. 3(Suppl 1), S22 (2008)

15. Svagård, Ingrid, Farshchian, Babak A.: Using business process modelling to model integrated care processes: experiences from a european project. In: Omatu, Sigeru, Rocha, Miguel P., Bravo, José, Fernández, Florentino, Corchado, Emilio, Bustillo, Andrés, Corchado, Juan M. (eds.) IWANN 2009, Part II. LNCS, vol. 5518, pp. 922–925. Springer, Heidelberg (2009). http://link.springer.com/chapter/10.1007/978-3-642-02481-8_140

A Process-Oriented Methodology for Modelling Cancer Treatment Trial Protocols

Aisan Maghsoodi[1,2(✉)], Anca Bucur[2], Paul de Bra[1], Norbert Graf[3], and Martin Stanulla[4]

[1] Technical University of Eindhoven, Eindhoven, The Netherlands
{A.maghsoodi,Debra}@tue.nl
[2] Philips Research, Eindhoven, The Netherlands
{Aisan.maghsoudi,Anca.Bucur}@philips.com
[3] Saarland University, Homburg, Germany
Norbert.Graf@uniklinikum-saarland.de
[4] University Medical Center Schleswig-Holstein, Kiel, Germany
martin.stanulla@uk-sh.de

Abstract. Cancer-patient management in the context of a multi-center treatment trial requires following a complex detailed process involving multispecialty patient treatment as well as study-related tasks, described in free-text protocol documents. We present a process-oriented approach for modelling clinical trial treatment protocols (CTTPs) to be used for enabling applications that support protocol-based care process delivery, monitoring and analysis. This modelling approach provides an intuitive visual representation of the protocol document catering for change management, intra-center and national adaptations to the master protocol, and multi-level share-ability. The methodology can be re-used in CTTPs of different cancer domains due to the similarity of the CTTPs in terms of required content.

Keywords: Clinical trial protocols · BPMN · Process modelling · Procedural knowledge representation · Change management · Workflows · Master protocol

1 Introduction

Cancer care is a complex multidisciplinary process that runs throughout a long period of time and is carried out in different clinical settings. Some cancer patients are being treated in the context of a clinical trial. Clinical trials are usually conducted in multiple participating centers. The results of the study are later evaluated to validate hypotheses and include new findings in the care process. They are also the basis for the generation of new hypotheses.

To standardize the management of the trial among centers, protocol documents are generated by a panel of experts aiming at explaining the different aspects of the trial. Cancer Treatment Trial Protocols (CTTPs) are documents sharing evidence-based method of patient treatment in the context of the study among participating institutions. They include information about the study description such as design, objective,

© Springer International Publishing Switzerland 2014
S. Miksch et al. (Eds.): KR4HC 2014, LNAI 8903, pp. 133–146, 2014.
DOI: 10.1007/978-3-319-13281-5_10

rationale and patient enrolment criteria, as well as detailed explanation of patient treatment designed to answer study questions. Guidelines and sub-protocols for each medical discipline involved in the care process are often included in the protocol.

The complex narrative format of the protocol documents hinders their routine and efficient use. In order to benefit from the protocol document in applications providing support for clinicians and care personnel, the first step would be converting them to a computer processable format from which required information and functionalities can be derived. Inconsistencies, lack of proper structure, ambiguities, scattered information, incompleteness, and statements open for interpretation are inherent problems of the protocol text itself that aggravates the problem.

For clinical guidelines, different representation languages have been introduced over the past decades belonging to the major categories of task network models (TNMs) and document-based models. Computer-interpretable guidelines (CIGs) are referred to the resulting formalized guidelines generated with the goal to enable building of CIG-based clinical decision support systems (CDSSs) through execution of these models [1].

Many studies have pointed out that integration into the workflow of clinicians is a key factor in CDSS success, while management of change and updates, support for local adaptations and settings and share-ability are the critical factors for a successful representation model [2]. However, the current formalisms introduced have not been widely adopted due to lack of one or more of the above-mentioned success factors. Moreover, due to the need of local execution of guidelines and protocols, the process support is gaining more attention.

Need for supporting complex multidisciplinary care processes along with study-related processes are more stringent in the context of CTTPs. Acquiring comparable results from the data collected by participating centers calls for the standardization of the processes while allowing local adaptations and justified deviations. Having to deal with a long-run and complicated care process during which patients have multiple encounters with care givers from different disciplines entails the need for monitoring where in the process the patient is, what comes next and who is responsible for each step in the care process.

There is a need to integrate the various theoretical frameworks and formalisms for modeling clinical guidelines, workflows, and pathways in order to move beyond providing support for individual clinical decisions and toward the provision of process-oriented, patient-centered, health information systems (HIS) [3].

In this paper, we present a process-oriented methodology for modelling CTTPs. We worked with participating centers in the SIOP[1]'s Nephroblastoma and AIEOP-BFM[2]'s Acute Lymphoblastic Leukemia (ALL) trial as part of an effort related to the P-medicine[3] project to facilitate the development of applications to support the protocol-based treatment process. This work is partially funded by the European Commission under the 7th Framework Programme (FP7-ICT-2009-6- 270089).

---

[1] International Society of Paediatric Oncology (SIOP), http://www.siop-online.org/

[2] http://www.bfm-international.org/aieop/aieop_index.html

[3] www.p-medicine.eu/

While devising our modeling methodology, we had in mind the potential applications of the modeled document and the following needed characteristics of a CTTP model: Reuse in other cancer domains, Support for local adaptations while enforcing certain critical processes and activities, Ability to incorporate change and update, Shareability, and Facilitating the monitoring of the care processes for patients at real-time providing different views over the process for different participants along with retrospective execution analysis.

1.1   Related Work

The cancer treatment trials can run for several years and the data collection continues as follow up long after the end of the treatment. The data collected over years will be analyzed to find answers to the study questions and further analyzed form new hypotheses. Thus, the quality of data collected over a long period of time through treatment of enrolled patients by multiple centers participating in a study is of major importance and directly related to the fact that the patient treatment needs to be carried out in a standardized and controlled way and the documentation and data collection should be accurate and complete.

CTTPs are extensive knowledge-rich documents focused on the detailed description of methods to perform complex care processes, while guidelines are usually less extensive and detailed. Most guideline-based CDS systems are focused on individual decisions at a certain time point and tasks rather than processes such as care plans extending over a period of time and multiple care settings [4]. Some studies aimed to model guidelines for integration into clinical workflow as a reactive system to the workflow management system in place, as opposed to some multi-step guideline modeling formalisms either have no explicit representation for clinical care processes or assume that the guideline system is in control of a workflow management [5].

In the context of CTTPs, we analyzed the content of protocols and carried out interviews with clinicians. This led us to conclude that supporting and monitoring the process delivery, for instance, through a visualized overview of patient(s)' progress with respect to the protocol-based care process is highly demanded and valuable to the clinicians. CTTPs have no explicit ordering of tasks involved in care processes, neither do they aggregate the scattered information about a specific process and direct it to the clinical actor responsible for performing it. Thus, process-oriented modelling can transform the protocol content to reflect the perspective of the workflow of the clinical actors involved in the treatment process.

Process modelling techniques, specifically business process modelling notation (BPMN)[4] has been recognized as a promising candidate for representing healthcare processes [6]. BPMN 2.0 is considered as the de facto standard for the process modeling languages. It is an open and free standard accompanied by a variety of supporting tools. BPMN has been adopted in various studies dealing with problems involving modeling of the healthcare processes. For instance, it was used in process-oriented

---

[4] http://www.bpmn.org/

modeling of clinical pathways (CP) by introducing a semantic mapping between CP and BPMN ontology [7]. Some studies have addressed the shortcomings of BPMN for modeling shared tasks [8].

Wang et al. [9] have studied eleven guideline representation models and have found primitives such as actions, decisions and their synchronization as well as nesting feature necessary for encoding guidelines. They conclude that data collection, decision, patient state, and intervention constitute four basic types of primitives in a guideline's logic flow.

BPMN has elements that can be mapped to the required primitives recognized critical for modeling guideline procedural knowledge. On the other hand, it facilitates modeling of different events and exceptions for routing a process [10]. These sets of features specifically correspond to the nature of healthcare processes which involve various events, exceptions and scenarios. Support for modeling resource assignment, messaging, collaboration are a critical aspect of modeling the healthcare processes. Thus, we adopted BPMN as our modeling notation and we used it in our methodology together with an entity model to facilitate the implementation of protocol-based applications.

Section 2 describes the methodology for the modeling approach as well as model validation, execution and analysis. Discussion and future work are presented in Sect. 3, followed by conclusion and references.

2   Methodology

In this section we describe our proposed methodology for process-oriented modeling of the cancer trial protocols. The next section will describe the requirements for the model then in Sect. 2.2, we describe the methodology steps for modeling the protocols from the process-oriented and entity-oriented aspects.

2.1   Model Requirements

While devising the methodology we had two major aspects in mind. Firstly, the potential applications of the model some of which were projected through the requirements of the clinicians we had collaborated with, and secondly, the required characteristics of a successful model that properly captures the needs for modeling the cancer trial and study treatment protocols.

A shared requirement for both of the explored cancer domains is providing the treating clinicians with an overview over their patients at any given time, enabling them to find answers for questions like: Where the patient is in the course of the therapy? What are the next steps according to the protocol? What are the needed arrangements and communication at a certain point? Who is the responsible actor for the next steps? How long did a certain process or task take to be completed? What were the exception events/flows that happened during the care processes and how were they managed?

Thus, considering the support for the applications the model should be devised in a way that facilitates:

1. Workflow-based execution of protocols:

   – Directing the protocol-based tasks, recommendations and evidence to the relevant clinical roles responsible for performing process-related tasks, thus sparing the clinical users from the exposure to irrelevant, redundant information. Tasks can either be directly related to the care or required by the study for example, reporting.
   – Support the clinical performer assigned to a task by presenting the protocol-based requirements and guidelines for performing it, such as pre and post conditions, recommendations and the link back to available evidence.

2. Visualization:

   – Representing the trial protocol in a visual way would render the model understandable and insightful for the clinicians and thus encourage adoption and usage.
   – The execution progress should be visualized in order to provide an overview over the progress of patient(s) in the total course of protocol-based care process or at different level of sub-processes for different roles involved in patient care. Different views over the process tailored for different involved actors provides understanding of the positioning of the activity with respect to the whole process and promotes clarity to what has so far been done and what needs to be performed.

3. Analysis of the execution:

   – Monitoring the adherence to the master and local protocol while accommodating justified deviations.
   – Identification of the incomplete decision branches or the points that are left for interpretation in order to provide a support mechanism or feedback to the authoring committee.
   – Identification of the points of delay, bottlenecks and their cause.

Second consideration was the needed characteristics of the model to be successfully adopted for modeling cancer trial and study treatment protocols. To accommodate the needs for modeling the cancer protocols, support for modeling complex detailed processes expanded over a long period of time, multiple participants in the care process and collaborations between them, exceptions and events, study-related activities as well as care-related activities is critical. Thus, our methodology puts the modeling in the perspective of the workflow as well as the study requirements.

Moreover, we aimed at proposing a modeling approach that could be reused for CTTPs in different cancer domains. Therefore, we looked into CTTPs from two different domains namely, SIOP's Nephroblastoma and AIEOP-BFM's Leukemia study and treatment protocols, and discussed the requirements and the proposed modeling approach with the clinicians from both domains. Furthermore, the multi-centric and international nature of the studies called for a modelling approach that could accommodate local and national adaptations to the model. To understand the types and extent of local requirements we compared the SIOP protocol from UK and the one from Germany and devised means to enable the customization while respecting the framework defined by the master protocol which is the standard base needed to be complied with by all participating centers. Figure 1 shows the CTTP model requirements aimed to be supported by our modelling approach.

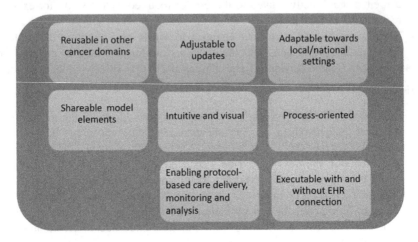

Fig. 1. CTTP model requirements

2.2 Process-Oriented Modeling Methodology

In this section, the two main aspects of our proposed modeling methodology are described. Aligned with our model requirements, we modeled the protocol from the process-oriented and entity-oriented aspects. We describe the steps necessary to build the protocol-based process-model so that the model requirements described in the previous section are catered for. Next, the types of entities relevant for capturing the content of protocols and implementing the processes are defined and methods for their identification and extraction are presented.

In our methodology, modeling starts using the protocol document and then the local adaptations are included to the defined model by discussing it with the clinicians and looking into the local protocol.

Building the Process Model. We noticed that CTTPs regardless of their domain, share certain types of information required for establishing a study, for example detailed description of the study design, inclusion and exclusion criteria, outcome measures, study questions, reporting, types of adverse events and their management, ethical requirements, etc. The care processes extracted from cancer CTTPs have activities related to the following main groups:

- Design and conducting of the study,
- Domain-specific patient care such as administration of a medication or surgery.

As mentioned in the Sect. 1.1, we have used BPMN for modeling the processes involved in the protocol-based treatment of patients. The process-modeling approach includes the following steps:

- Identification of the main processes, sub-processes and tasks from the protocol. Sub-processes are decomposition of processes and tasks are decomposition of sub-processes in BPMN.
- Identifying the resources mentioned in the protocol and assigning the resources for each process identified according to the protocol. Resources can be human resources such as pathologist or surgeon that can be the performer of a process.
- Define protocol-based collaboration between resources such as a surgeon and pathologist, and identify the form of collaboration like: messaging, data/form exchange, communication, etc. That are used to realize that collaboration. Collaboration between multiple resources can be represented by using *pools* and *message* flows in BPMN. This step provides a useful understanding for the entity definition as well.
- For each (sub) process, identify the tasks, synchronization needs, and decision points. Synchronization and decision points can be modelled using different type of *gates* in BPMN. After defining the entity model, which contains the data, for each branch rules will be defined using process-related entity properties to enable execution.
- Identify *events* including their type and where they occur. *Events* are a very useful element in BPMN that can represent anything than "happens" inside, outside or at the border of each process and can be adjusted how to affect the process flow. Some of the event types used for our modelling purpose include: message, timer, cancel, signal, error and link. Start, end and intermediate events, such as wait event, which is a common event for healthcare processes-, are defined in this step. A wait event can be a required period, for instance, in case of the intervals between administrations of medication, or can be an unknown period of time of a maximum range so that a state is changed, for example, surgery is done.
- After modeling the "sunny day scenarios" which are the normal flow of processes and events, look for the possible exceptions and other events that are either stated in briefly in the protocol, or just can happen in real-life settings. For example, an ordered drug might not arrive on time affecting the timely start of a regimen. For each process, errors, exceptional or less frequent outcomes and events are modeled by asking what can go wrong during execution of each process.
- Identification of re-usable domain-specific processes. Domain-specific process entities will also be recognized in the entity model definition. These are the part of the model that can be shared among participating centers. The name of these processes and entities should be defined in a standard way. For each process, there is an entity defined. Every domain knowledge entity, has a property containing the UMLS class type, and a medical named entity category and synonyms.
- Marking the critical processes and entities is the next step. The processes, entities and properties in the master protocol that should not be changed in local adaptations are identified and marked in order to ensure standardization required for conducting the study. Although, even this limitation will be modelled in a way that the need to

inform the related committee and ask for approval is enforced rather than strictly prohibiting. The changes are accepted if they prove not to be affecting the study questions. The unjustified divergences can be detected after execution of the model during analysis. Also, our model supports justified divergences since provided that the reasons are known, aggregation of types and reasons of divergences can be very insightful. Therefore, some divergences are permitted by providing extra exit to the decision gates or defining process abortion events that can be activated on purpose by the actor given that it is accounted for. This is an explicit form of gathering the divergences along with the reasons for them.

- For incorporation of change, first the change needs to be associated with a process. Then the process elements and/or entities affected by the change are identified. Change propagation is more explicit and understandable due to the visualization and the view of change in the context of processes. After locating the change, all the entities and processes connected to the affected model element is checked and updated to ensure that the change is managed. The evidence entity for affected model elements is updated and the link to new evidence. Ideally in future, changes and updates can provided the process-model change along with the written format.
- Posing questions is possible by enabling events from every step of the process. The actor can point out incomplete branches, need for extra information in case of ambiguity at any point in the process. This is especially needed in case of occurrence of some adverse events that are rare or those the management of which has not been elaborated in the protocol and thus, are not modeled. Although, the adverse events need to be reported but they also need to be handled in real-time. In these case, communication happens and guidance will be provided by the study center usually though a phone call. Despite receiving repeated questions these cases are not documented and made accessible to all. Our model accommodates the capturing of the questions to be used ultimately for creation of a search-able FAQ after execution or can be later integrated as part of the adverse event management process in the model.

Entity Model Definition and Extraction. To define the *entity model* we selected the entities using two major sources: the protocol document and the process model. Entities represent the knowledge aspect of the protocol. They can be consumed or affected by the process model. Entities can be *parametric*, thus, containing static information or they can be *variable* so that while execution of the process model, they can be instantiated and information can be stored about them. In the latter case, they are referred to as *process-related* entities.

Entities have attributes and can have relations to other entities. For example, an entity of type "medication" can have attributes such as name and maximum dosage. This entity can be in a composition relationship with the entity "regimen" meaning that a regimen is composed of multiple medication.

In order to encapsulate the knowledge content, we classified entities into the following types:

- Domain entities consists of medical named entities and their attributes. A process such as "surgery" is also a medical named entity since the term contains domain knowledge and can have attributes such as the "body location". The domain entities affected by a process and the entities of the procedural nature can have an attribute "state" which is used to mark their execution state.

- Study entities: These are mostly conceptual and parametric entities used to mark the information used to define the study and study-related processes, such as endpoints, investigational product, etc. We have only focused on study-related entities and processes when it was used in part of the care flow.

- Information entities: We define a class for the entities that are used to provide information between processes or for a given process or action. Collaborative information entities also include BPMN artefacts such as data forms. Forms consist of other entities or combination of their attributes. Another protocol-specific information entity is *evidence,* defined to enable linking of the evidence, being a link to the protocol text at sentence level for an activity, a process or recommendation. We also defined an information entity for capturing the deviations. This entity would hold the reasons for deviation as a property.

Pre-processing and Medical Named Entity Extraction. We implemented a tool for pre-processing and iteratively structuring the protocol documents. First, the HTML source of the document was automatically processed to capture its structure such as headings, sections, figures, charts, lists, paragraphs, sentences and word tokens. We created an XML element for each structural element. The link between the XML output and the original text has been enabled by maintaining the position of the sentences, sections and terms.

Next, for every section, further processing was carried out by ontology-based automatic extraction of medical named entities (MNEs). This was performed by mapping the nested noun-phrases (NNP) extracted to categories defined based on a selection of UMLS semantic types. The annotated SNOMED concept and UMLS type (s) of each NNP chunk was recorded as XML attributes of NNP elements. Using the standard terminology and semantic annotation would be useful for linking of the relevant evidence and connection to patient data.

The automatic extraction of MNEs is to be regarded as a source for recognizing the MNEs that can be used in the entity model as well as annotating them with standard annotations. Another use of this tool is to enable annotation of text as evidence and assigning the evidence to an entity or a process, maintaining the location of the evidence in the original document. Thus, the XML output of the tool can be linked to the process model. The automatic extraction step is only optional in the proposed modeling methodology and thus implementation details are not in the scope of this paper (Fig. 2).

Model Validation. This category of activities comprises: Validation of the process-model and of the entity model with clinicians, validation of the model characteristics (including share-ability, reuse in other cancer domains, and accommodation of change), and evaluation of the output of the annotator tool including the automatic medical entity extraction. So far, we are performing the validation of the protocol-based process and entity model together with the clinicians.

As for model characteristics, we provided the experiment settings to evaluate the extent to which each of the model characteristics are valid. We devised our

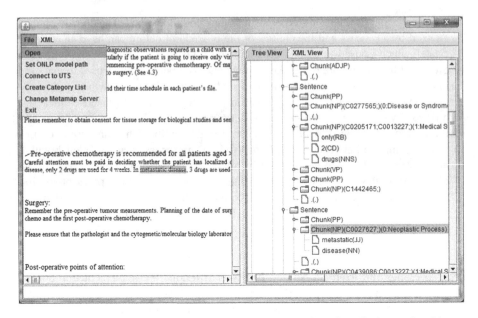

Fig. 2. A snapshot of the tool created for automatic extraction of medical named entities.

methodology using CTTPs from two distinct cancer domain one of which has surgery and a body location, namely kidney, involved while the other does not include surgery and deals with blood, to evaluate the possibility of re-use of the methodology towards modeling the protocols from different study domains. We noticed that in both domains the process-oriented modeling approach can be applied.

We have implemented a tool (Fig. 3) for acquiring the manual annotation of the clinicians in order to be compared with the automatic extraction tool. We aim at providing automated support for identification of entities and processes. However, the methodology can also be used without the automatic extraction module.

Execution and Analysis. We report on a process-oriented methodology for modeling CTTPs using BPMN. In this section we discuss the model execution and validation method.

The process-based model generated using our methodology can be executed at different levels. For example, it can be executed by introducing check points that mark the successful fulfilment of tasks and satisfaction of the pre- and post-conditions so that activities can be assigned to roles introduced in the resources, and tasks such as communication, reporting, administration of medication, performing a test can be directed to the responsible persons (for instance when they logs into the system). Moreover, the evidence related to those tasks and recommendations will be made accessible to the performer role defined in the model.

At current stage connection to patient data is not covered but we provided the hooks for including it in the methodology in the future. Mapping the entity model (being a relational model) to a data model is possible and the use of standard terminology can further facilitate that.

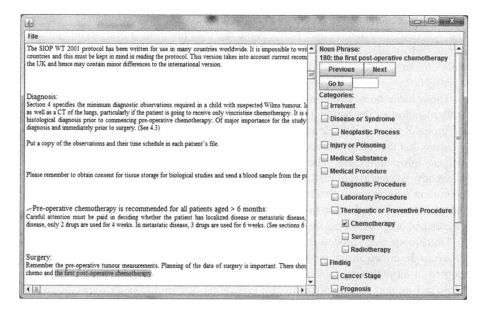

Fig. 3. Evaluation tool for medical named entity extraction

After the execution of the process-oriented protocol model, the result of the execution can be analyzed. The analysis of the event logs from the event monitoring points defined while execution is a type of evaluation that can be performed using process mining techniques to find out the deviations, delays and bottlenecks.

Finding deviation points provides an interesting insight. However, finding the reasons for those deviations is also highly relevant and worthy of further investigation. Deviations happening frequently at certain points in the process over multiple centers for example, can lead to modification of the protocol. Thus, in our modeling approach we have allowed for inclusion of deviations by providing an extra exit to the decision gates or defining process abortion events that can be activated by the performer, but to comply with the protocol he needs to justify it in writing. This is an explicit form of gathering the deviations together with the reasons for deviation that can be analyzed after the execution.

Identification of sources of ambiguity and interpretation, and the incomplete paths can be evaluated by investigation of the questions posted by clinical performers which is enabled in the model. Answers can be provided as searchable FAQs that serve as a form of decision support evidence since the answers will be provided by expert clinicians.

3   Discussion and Future Work

Bringing the cancer trial protocols as a source of process and decision support to the perspective of workflow of actors involved in care process can facilitate guidance, monitoring, and consequently deriving more insightful knowledge from the multi-center long term execution of the trial-based care processes. The process-oriented modeling approach described in this paper provides the basis for performing analysis and gaining as much information as possible from the performers about each step of the care process while directing to them needed information about the handling of care process during execution.

There have been efforts such as SPIRIT 2013 [11] to provide a template for standardization of the cancer clinical trial protocols in terms of content requirements and protocol items. SIOP has also started providing such as template (master protocol) to ensure that the future protocols would meet the regulatory requirements and include adequate information. We believe that the modeling of the protocols as post-processing of already written documents should be linked at some point with the authoring. Integration of a minimal level of structure while authoring as well as introducing an understandable and flexible process-oriented modeling approach that accommodates updates and adaptations can be a step forward to enabling protocol-based applications.

Domain-specific processes, medical named entities and their attributes, and resources described in the methodology are among the information items that can be adopted in an authoring tool. This would enable process-based authoring of the protocols and support sharing of content for generating new protocols for a specific cancer domain. Subsequently, providing more structure at the authoring phase would positively impact the automatic post-processing and the shareability of the model.

Similarly to the reasons provided for frequent points of deviations and the analysis result of the execution at participating centers can be communicated back to authoring committee for investigation of the potential hypotheses or required process modification.

With respect to modeling, we will work on defining patterns for process-oriented modeling of the cancer trial protocols to further streamline the use of the introduced methodology. Similar to the business process modeling in which the re-use of relevant parts of existing models can help modelers to create high-quality models [12], there are patterns that occur in the course of protocol-based care processes that can be re-used when identified. We are also extending our annotator tool to (semi)automatically identify process elements and temporal expressions to be used in a treatment plan extraction application.

4   Conclusion

In this paper we described a process-oriented modeling approach that can be reused for different cancer treatment trial protocols (CTTPs). CCTPs are detailed descriptions of methods and are aimed at standardization of the evidence-based multidisciplinary care process in multiple participating centers with the goal to answer the study questions from the results collected. We proposed a process-oriented modeling methodology for representing such documents with the objective to enable applications to support the protocol-based care process delivery, monitoring, and analysis. Such modelling approach when linked to an executable flow can provide an overview of the status of each patient in the care process as well as support the forwarding of the process-based requirements and advice to the right clinical actor.

Process-oriented modeling performed in BPMN provides a comprehensible visual model of the protocol that makes the ordering of the tasks and their needed resources explicit. By associating changes to affected model elements and maintaining position of each extracted piece of evidence in the original text, changes and updates can be addressed. The model of the master protocol can be shared among centers - at least at the level of domain-specific processes and entities- and adaptation to local and national settings can be implemented in the model by marking critical paths and allowing non-prohibited modifications. Interoperability with the EHR systems is not directly addressed, but the relational entity model can be mapped to a relational data model and the standard vocabularies used in the entity model provide the basis for linkage to patient data.

Free-text and the challenges associated to information extraction have hindered the effective use of protocols content but some other challenges originate from the poor authoring of the protocols. The modeling methodology can be used to facilitate the creation of a process-oriented authoring tool supporting the process-oriented modeling. This will enable further automatic extraction of model elements from free-text.

References

1. Peleg, M., Tu, S., Bury, J., Ciccarese, P.: Comparing computer-interpretable guideline models: a case-study approach. J. Am. Med. Inform. **20**(3), 470–476 (2003)
2. Peleg, M.: Computer-interpretable clinical guidelines: a methodological review. J. Biomed. Inform. **46**, 744–763 (2013)
3. Gooch, P., Roudsari, A.: Computerization of workflows, guidelines, and care pathways: a review of implementation challenges for process-oriented health information systems. J. Am. Med. Inform. **18**, 738–774 (2011)
4. Patkar, V.: From guidelines to careflows: modelling and supporting complex clinical processes. In: ten Teije, A., Lucas, P., Miksch, S. (eds.) Computer-Based Medical Guidelines and Protocols: A Primer and Current Trends, vol. 139, pp. 44–62. IOS Press, Amsterdam (2008)
5. Huff, S., McClurec, R.: Modeling guidelines for integration into clinical workflow. In: MEDINFO 2004: Proceedings of the 11th World Congress on Medical Informatics (2004)
6. Stefanelli, M.: Knowledge and process management in health care organizations. Methods Inf. Med. der. Info. Med. **43**(5), 525–535 (2004)
7. Hashemian, N., Abidi, S.: Modeling clinical workflows using business process modeling notation. In: 25th IEEE International Symposium on Computer-Based Medical Systems (CBMS) (2012)
8. Müller, R., Rogge-Solti, A.: BPMN for healthcare processes. Serv. und ihre Komposition (2011)
9. Wang, D., Peleg, M., Tu, S.W., Boxwala, A.A, Greenes, R.A, Patel, V.L., Shortliffe, E.H.: Representation primitives, process models and patient data in computer-interpretable clinical practice guidelines: a literature review of guideline representation models. Int. J. Med. Inform. **68**, 59–70 (2002)
10. Silver, B.: BPMN Method and Style. Cody-Cassidy Press, Aptos (2009)

11. Chan, A.-W., Tetzlaff, J.M., Altman, D.G., Laupacis, A., Gøtzsche, P.C., Krleža-Jerić, K., Hróbjartsson, A., Mann, H., Dickersin, K., Berlin, J.A., Doré, C.J., Parulekar, W.R., Summerskill, W.S.M., Groves, T., Schulz, K.F., Sox, H.C., Rockhold, F.W., Rennie, D., Moher, D.: SPIRIT 2013 statement: defining standard protocol items for clinical trials. Ann. Intern. Med. **158**, 200–207 (2013)

12. Minard, A.-L., Ligozat, A.-L., Ben Abacha, A., Bernhard, D., Cartoni, B., Deléger, L., Grau, B., Rosset, S., Zweigenbaum, P., Grouin, C.: Hybrid methods for improving information access in clinical documents: concept, assertion, and relation identification. J. Am. Med. Inform. Assoc. **18**, 588–593 (2011)

Training Residents in the Application of Clinical Guidelines for Differential Diagnosis of the Most Frequent Causes of Arterial Hypertension with Decision Tables

Francis Real[1], David Riaño[1]([⊠]), and José Ramón Alonso[2]

[1] Research Group on Artificial Intelligence,
Universitat Rovira i Virgili, Tarragona, Spain
{francis.real,david.riano}@urv.net
[2] Emergency Department, Hospital Clínic de Barcelona, Barcelona, Spain

Abstract. Arterial hypertension (AH) is an abnormal high blood pressure in the arteries with many possible etiologies. Differential diagnosis of the causes of AH is a complex clinical process that requires the simultaneous consideration of many clinical practice guidelines.

Training clinicians to manage, assimilate, and correctly apply the knowledge contained in the guidelines of the most frequent causes of AH is a challenge that we have addressed with the combined use of different sorts of decision tables. After extracting the diagnostic knowledge available in eight clinical practice guidelines of the most frequent secondary causes of hypertension, we have represented this knowledge as decision tables, and have used these tables to train 23 residents at the Hospital Clínic de Barcelona. During the training, the decisions of the residents along the differential diagnostic steps were compared with the decisions provided by the decision tables so that we could analyze the progressive adaptation of clinicians' decisions to the guidelines' recommendations.

The study shows a progressive improvement of the adherence of the residents to the guidelines as new AH cases are considered, reaching full adherence after a training with 30 clinical cases.

1 Introduction

Diagnosis is seen as one of the most demanding professional activities of physicians. For some patients, reaching a final diagnosis is a complex process that requires one or more intermediate steps in which physicians schedule some tests in order to obtain results that eventually could confirm or refute one or several suspected diseases [1]. This process is called *differential diagnosis* [2]. From this description we can observe that differential diagnosis entails two sorts of decisions (see Fig. 1): on the one hand, given all the currently available findings about the patient (i.e., *signs and symptoms*), decide which are the possible diseases (i.e., *hypotheses*) that could explain these findings. On the other hand, given the suspected hypotheses, decide which are the diagnostic actions (i.e., *medical tests*) that may confirm or refute these hypotheses.

© Springer International Publishing Switzerland 2014
S. Miksch et al. (Eds.): KR4HC 2014, LNAI 8903, pp. 147–159, 2014.
DOI: 10.1007/978-3-319-13281-5_11

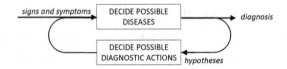

Fig. 1. Differential diagnosis loop [1]

Clinical Practice Guidelines (CPG) contain the evidence-based knowledge required to make these decisions during differential diagnosis, but this knowledge is scattered across the guidelines of all the multiple diseases that can explain the patient condition. The seamless integration of all this knowledge for practical use is an intellectual complex learning process that residents have to train for internal medicine specialization at the Hospital Clínic de Barcelona (HCB).

In this paper we introduce a new medical software that we have developed to help HCB residents in this purpose. The software works with the knowledge available in a incremental library of decision tables. These tables are elicited from the CPGs that are recommended at the hospital. The system implements a case-based training process for differential diagnosis in which the clinical actions and disease suspicions of the residents are compared with the evidences in the respective CPGs, providing a personal feed-back that fosters a progressive improvement of the adherence of students to the hospital guidelines. The system was tested for differential diagnosis of the main causes of arterial hypertension.

Arterial Hypertension (AH) is an abnormal high blood pressure in the patient's arteries [3] that can be considered a disease (i.e., essential hypertension) or a clinical condition induced by other causes or diseases (i.e., secondary causes). The CPG of AH [3] identifies *achromegaly, adrenal Cushing's syndrome, coarctation of the aorta, glomerulonephritis, hyperparathyroidism, pheochromocitoma, renovascular disease, and sleep apnea* as eight of the main secondary causes of AH. In this paper we call these causes the 8-SCAH.

The CPGs [3–11] corresponding to AH and the 8-SCAH were analyzed with the help of two senior GPs of the health care centers HCB and SAGESSA. The diagnostic knowledge available in these guidelines was converted to the SNOMED-CT codification and stored as 17 decision tables [12]. This process, and the alignment of knowledge in decision tables with the clinical guidelines was supervised by a senior GP of SAGESSA, and double-checked by a senior internal medicine doctor from the HCB. Finally, these tables were used to train 23 residents at HCB in the differential diagnosis of AH with 30 clinical cases. The results of this training process are reported in this paper.

Section 2 summarizes the knowledge engineering process and the three sorts of decision tables that we used to represent all the knowledge obtained after the process. Section 3 describes the training system, and Sect. 4 the use of this system as an exercise to train 23 residents of the HCB, and the main results obtained. In Sect. 5 we conclude with some final remarks and a short comparison of our system with other clinical training tools.

Table 1. Signs and symptoms, and diagnostic tests related to AH [3–11]

Signs and Symptoms	Diagnostic tests
Achromegaly	Achromegaly
Acquired skeletal deformity	*Plasma IGF 1 measurement, Plasma growth hormone measurement, Magnetic resonance imaging of head, Computed tomography of chest and abdomen*
Adrenal Cushing's syndrome	
Edema, Amenorrhea, Hirsutism, Insomnia, Anxiety, Muscle weakness, Skin striae, Bone pain	Adrenal Cushing's syndrome
Coarctation of the aorta	*Plasma cortisol measurement, Measurement of hydrocortisone in saliva, Dexamethasone suppression test, Cortisol rhythm measurement*
Headache, Unequal pulse, Heart murmur, Epistaxis, Muscle weakness	Coarctation of the aorta
Glomerulonephritis	*Magnetic resonance imaging*
Edema, Nausea and vomiting, Oliguria	Glomerulonephritis
Hyperparathyroidism	*Urine protein test, Urine blood test, Kidney biopsy, Immunology and serology blood test, Immunosuppressive antiviral therapy trial*
Abdominal pain, Muscle weakness, Nausea and vomiting, Polyuria, Excessive sleepiness	Hyperparathyroidism
Pheochromocitoma	*Plasma parathyroid hormone level, Blood calcium level*
Abdominal pain, Constipation, Fever, Tachycardia, Acute necrosis	Pheochromocitoma
Renovascular disease	*Metanephrines*
NOT Progress satisfactory, NOT Age more than 50 years	Renovascular disease
Sleep apnea	*Doppler studies, Computed tomography angiography*
Excessive sleepiness, Snoring, Apnea	Sleep apnea
	Polysomnography

2   Knowledge Sources and Representation

For the 8-SCAH identified in [3], the clinical guidelines [4–11] were used to identify their respective signs and symptoms (SS) and related diagnostic tests (DT). Table 1 summarizes the SS and DT of the respective 8-SCAH.

All these concepts and the evidences of the CPGs were used to create three sorts of decision tables.

Decision tables [13,14] are knowledge structures in which columns represent rules, and rows represent either conditions (in the antecedent of the rules) or actions (in the consequent of the rules). In decision tables for differential diagnosis, conditions are signs and symptoms, and actions can be diagnostic hypotheses, diagnostic tests, or ACCEPT/REFUTE diagnostic decisions [12].

In order to extend the ability of decision tables to represent clinical variability with a low impact in the amount of rules, we have incorporated the YES#n grouping constructor, with n being a group identifier. This constructor is used to represent non exclusive disjunctive clinical conditions such as *"Respiratory*

Table 2. Decision table to identify possible 8-SCAH

Abdominal pain	Yes#1				Yes#1			
Acquired skeletal deformity						Yes#1		
Acute necrosis	Yes#1							
Amenorrhea		Yes#1						
Anxiety		Yes#1						
Apnea							Yes#1	
Constipation	Yes#1							
Edema		Yes#1	Yes#1					
Epistaxis								Yes#1
Excessive sleepiness					Yes#1		Yes#1	
Fever	Yes#1							
Headache								Yes#1
Heart murmur								Yes#1
Hirsutism		Yes#1						
Hypertensive disorder	Yes	Yes	Yes	Yes	Yes	Yes	Yes	Yes
Insomnia		Yes#1						
Muscle weakness		Yes#1			Yes#1			Yes#1
NOT Age more than 50 years				Yes#1				
NOT Progress satisfactory				Yes#1				
Nausea and vomiting			Yes#1		Yes#1			
Polyuria					Yes#1			
Snoring							Yes#1	
Tachycardia	Yes#1							
Unequal pulse								Yes#1
Acromegaly						X		
Adrenal Cushing's syndrome		X						
Coarctation of aorta								X
Glomerulonephritis			X					
Hyperparathyroidism					X			
Pheochromocytoma	X							
Renovascular hypertension				X				
Sleep apnea							X	

events which can have a patient with *Sleep Apnea* are hypopneas, obstructive apneas, central apneas and mixed apneas associated with falls in oxygen saturation" (translated from [11]). For a column, all the row conditions with value YES#n with the same n describe a group of conditions among which at least one of them has to be satisfied in order to trigger the rule. Several YES#n groups are possible (with different n's) in the same column or decision table.

2.1 Decision Table 1: Deciding the Initial Hypothesis

The first decision in a differential diagnosis process is to determine the feasible diseases that may explain the condition of the patient. A single decision table was made containing all the possible combinations of signs and symptoms that could explain each one of the 8-SCAH. This is Table 2, in which alternative signs and symptoms are joined in YES#n groups, and the sign *hypertensive disorder* is forced to be present (value Yes).

When a patient with an hypertensive disorder arrives, the signs and symptoms of the patient are used to evaluate which columns in the table are satisfied.

Table 3. Decision table to recommend diagnostic tests for achromegaly.

```
+-----------------------------------------------+-----+-----+-----+-----+
| Acromegaly                                    | Yes | Yes | Yes | Yes |
| Computed tomography of chest and abdomen      |     |     |     |  ?  |
| Magnetic resonance imaging of head            |     |     |  ?  | No  |
| Plasma IGF 1 measurement                      |  ?  | Yes | Yes | Yes |
| Plasma growth hormone measurement             |     |  ?  | Yes | Yes |
+===============================================+=====+=====+=====+=====+
| Computed tomography of chest and abdomen      |     |     |     |  X  |
| Magnetic resonance imaging of head            |     |     |  X  |     |
| Plasma IGF 1 measurement                      |  X  |     |     |     |
| Plasma growth hormone measurement             |     |  X  |     |     |
+-----------------------------------------------+-----+-----+-----+-----+
```

A column is satisfied if the patient has all the signs with a Yes value, and at least one of the signs with a Yes#1 value.

The satisfied columns point to the possible causes of these signs and symptoms (see the X values in the conclusions). The union of all the possible causes configure the diagnostic hypothesis. For example, a patient with an hypertensive disorder, edema, and amenorrhea would cause the second and third rules of Table 2 to fire and suggest a hypothesis of adrenal Cushing's syndrome, or glomerulonephritis, or both, as possible diagnoses.

2.2   Decision Tables 2: Deciding the Diagnostic Tests

The second decision of differential diagnosis is to select the appropriate diagnostic tests in order to confirm or refute one or several diseases of the current hypothesis. For each one of the 8-SCAH, a decision table was made to describe the set of diagnostic tests recommended by the corresponding CPG, depending on the patient's current signs and symptoms and the results of previous diagnostic tests. For example, Table 3 describes the patient conditions under which the CPG [4] recommends the different diagnostic tests related to achromegaly. Rule 4 in the table is telling us that if the patient is suspected of suffering from acromegaly (Yes value), and the tests plasma IGF 1 measurement and plasma growth hormone measurement have both been performed with positive results (respective Yes values), but magnetic resonance provided a negative result (No value), and a computed tomography of chest and abdomen has not been performed or the result is uncertain (? value), then perform a computer tomography of chest and abdomen (the test with an X value).

2.3   Decision Tables 3: Deciding the Next Hypothesis

In order to close the differential diagnosis loop depicted in Fig. 1, a third sort of decision table was implemented. These tables capture the CPG knowledge related to the clinical conditions that we must observe so that the diseases in the hypothesis could be confirmed, discarded, or maintained. If a hypothesis

Table 4. Decision table to reconsider acromegaly as possible diagnosis.

```
+-------------------------------------------------+-----+-----+-----+-----+-----+-----+-----+-----+
| Acromegaly                                      | Yes | Yes | Yes | Yes | Yes | Yes | Yes | Yes |
| Computed tomography of chest and abdomen        |     |     |     |     |     |  ?  | Yes | No  |
| Magnetic resonance imaging of head              |     |     |     |  ?  | Yes | No  | No  | No  |
| Plasma IGF 1 measurement                        | No  | Yes | Yes | Yes | Yes | Yes | Yes | Yes |
| Plasma growth hormone measurement               |     |  ?  | No  | Yes | Yes | Yes | Yes | Yes |
+=================================================+=====+=====+=====+=====+=====+=====+=====+=====+
| Acromegaly                                      |     |  ?  |     |  ?  |  X  |  ?  |  X  |     |
+-------------------------------------------------+-----+-----+-----+-----+-----+-----+-----+-----+
```

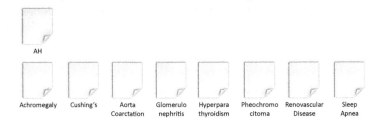

Fig. 2. Disease knowledge library for differential diagnosis

disease is confirmed then it will be part of the final diagnosis. If it is discarded it will not be in the final diagnosis. Otherwise, the disease remains as part of the hypothesis in the differential diagnosis loop.

For example, Table 4 describes the patient conditions and test results that should be observed in order to keep acromegaly as part of the final diagnosis of the patient (columns concluding X), the patient conditions and test results that justify acromegaly to remain as part of the current hypothesis (columns ?), and patient conditions and test results that discard acromegaly as cause of the patient high blood pressure (columns with an empty conclusion).

2.4   The Library of Decision Tables

All the decision tables that we developed were organized a knowledge library in which, for each disease (or CPG), there are three decision tables that we grouped under the same disease name (see Fig. 2).

The first decision table of type 1 (see Sect. 2.1) describes the conditions under which there is some evidence that a patient could have the disease. The second decision table of type 2 (see Sect. 2.2) describes the conditions under which the diagnostic tests related to the disease are recommended, according to the CPG. The third decision table of type 3 (see Sect. 2.3) describes under which conditions a disease can be confirmed, refuted, or retained as hypothesis. The confirmed diseases will be part of the final diagnosis. The diseases that remain in the hypothesis will require additional tests to get confirmed or refuted, along the differential diagnosis process.

3   The Training System

The above explained decision tables are used to implement a software to train physicians for differential diagnosis. The general procedure of this training system is to provide residents with partial probably modified information of a clinical case and let them to progressively refine their initial hypotheses until they accept a final diagnosis or the case is closed without a diagnosis. At this point, the system shows the diagnosis procedure that the user has followed, confronted to the diagnosis procedure recommended by the decision tables, according to the indications in the CPGs. So, the residents are allowed to compare both approaches and realize whether their decisions are similar or not to the recommendations that the CPGs provide for the same case. After that, a new medical case for differential diagnosis is suggested.

Table 5. Base-line characteristics of (a) the AH cases, and (b) the residents

Variable	No. of cases
Signs & Symptoms	
Abdominal pain	6
Acquired skeletal deformity	8
Acute necrosis	5
Age more than 50 years	1
Amenorrhea	4
Anxiety	6
Apnea	3
Bone pain	6
Constipation	4
Edema	6
Epistaxis	6
Excessive sleepiness	6
Fever	2
Headache	4
Heart murmur	3
Hirsutism	4
Hypertensive disorder	30
Insomnia	2
Muscle weakness	9
Nausea and vomiting	9
Oliguria	5
Polyuria	3
Progress satisfactory	1
Skin striae	4
Snoring	5
Tachycardia	5
Unequal pulse	5
...	

...

Diagnosis	
essential AH	5
achromegaly	4
adrenal Cushing's syndrome	5
coarctation of the aorta	4
glomerulonephritis	4
hyperparathyroidism	4
pheochromocitoma	5
renovascular disease	4
sleep apnea	4
Co-Morbidities	
none	5
1	18
2	5
3	2

(a)

Specialty	Residency year	Qtty	No. of Cases
generic	1	2	9.0±1.0
generic	2	4	31.5±8.5
generic	3	1	40±0.0
generic	4	2	23.5±16.5
generic	jr assoc	1	21±0.0
specialized	1	9	30.3±9.7
specialized	2	3	30.7±9.3
specialized	3	1	40±0.0

(b)

3.1   The Case Base

A case-base was made with 30 initial cases describing patients suffering from high blood pressure (see Table 5a). Five of these cases were patients with essential AH, 18 cases were patients having a single disease causing AH, 5 cases described patients with two secondary causes of AH, and 2 of them were patients with three co-morbidities causing AH. All the cases were modified to force difficulty of differential diagnosis. With the help of two GPs, these modifications were designed to attend two principles: (1) modifications must keep the case a realistic patient, and (2) modifications must keep the case a valid example of the originally diagnosed disease.

Two sorts of modifications were implemented: hiding signs and symptoms, and adding signs and symptoms. *Hiding signs and symptoms*: for each case, some of the signs and symptoms related to the diseases of the case were hidden. The number of hidden symptoms was selected according to a standard normal distribution, and the symptoms to be hidden according to a uniform distribution. *Adding signs and symptoms*: for each case, between 0 and 4 signs and symptoms from other 8-SCAH that the case do not have were incorporated. A uniform distribution function was used to randomly select which signs or symptoms had to be added.

For the diagnostic tests the CPGs recommend for each case, a new distortion process was applied. According to the published reliability of each diagnostic test, the results of the test (either positive or negative) were assigned a *probability of wrong test result* between 2 % and 32 %. This probability of error was applied to the results obtained the first time that the tests were requested, but not to repeated tests. Note that during the study, residents were able to order the same test one or more times.

A case-base of 30 distorted cases suffering from hypertensive disorder was obtained. Table 5a shows the distribution of cases for all the signs and symptoms related to the 8-SCAH.

3.2   The Learning Loop

The training system was designed to repeat a learning loop for each case in the case-base. During the learning loop (see attached algorithm) the user is informed of the signs and symptoms of the case. Recall that some signs and symptoms are hidden in the case, and some others related to 8-SCAH but that do not correspond to the patient are added to the case.

```
for each case in the case-base
  show the signs and symptoms of the case (*)
  loop until there are not tests to perform or final diagnosis confirmed
    wait for the user to choose a hypothesis (D1)
    wait for the user to order some diagnostic tests (D2)
    recover the results of the ordered tests from the case-base (*)
  end loop
  show user's diagnostic process confronted to guidelines' suggested process
end for
(*) modifications in the case can be forced as indicated in 3.1.
```

After the observation of the signs and symptoms of the case, the user of the system (i.e., the resident) is allowed either to provide a final diagnosis or a hypothesis for the causes of AH (decision D1). Hypotheses need to be confirmed with additional diagnostic tests that the user is asked to order (decision D2). The system recovers the results of the tests from the available information about the case in the case-base, and shows this information to the user, before a new learning loop is started.

At the end of the process, either if a final diagnosis is indicated or the case is dismissed, the system shows the user the whole differential diagnosis process followed by the user, confronted to the differential diagnosis process suggested by the decision tables representing the CPGs.

4   Running the Study

The 30 cases in the case-base were used as baseline for the training of 23 residents in the Emergency Department at the Hospital Clínic de Barcelona. These cases were shuffled and presented in a different order to the different residents to avoid case discussions between the users of the training system. For each resident, ten additional cases were taken at random from the case-base with the purpose of evaluating the achievements of the learning system when the users were asked to diagnose repeated different cases. This way, all the cases in the case-base were shown to all the residents in different order, so that cases with different diagnostic difficulties could appear at different moments during the training. And the groups of ten additional cases were different for each resident, so that case difficulty was randomized during the evaluation of performance in front of repeated cases, once the training process was concluded.

The cases were exposed one by one to the residents by means of a web server. The profile of the residents was diverse in terms of specialty (specialist versus GPs), and number of years of residency (between 1 and 4), see Table 5b. Two weeks were left for residents to complete the training, allowing them blind free access 24×7 to the training system. The system stored the information after each case was closed, so residents could interrupt their training at any time and continue with the following training cases whenever they wanted, later. Every time a case was closed, the system showed the resident his/here differential diagnosis process confronted to the differential diagnosis that the CPGs recommends for the case (learning feed-back). Textual CPGs [3–11] were available in the training system for residents consultation at any time. Residents were informed of the starting and ending date of the training exercise, but not of the cases, their number, or their types.

After two weeks, the web access to the system was blocked with the amount of cases reported in Table 5b. The stored information was used to compare the training of residents in terms of improvement and stabilization. For the analysis of *training improvement* we compared the mean user's adherence to CPGs in the first 5 cases of the training (cases 1 to 5), with the user's adherence to CPGs in the last 5 cases (cases 26 to 30).

Cases 1 to 5 were different for each resident, and they represented the first cases that each resident had to diagnose during the training. That is to say, the cases that the residents diagnosed when they are still not familiar with the diagnostic procedures in the CPGs. Cases 6 to 25 were also different for each resident, and they were the intermediate cases used to train the residents to assimilate the CPGs. Finally, cases 26 to 30 were again different for each resident and they represent the cases diagnosed when the resident was expected to be familiar with the diagnostic procedures in the guidelines, at the end of the training.

For the analysis of *training stabilization* we compared the mean adherence to CPGs in the last 5 training cases (cases 26 to 30), with the mean adherence to CPGs in the repeated additional 10 cases (cases number 31 to 40). For all the residents, cases 31 to 40 were cases already seen during training but distinct from one resident to another. These were used as control group to check whether each resident had correctly assimilated the CPGs (i.e., adherence to CPGs).

Four sorts of adherence were considered: adherence in the *initial hypothesis*, adherence in the *final diagnosis*, and mean adherence to *hypothesis selection* (decision D1 in the algorithm) and mean adherence to *test selection* (decision D2 in the algorithm), along the differential diagnosis process. In all the analyses we calculated the accuracy, sensitivity, specificity, and positive and negative predictive values of residents' decisions, and performed t-Student's tests[1] to obtain the p-values in Table 6.

Evidence was found that the training system improved the sensitivity, negative predictive value and the accuracy of residents at the time of suspecting initial hypotheses[2] (p-values 0.001, 0.009, and 0.026, respectively). Moreover, there is not a clear evidence that this improved ability was lost after training (P > 0.28). For the final diagnosis, there was not a significant change in the diagnostic capacities of the residents (P ≈ 0.8), that remained high (*accuracy* ≥ 0.9). An improvement in the accuracy, specificity, and negative predictive value of residents' in hypothesis selection along the differential diagnosis process was also detected with P=0.01, P=0.02, and P=0.003, respectively. That is to say, with the use of the system, residents learned to disregard unfounded hypotheses. However this acquired ability did not last (P < 0.04). Finally, we observed a lasting improvement of residents accuracy, sensitivity, specificity, and positive predictive value at the time of selecting diagnostic tests along differential diagnosis (P=0.03, P=0.03, P=0.04, and P=0.01, respectively).

In other words, there is a sound evidence that residents improved their ability to order the proper tests, and only the proper tests, in accordance to the indications in the CPGs, but we could not find evidence that these abilities could be lost after training.

---

[1] Bilateral dependent samples t-Student's hypothesis tests of residents performance comparing mean accuracy, sensitivity, specificity, and positive and negative predictive values between (1) the first five cases during training and the last five cases during training, and also between (2) the last five cases during training and the ten additional control cases after training.

[2] An initial hypothesis is the one suspected after the first contact with the patient, and before performing any diagnostic test.

Table 6. Estimates of mean improvement after the use of the training system

Variable	Cases 1-5	Cases 26-30	Cases 31-40	Improvement P Value	Stabilization P value
Initial hypothesis					
Accuracy	0.64	0.71	0.72	**0.026**	**0.98**
Sensitivity	0.43	0.57	0.56	**0.001**	**0.64**
Specificity	0.83	0.82	0.86	0.795	0.42
Positive Predictive Value	0.65	0.67	0.72	0.544	0.43
Negative Predictive Value	0.67	0.77	0.74	**0.009**	**0.28**
Final Diagnosis					
Accuracy	0.90	0.92	0.90	0.90	0.36
Sensitivity	0.58	0.60	0.62	0.87	0.85
Specificity	0.95	0.96	0.94	0.49	0.38
Positive Predictive Value	0.67	0.68	0.66	0.94	0.71
Negative Predictive Value	0.94	0.95	0.95	0.96	0.48
Mean Adherence (*hypothesis selection* - decision D1)					
Accuracy	0.90	0.93	0.90	**0.01**	0.008
Sensitivity	0.40	0.57	0.51	0.58	0.77
Specificity	0.91	0.93	0.91	**0.02**	0.04
Positive Predictive Value	0.40	0.56	0.48	0.65	0.68
Negative Predictive Value	0.98	0.99	0.98	**0.003**	0.004
Mean Adherence (*test selection* - decision D2)					
Accuracy	0.89	0.94	0.93	**0.03**	**0.14**
Sensitivity	0.69	0.79	0.79	**0.03**	**0.57**
Specificity	0.90	0.95	0.94	**0.04**	**0.22**
Positive Predictive Value	0.53	0.71	0.67	**0.01**	**0.22**
Negative Predictive Value	0.97	0.98	0.97	0.12	0.20

5   Antecedents and Conclusions

INTERNIST-1 [15] was one of the first software approaches to medical diagnosis that was followed by other systems such as QMR, MYCIN, PIP, or CADUCEUS. These systems applied alternative data and knowledge structures such as weighted dependencies between symptoms, or deductive rules to represent the medical skills required to recommend diagnoses (and treatments) in front of specific cases that the user of the system had to introduce. Other following systems approached medical diagnosis with probabilistic and Bayesian Network technologies (e.g., ILIAD or DXPLAIN). Currently there are interesting differential diagnostic systems available; e.g., ISABEL, ESAGIL, or DXPLAIN, among others [16].

Leaving their internal implementation apart, all these systems provide equivalent user interfaces for differential diagnosis: (1) they receive a case description (symptomatology) and (2) propose a ranking of possible diseases, (3) they rarely provide advice on diagnostic tests, the medical knowledge captured in their internal structures is (4) private, and from their vague explanations we can conclude that they are (5) difficult to extend or update. When they are used to train differential diagnosis, all these systems act as *case checkers* rather than as tools to help residents to guess possible diseases, decide appropriate tests, iterate the diagnostic process, and conclude with a final diagnosis. Except ILIAD[17], have not been used to train junior physicians with synthetic cases, or trustworthy conclusions on their capacity to train are not always available. They do not explicitly manage multi-morbidity, thought the ranking of diseases allows users to think of possible simultaneous diseases. To our knowledge, they are not based on diagnostic procedures described in CPGs but their internal knowledge is based on sign-disease/sign-sign medical relationships whose information sources are not always clear.

On the contrary, the tool that we propose in this paper is CPG-directed (i.e., adaptable to CPG evolution and localization -e.g., rural CPGs, developing countries CPGs, etc.); it is based on public available CPGs [3–11]; it involves knowledge on signs and symptoms, diseases, and diagnostic tests; it leaves the user all the decisions of the diagnostic process (and therefore it trains the user in all these decisions); it proposes clinical cases to train diagnostic skills of the user; it allows continuous comparison of user diagnostic actions with CPG evidences (i.e., it helps increasing the adherence of user actions to CPG indications). Moreover, extending the system with additional diseases is simple and independent of previous decision tables, and it manages multi-morbidity naturally.

The system was used to train 23 ER residents in the diagnosis of eight of the most frequent causes of arterial hypertension. Statistical evidence was found that the system improved and consolidated the ability of residents to make a correct initial diagnostic hypothesis, but also their ability to order the right diagnostic tests along all the diagnostic process. An improvement was also observed in the way that users change the suspected diseases (hypotheses) as new findings are detected. Surprisingly we could not find statistical evidence that this last acquired ability remained in the last 10 control cases of the experiment.

The results are promising, however further work is required before this system could be used as a regular tool for residency training at the Hospital Clínic de Barcelona, as we expect. At the moment we are working to improve the system in three senses: extending the corpus of diseases in the library to make it attractive for ER residency training, incorporating electronic health care record statistical information to attach probabilities to the rules in the decision tables [14] and thus allowing the exploitation of evidence-based and experience-based dual knowledge, and running a questionnaire on the satisfaction of the users of the system in order to detect issues that could make the tool more attractive and useful.

We would like to acknowledge Dr. Antoni Collado, who worked in the first versions of decision tables extracted from the CPGs [3–11], and Dr. Carme Olivé for her help supervising the statistical study.

References

1. Riaño, D., Bohada, J.A., Collado, A., Lopez-Vallverdu, J.A.: MPM: a knowledge-based functional model of medical practice. J. Biomed. Inform. **46**(3), 379–387 (2013)
2. Siegenthaler, W.: Differential Diagnosis in Internal Medicine: From Symptom to Diagnosis. Thieme Medical Publishers, New York (2007)

3. James, P.A., Oparil, S., et al.: 2014 evidence-based guideline for the management of high blood pressure in adults: report from the panel members appointed to the Eighth Joint National Committee (JNC 8). JAMA **311**(5), 507–520 (2014)
4. Duran Rodriguez-Hervada, A., Diaz Perez, J.A., Martin Rojas-Marcos, P., Charro Salgado, A.L.: Acromegalia. Medicine **09**, 766–773 (2004)
5. Miralles Garcia, J.M.: Hipercortisolismo de origen suprarrenal: sindrome de Cushing. Medicine **10**, 967–975 (2008)
6. Hurtado Martinez, J.A., Teruel Carrillo, F., Garcia Alberola, A., Valdes Mas, M., Valdes Chavarri, M.: Cardiopatias congenitas en el adulto. Medicine **09**, 2463–2470 (2005)
7. Egido, J., Rojas-Rivera, J.: Consideraciones generales y diagnostico del sindrome nefritico. Medicine **10**, 5584–5586 (2011)
8. Amado Señaris, J.A.: Trastornos de las paratiroides. Medicine **10**, 1057–1062 (2008)
9. Tebar Masso, F.J., Rodriguez Gonzalez, J.M.: Feocromocitoma. Medicine **10**, 997–1005 (2008)
10. Gago Fraile, M., Fernandez Fresnedo, G., Arias Rodriguez, M.: Protocolo diagnostico de la patologia vascular renal. Medicine **10**, 5515–5517 (2011)
11. Martinez-Ceron, E., Fernandez Navarro, I., Fernandez Lahera, J.: Sindrome de apneas hipopneas del sueño. Medicine **10**, 4345–4353 (2010)
12. Riaño, D.: A systematic analysis of medical decisions: how to store knowledge and experience in decision tables. In: Riaño, D., ten Teije, A., Miksch, S. (eds.) KR4HC 2011. LNCS, vol. 6924, pp. 23–36. Springer, Heidelberg (2012)
13. King, P.J.H.: Decision tables. The Comput. J. **10**, 135–142 (1967)
14. Shiffman, R.N.: Representation of clinical practice guidelines in conventional and augmented decision tables. J. Am. Med. Inform. Assoc. **4**(5), 382–393 (1997)
15. Miller, R.A., et al.: INTERNIST-1: An experimental computer-based diagnostic consultant for general internal medicine. New Eng. J. Med. **307**, 468–476 (1982)
16. Wagholikar, K.B., Sundararajan, V., Deshpande, A.W.: Modeling paradigms for medical diagnostic decision support: a survey and future directions. J. Med. Syst. **36**(5), 3029–3049 (2012)
17. Lincoln, M.J., Turner, C.W., Haug, P.J., et al.: Iliad training enhances medical students' diagnostic skills. J. Med. Syst. **15**(1), 93–110 (1991)

Exploiting the Relation Between Environmental Factors and Diseases: A Case Study on Chronic Obstructive Pulmonary Disease

David Riaño[1](✉) and Agusti Solanas[2]

[1] Banzai Research Group, Department of Computer Engineering and Mathematics, Universitat Rovira i Virgili, Tarragona, Spain
david.riano@urv.net
[2] Smart Health Research Group, Department of Computer Engineering and Mathematics, Universitat Rovira i Virgili, Tarragona, Spain
agusti.solanas@urv.net

Abstract. The raise of chronic diseases poses a challenge for the health care sector worldwide. In many cases, diseases are affected by an environmental component that, until now, could be hardly controlled. However, with the recent advances in information and communication technologies applied to cities, it becomes possible to collect real-time environmental data and use them to provide chronic patients with recommendations able to adapt to the changing environmental conditions.

In this article, we study the use of the sensing capabilities of the so-called smart cities in the context of the recently proposed concept of Smart Health. In this context, we propose a way to exploit the relation between environmental factors and diseases, and we show how to obtain a comfort level for patients. Moreover, we study the application of our proposal to outdoor exercises and rehabilitative activities related to the treatment of Chronic Obstructive Pulmonary Disease.

Keywords: Smart health · e-Health · m-Health · COPD · Smart cities

1   Introduction

In modern health care systems, the treatment of chronic patients comes represented by outpatient therapies in which the patient is encouraged to take a relevant, participatory role. Many chronic diseases, particularly cardiovascular and respiratory ones, involve physical exercise and rehabilitative activities, some of which can be done outdoors. For example, pulmonary rehabilitation of Chronic Obstructive Pulmonary Disease (COPD) recommends regular exercise in order to reduce heart rate and blood pressure, and also to improve breathing. Some guidelines provide clinical evidence that regular (e.g., daily) walks are beneficial in the treatment of COPD. They also argue that, for some patients, this exercise can cause shortness of breath and other COPD signs if it is not correctly practised, and outline the importance of gradually increasing the level of exercise

© Springer International Publishing Switzerland 2014
S. Miksch et al. (Eds.): KR4HC 2014, LNAI 8903, pp. 160–173, 2014.
DOI: 10.1007/978-3-319-13281-5_12

under the supervision of health care experts. For outdoor exercise, however, the patient cannot always count with such expert supervision.

Outdoor exercise also entails considering environmental factors, such as pollution, temperature or seasonal allergens concentration, that can negatively affect fragile patients. Some studies have shown the correlation between pollen concentration and the number of arrivals at hospital emergency departments [8], hospitalizations [7], or deaths [4] because of respiratory problems, but also between pollution and hospital respiratory admissions [3,11,18], and between heat and respiratory problems exacerbation [2].

Future perspectives in the treatment of COPD [1] conclude that understanding such a complex disease is possible only if we consider four levels of complexity, namely genetic, biological, clinical, and environmental. The *genetic level* identifies genetic markers in order to assess the risk of developing COPD; the *biological level* deals with intermediate phenotypes in order to obtain diagnostic biomarkers and therapeutic targets; the *clinical level* works with clinical phenotypes to achieve integrated care and personalized medicine, and the *environmental level* is focused on the patient life style and the modifiable factors that may affect the COPD treatment, amongst which we can find some that may affect patient's outdoor activities (e.g., pollution, allergens, humidity, or temperature).

Until now it has been pretty difficult to analyse those environmental factors in real-time and provide patients with advise. However, this is steadily changing due to the emergence of smart cities. Although the concept of smart city is still new, we can already find several examples of cities that have adopted it, namely Amsterdam, Vienna, Toronto, Paris, New York, London, Tokyo, Copenhagen, Hong Kong and Barcelona, to name a few. Each smart city tends to concentrate on specific aspects like sustainable living, sustainable working, mobility, reduction of emissions, reduction of public services and transportation, improving the interaction of the society with the administration, or simply improving the experience of tourists. According to the definition of Caragliu et al. [5] extended in [19], smart cities are *"cities strongly founded on ICT that invest in human and social capital to improve the quality of life of their citizens by fostering economic growth, participatory governance, wise management of resources, sustainability, and efficient mobility, whilst they guarantee the privacy and security of the citizens"*. Smart cities can contribute to the improvement of health care systems and their infrastructure can be used to provide better health care. In this line, Solanas et al. [21] proposed the concept of Smart Health (s-Health) as a new paradigm of health in the context of smart cities. In this paper we describe an application of smart health to compute a comfort level for patients. According to Merriam-Webster, comfort is *"a state or situation in which you are relaxed and do not have any physically unpleasant feelings caused by pain, heat, cold, etc."* Inspired in this definition, we have proposed the concept *comfort level* as a quantification of the patient's comfort, we have implemented a procedure to calculate it in terms of the patient and the environmental variables, and have applied this procedure to the case of COPD patients as a first step previous to personalizing the prescribed COPD rehabilitative outdoor activities (i.e., COPD treatment at the environmental level), according to the environmental measures registered by smart city sensors.

The rest of the article is organised as follows: In Sect. 2 we recall the fundamental elements that support our proposal, namely e-health, m-health and s-health. Also, we briefly introduce COPD. Next, in Sect. 3 we describe our proposal, first, from a general perspective and, later, by concentrating on its application to the specific case of COPD. The article concludes in Sect. 4 with some final remarks and pointing out some open research lines that will be studied in the near future.

2   Background

2.1   e-Health and m-Health

e-Health was defined by Eysenbach in 2001 [10] as *"an emerging field in the intersection of medical informatics, public health and business, referring to health services and information delivered or enhanced through the Internet and related technologies."* In a broader sense, Eysenbach also stated that *"the term characterizes not only a technical development, but also a state-of-mind, a way of thinking, an attitude, and a commitment for networked, global thinking, to improve health care locally, regionally, and worldwide by using information and communication technology."*

Information and communication technology (ICT) are applied to a bunch of health-related tasks, such as patient-doctor communication, distant provision of care, support to diagnostic, health information storage in the form of electronic health care records (EHR), medication adherence control, etc. ICT was introduced in the health care sector to contribute to the reduction of management costs and to increase efficiency. It could be said that efficiency has been improved but it is quite controversial whether ICT has actually reduced cost since their deployment is significantly costly. However, the use of ICT in the health care sector has contributed to substantially reduce the displacements of professionals and patients, and has made treatments and health watchfulness more comfortable to patients.

Although the adoption of e-Health is a clear step forward for the health care sector, the generalisation of mobile technology has opened the door to an even more important conception: mobile health (m-health) that could be defined as the delivery of health care services via mobile communication devices, or as Istepanien et al. more succinctly put it in [12] as *"emerging mobile communications and network technologies for health care systems"*.

m-Health benefits the remote monitoring of patients and the communication between all the actors of the health care system (e.g. professionals, relatives, patients, administrative staff, etc.) Moreover, m-health allows the quick gathering of data from patients, and provides doctors and researchers with a large amount of information that can be used for a variety of purposes and health care services:

– Due to the ubiquity of mobile devices, many services might be accessed everywhere, any time.
– The focus is on the patient, who plays a key role in an m-health service. Services are provided wherever the patient is, and the approach is clearly patient-centric.
– Patients receive personalised services that better fit their needs.

For the most recent advances on e-health and m-health, the interested reader can refer to [20].

2.2   Smart Health and Smart Cities

With the growing interest in Smart Cities (i.e. cities that are equipped with ICT able to collect data for multiple variables, namely energy consumption, temperature, humidity, pollution, etc.) the concept of smart health (s-Health), proposed by Solanas et al. [21], appears as a natural evolution of e-health and m-health in this recently developed context. The definition of the concept of smart health is the following: *"Smart health (s-health) is the provision of health services by using the context-aware network and sensing infrastructure of smart cities."*

Smart cities are equipped with sensors able to analyse many features that affect our health. The following are only a few indicative examples:

– Temperature and humidity sensors: It is well known that temperature and humidity affect perspiration. In this sense, this information could be used to help patients decide the right quantity of liquids to drink during their daily activities. This is specially important for fragile sectors of the population like elderly and children, and people suffering from congestive heart failure (CHF) [22] and similar diseases.
– Pollution and allergens sensors: due to traffic conditions and nearby polluting industries, cities might be affected by variable degrees of air pollution. Pollution sensors distributed in the city could provide specially important data for people with respiratory problems like COPD [17]. Also, sensors that can detect allergens could help people who suffer from allergic rhinitis and similar conditions [9].
– Luminosity sensors: At night, light conditions vary from one street to another. Citizens with visual impairments [6] or photosensitivity could be highly affected by these light conditions and the information from luminosity sensors could help them decide the best route to take.

This sensing infrastructure empowers s-health and provides it all its potential. However, it is even more powerful because it can be used to augment the capabilities of m-health [12]. Also, it is important to stress that the above examples are focused on the citizen/patient. Any health care service based on the smart city infrastructure could be considered smart health. Clearly, s-health is a subclass of e-health because it is founded on ICT like m-health. However, it differs from m-health in that the infrastructure of the smart city is not necessarily mobile and in most cases it will be static. In addition, from the city perspective we could understand s-health in two ways:

- Passively: s-Health services are passive when they only use the information gathered from the sensing infrastructure of the smart city. For example, if pollution sensors detect a dangerous concentration of contaminants, a service could recommend the population to stay indoors.
- Actively: s-Health services are active when the actuators of the city (e.g., water sprays, traffic lights, metropolitan buses) are used to provide the service. For instance, if high concentrations of pollen are detected in a park, the city can activate water sprays to drag them from the air.

2.3 Chronic Obstructive Pulmonary Disease

Chronic obstructive pulmonary disease (COPD) is a major chronic respiratory disease with a high prevalence, remarkable mortality and morbidity ratios, and significant socioeconomic costs [17]. It is described as a *"persistent airflow limitation that is usually progressive and associated with an enhanced chronic inflammatory response in the airways and the lung to noxious particles or gases"*. Among the most frequent signs of COPD, we can find *cough, shortness of breath, wheeze*, and *chest tightness*. The treatment is defined at multiple levels [1] and, for mild-moderate COPD, physical exercise and rehabilitative activities such as outdoor walks are recommended.

In spite that the implication of environmental factors such as pollution in COPD causes and evolution remains unclear [17], their association to COPD signs is supported by multiple studies such as [3,13]. Among these factors that affect patient's cough, shortness of breath, wheeze, and chest tightness, we can find ambient air *pollution* (AAP) [18], allergens such as *pollen* (P) [8], and ambient *temperature* (T) [16].

3   Our Approach

3.1   Rationale

In the context of smart cities that struggle to foster healthy habits amongst their citizens and promote smart health, we propose a new way of using the sensing capabilities of smart cities. We observe that many citizens/patients have to perform physical activities in the city, namely walking, jogging, running, etc. To promote such healthy habits, it would be desirable to count with a system that could dynamically adapt to the needs of the citizens. Hence, our aim is to provide a way of exploiting the existent relation between environmental factors (analysed by smart city sensors) and diseases (suffered by citizens). In particular we focus on the computation of patient's comfort level as a measure to personalize the prescribed COPD rehabilitative outdoor activities, to be performed in later steps. For the sake of specificity, in this paper we concentrate on COPD under a passive s-health framework.

3.2 General Scheme and Main Components

Our approach considers the following main components:

- Smart City Infrastructure: We assume that we can collect real-time information from already deployed sensors in a smart city. Those sensors can provide us with information on environmental variables such as, temperature, humidity, and concentration of pollution and allergens.
- Diseases: Those that are suffered by citizens/patients. Each disease can have related a number of symptoms, and these symptoms could have relations with the environmental variables sensed by the city infrastructure.
- Patients/Citizens: Those are the subjects to which we apply our approach. We assume that patients react differently to the environmental factors and, also, that their symptoms could vary. All in all, patients would feel more or less comfortable depending on the environmental factors and their effect on the symptoms of their diseases.

As it is depicted in Fig. 1 (from left to right), we are in the context of a smart city able to collect environmental information (i.e., passive s-Health). These environmental variables are related to diseases in the sense that they could contribute to reduce or to increase the appearance of several symptoms. Next, those symptoms may affect patients in different individual ways, affecting their level of comfort which may vary accordingly.

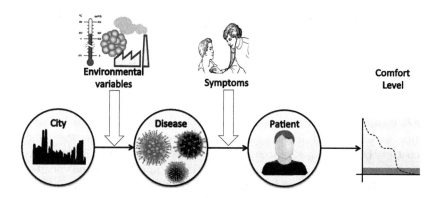

Fig. 1. Conceptual scheme

3.3 Application to COPD

The general model in Fig. 1 can be personalised to the care of COPD patients during outdoor activities, as Fig. 2 represents. In this new scheme, we observe how environmental variables are captured by the smart city sensors. Some of these variables, such as *pollution, pollen concentration,* and *temperature,* may influence one or more of the signs that COPD guidelines relate to this disease, for example, *cough, shortness of breath, wheeze,* and *chest tightness.* The degree of influence of city information in COPD signs comes modulated by a set of incidence functions of the sort $f_{v,s} : D_v \to D_s$, with v an environmental variable (e.g., temperature), D_v the domain of v (e.g., degrees Celsius), s a COPD sign (e.g., shortness of breath) and D_s its domain (e.g., Borg scale [15]). These $f_{v,s}$ functions can be extracted from published environmental or health care studies or derived from the accumulated data of the s-Health history records.

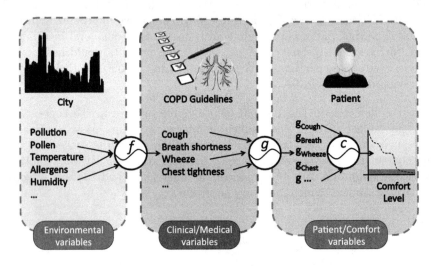

Fig. 2. Our scheme applied to COPD

The incidence of an environmental variable v with a smart city measurement $m \in D_v$ in a COPD symptom s (i.e., $f_{v,s}(m)$) is an objective statistical value that may have different impact in different patients. Moreover, the incidence in each COPD sign comes represented in different scales. For example, cough may be measured in number of coughs per minute, in cough seconds or in cough epochs [14], but shortness of breath is often represented in the modified Borg scale [15]. Scale homogeneisation and patient personalisation of the incidence of environmental variables is achieved with patient comfort level functions of the sort $g_s : D_s \to C$, with s a COPD symptom with domain D_s, and C our concept of *level of comfort.* These g_s functions are subjective and they may get dynamically adapted as the patient (or the patient worn sensors) report on the evolution of outdoor activities.

In order to get a final adaptation of health care outdoor exercise to each patient, all the comfort level values $g_s \circ f_{v,s}(m)$ related to the environmental variable v and the COPD sign s, are integrated with a combination function c that provides the global comfort level predicted for the outdoor activities of the patient, according to the current environmental factors. In this particular paper, the *min* function is used. So, the influence of environmental factors in a concrete COPD patient is calculated as $comfort = \min_{v,s} f_{(v,s)}$.

Selecting Incidence Functions for COPD. Historical information on the smart city sensor's measurements can be crossed with information of the patient admissions of the hospitals in that city. So, for the same time interval (e.g., one concrete day) we can recover from the smart city records, for example, how many mg/m^3 of pollen were present in a given city area and the degree of wheeze of all the COPD patients assisted in the hospitals of this area in that particular time interval. All this information can be accumulated, as the plot in Fig. 3 depicts, and used afterwards to predict the expected wheeze value (w_p) of a COPD patient when the smart city registers a pollution value p (i.e., $f_{(pollution,\ wheeze)}(p)$). This kind of procedure can be thoroughly found in previous health-environmental studies for *air pollution* factors conditioning *cough, wheezing,* and *shortness of breath* [13] (i.e., functions $f_{(pollution,\ cought)}$, $f_{(pollution,\ wheezing)}$, and $f_{(pollution,\ breathshortness)}$, respectively); *pollen* conditioning *wheeze* [8] (i.e., $f_{(pollen,\ wheeze)}$), and ambient *temperature* conditioning *cough, wheeze,* and *chest tightness* [16][1] (i.e., functions $f_{(temp,\ cought)}$, $f_{(temp,\ wheeze)}$, and $f_{(temp,\ chest\ tightness)}$, respectively), among others.

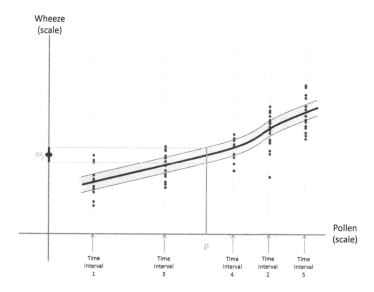

Fig. 3. Objective incidence of outdoor environmental factors (e.g., pollen) in COPD signs (e.g., wheeze), or $f_{(wheeze,\ pollen)}$ function.

---

[1] This study is for children.

Recent studies [13] conclude that pollution may have incidence in COPD patient's shortness of breath, cough, wheezing and that it limits patients outdoor walking capability. This is particularly observed for PM10 (i.e., particulate matter smaller than 10 µm) and coarse pollutants (i.e., particulate matter between 2.5 and 10 µm). Other studies [8] also conclude about the incidence of pollen in wheeze and asthma, with an average incidence of 2–3 %, but reaching 10–15 % risk increase in the days of highest concentrations (5 % of the year days). Particularly this is observed for Poaceae and Quercus species of pollen.

The conclusions of all these studies are used to objectively determine the degrees of incidence of outdoor environmental factors in COPD signs. But these incidences (objective measures) must be converted into comfort indices for a concrete patient (subjective measures), before they can be used to tailor patient's outdoor exercises and rehabilitative activities.

Making Comfort Level Functions for COPD. We achieve the above mentioned conversion with a new kind of plot, see Fig. 4, that relates each COPD sign s which is influenced by an environmental factor, with a degree of patient's comfort g_s.

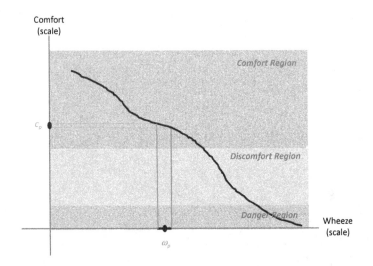

Fig. 4. Subjective conversion of degrees of COPD sign (e.g., wheeze) into patient comfort level, or g_{wheeze} function.

With these new plots we are able to transform the expected evolution of each COPD sign of the patient during outdoor walk, into a personal comfort value that can be categorized as *comfortable* (it is expected that the current environmental conditions will not affect patient's outdoor exercise), *discomfortable* (some sort of acceptable hazard is expected during the exercise), or *dangerous* (according to the current environmental conditions, outdoor exercise must be avoided).

For the sake of a correct management, we integrate all the values obtained by these plots (i.e., comfort levels) with a combination function that in this particular work is set to be the *min* function (i.e., the patient's global comfort is set to the lower level of comfort caused by the respective COPD signs). With this function, if any comfort value reaches the danger zone (see Fig. 4), the outdoor activity of the patient is considered dangerous and therefore recommended not to do it under the current environmental circumstances. If the comfort values of all the COPD signs remain in their respective comfort areas, the outdoor activity being part of the patient treatment is recommended. Finally, for uncomfortable values, the lowest one is reported and it is left to the patient to decide whether she feels like going out for outdoor exercise.

Example Figure 5 represents the influence of pollution and temperature in patient's cough and shortness of breath, respectively. A same patient p is considered for outdoor exercise in two different moments of the year: p_1 representing a warm spring day with a low pollution level[2], and p_2 representing a summer hot day with a medium air pollution level. Real values of temperature and pollution are observed by the smart city sensors and real-time captured by our system to calculate their influence in the COPD signs cough and shortness of breath with respective values $f_{(pollution,\ cough)}(p_1) = 3.5$ (see Fig. 5(a)) and $f_{(temp,\ shortness\ of\ breath)}(p_1) = 2$ (see Fig. 5(b)), for the spring case p_1, and $f_{(pollution,\ cough)}(p_2) = 10$ (see Fig. 5(a)) and $f_{(temp,\ shortness\ of\ breath)}(p_2) = 7$ (see Fig. 5(b)) for the summer case p_2. Values of cough are measured in number of coughs per minute, whilst values of shortness of breath are measured in Borg scale[3].

All these values are used by our system to calculate the patient's comfort functions depicted in Fig. 6. For the patient in the spring day (i.e., p_1) two levels of comfort are obtained: 70 % in the comfort region for the expected coughs during outdoor activities, and 85 % in the comfort region for the expected shortness of breath to be suffered during outdoor activities. Consequently, both comforts are assessed as comfortable, and the system recommends to follow the outdoor exercises in the patient treatment plan. For the same patient, but in the summer day, (i.e., p_2) the comfort levels obtained are 25 % in the discomfort region (which would cause our system to inform the patient of the feasible inconveniences of doing outdoor exercise), but with a 8.5 % comfort level with regard to shortness of breath. As this value clearly falls into the danger region (see Fig. 6(b)), the system concludes with a strong recommendation for not to go out for exercise that day. Other patients could have different resistance functions of comfort that, under the same environmental factors, could drive our system to provide a different recommendation.

---

[2] EU pollution scale (www.airqualitynow.eu) determines the pollution levels: *very low* (0–25), *low* (25–50), *medium* (50–75), *high* (75–100), and *very high* (>100).

[3] Borg scale [15] provides a scale of 10 values with 0 meaning no breathless at all, 10 maximal breathless, and values 2 and 7 representing slight breathlessness and very severe breathlessness, respectively.

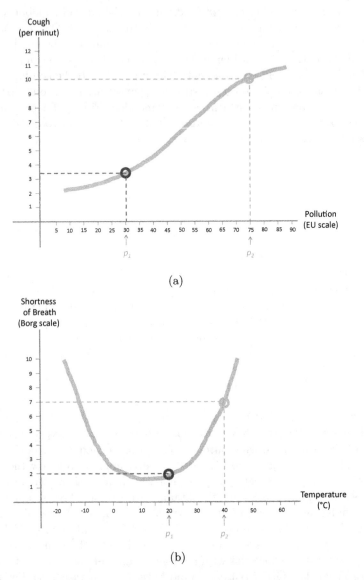

Fig. 5. Environmental functions affecting COPD signs: (a) $f_{(pollution,\ cough)}$, and (b) $f_{(temperature,\ shortness\ of\ breath)}$, with p_1 a patient under a spring day condition (pollution = 30 EU units and temperature = 20 °C), and p_2 the same patient under a summer day condition (pollution = 75 EU units and temperature = 40 °C). Figures are meant for illustration only

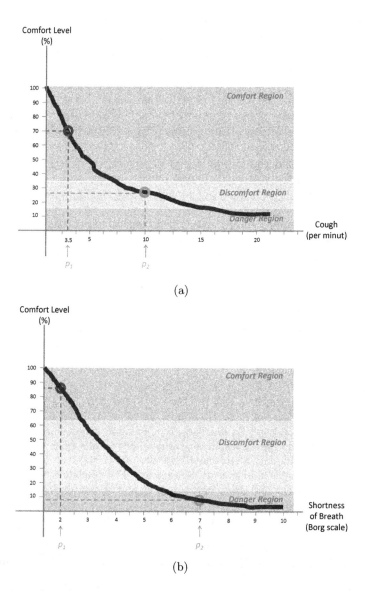

Fig. 6. Comfort level functions affecting COPD signs: (a) $g_{(cough)}$, and (b) $g_{(shortness\ of\ breath)}$, with p_1 a patient under a spring day condition (pollution = 30 EU units and temperature = 20 °C), and p_2 the same patient under a summer day condition (pollution = 75 EU units and temperature = 40 °C). Figures are meant for illustration only.

4   Conclusions

The urbanisation process and the raise of chronic diseases are two trends that pose serious problems to local governments and health care authorities. Most diseases have an environmental dimension that affects the comfort level of patients and might interfere with their treatments.

In this article, we have recalled the recently introduced concept of Smart Health and we have proposed a scheme that exploits the relation between environmental factors and diseases' symptoms to compute the comfort level of patients. Also, with the aim to show the usefulness of our approach, we have studied the application of our ideas to the special case of COPD.

We have established the ground for the study of the relation between the environmental variables and its transitive effect over patients comfort. Several research lines that will be studied in the near future remain open:

- Study the application of our approach to other chronic diseases
- Use the feedback of patients to tune the system
- Implement a real prototype of the scheme to be used by citizens.

References

1. Agustí, A., Vestbo, J.: Current controversies and future perspectives in chronic obstructive pulmonary disease. Am. J. Respir. Crit. Care Med. **184**(5), 507–513 (2012)
2. Anderson, G.B., Dominici, F., Wang, Y., McCormack, M.C., Bell, M.L., Peng, R.D.: Heat-related emergency hospitalizations for respiratory diseases in the medicare population. Am. J. Respir. Crit. Care Med. **187**(10), 1098–1103 (2013)
3. Atkinson, R.W., Ross Anderson, H., Sunyer, J., Ayres, J., Baccini, M., Vonk, J.M., Boumghar, A., Forastiere, F., Forsberg, B., Touloumi, G., et al.: Acute effects of particulate air pollution on respiratory admissions: results from aphea 2 project. Am. J. Respir. Crit. Care Med. **164**(10), 1860–1866 (2001)
4. Brunekreef, B., Hoek, G., Fischer, P., Spieksma, F.T.M.: Relation between airborne pollen concentrations and daily cardiovascular and respiratory-disease mortality. The Lancet **355**(9214), 1517–1518 (2000)
5. Caragliu, A., del Bo, C., Nijkamp, P.: Smart cities in Europe. In: CERS'09, 3rd Central European Conference in Regional Science, pp. 45–59, October 2009
6. Crews, J.E., Campbell, V.A.: Vision impairment and hearing loss among community-dwelling older Americans: implications for health and functioning. Am. J. Public Health **94**(5), 823 (2004)
7. Dales, R.E., Cakmak, S., Judek, S., Coates, F.: Tree pollen and hospitalization for asthma in urban Canada. Int. Arch. Allergy Immunol. **146**(3), 241–247 (2008)
8. Darrow, L.A., Hess, J., Rogers, C.A., Tolbert, P.E., Klein, M., Sarnat, S.E.: Ambient pollen concentrations and emergency department visits for asthma and wheeze. Int. Arch. Allergy Immunol. **130**(3), 630–638 (2012)
9. Dykewicz, M.S., Hamilos, D.L.: Rhinitis and sinusitis. Int. Arch. Allergy Immunol. **125**(2), S103–S115 (2010)
10. Eysenbach, G.: What is e-health? J. Med. Internet Res. **3**(2), e20 (2001)

11. Gan, W.Q., FitzGerald, J.M., Carlsten, C., Sadatsafavi, M., Brauer, M.: Associations of ambient air pollution with chronic obstructive pulmonary disease hospitalization and mortality. Am. J. Respir. Crit. Care Med. **187**(7), 721–727 (2013)
12. Istepanian, R., Laxminarayan, S., Pattichis, C.S. (eds.): M-Health: Emerging Mobile Health Systems. Springer, Berlin (2006). ISBN 978-0-387-26558-2
13. Karakatsani, A., Analitis, A., Perifanou, D., Ayres, J.G., Harrison, R.M., Kotronarou, A., Kavouras, I.G., Pekkanen, J., Hämeri, K., Kos, G.P., et al.: Particulate matter air pollution and respiratory symptoms in individuals having either asthma or chronic obstructive pulmonary disease: a European multicentre panel study. Environ. Health **11**(1), 75 (2012)
14. Kelsall, A., Decalmer, S., Webster, D., Brown, N., McGuinness, K., Woodcock, A., Smith, J.: How to quantify coughing: correlations with quality of life in chronic cough. Eur. Respir. J. **32**(1), 175–179 (2008)
15. Kendrick, K.R., Baxi, S.C., Smith, R.M.: Usefulness of the modified 0–10 borg scale in assessing the degree of dyspnea in patients with copd and asthma. J. Emerg. Nurs. **26**(3), 216–222 (2000)
16. Li, S., Baker, P.J., Jalaludin, B.B., Guo, Y., Marks, G.B., Denison, L.S., Williams, G.M.: An Australian national panel study of diurnal temperature range and children's respiratory health. Ann. Allergy Asthma Immunol. **112**(4), 348–353 (2014)
17. Pauwels, R.A., Buist, A.S., Calverley, P.M., Jenkins, C.R.: Global strategy for the diagnosis, management, and prevention of chronic obstructive pulmonary disease. Am. J. Respir. Crit. Care Med. **163**(5), 1256–1276 (2012)
18. Peacock, J.L., Anderson, H.R., Bremner, S.A., Marston, L., Seemungal, T.A., Strachan, D.P., Wedzicha, J.A.: Outdoor air pollution and respiratory health in patients with copd. Thorax **66**(7), 591–596 (2011)
19. Pérez-Martínez, P.A., Martínez-Ballesté, A., Solanas, A.: Privacy in smart cities - a case study of smart public parking. In: PECCS 2013 - Proceedings of the 3rd International Conference on Pervasive Embedded Computing and Communication Systems, pp. 55–59 (2013)
20. Ray P (ed.): Special issue on emerging technologies in communications - area 1 m-health. IEEE J. Sel. Areas Commun. **31**(9), 607–617(2013)
21. Solanas, A., Patsakis, C., Conti, M., Vlachos, I., Ramos, V., Falcone, F., Postolache, O., Pérez-Martínez, P., Di Pietro, R., Perrea, D., Martínez-Ballesté, A.: Smart health: a context-aware health paradigm within smart cities. IEEE Commun. Mag. **52**(8), 74–81 (2014)
22. Thom, M.T.J., Kannel, W.B.: Congestive heart failure. Dis. Manag. Health Outcomes **1**(2), 75–83 (1997)

Author Index

Printed in the United States
By Bookmasters